LOVE,

LAUGHTER &

DREAMS

LOVE, LAUGHTER & DREAMS

We Prayed
For Twelve Children

Bud & Gloria Vear

To order additional copies of this book, contact:
Xlibris Corporation
1-888-795-4274
www.Xlibris.com
Orders@Xlibris.com
14763

Contents

ACKNOWLEDGEMENTS

WE THANK GOD FOR HIS MANY BLESSINGS, ESPECIALLY HIS
ANGELS' HELP IN THE SURVIVAL OF OUR TWELVE CHILDREN.
WE THANK HIM FOR OUR LOVE AND LAUGHTER WHICH
HAS KEPT US REASONABLY SANE. WE ALSO THANK OUR CHILDREN
FOR PROVIDING US WITH MUCH OF THE MATERIAL FOR THIS BOOK,
AS WELL AS THOSE OF YOU WHO HAVE ENCOURAGED US TO WRITE
OUR STORY, AND THE MANY WHO HAVE SUPPORTED US
AS WE PURSUED OUR DREAMS.

WE ESPECIALLY THANK BILL KOSHELNYK, WHO SPENT MANY HOURS
ASSISTING US WITH HIS LITERARY EXPERTISE AND OUR DAUGHTER,
TERRY, FOR REVIEWING THE BOOK. THIS BOOK WOULD NEVER
HAVE PROGRESSED BEYOND THE TALKING STAGE WITHOUT THE HELP
OF BILL AND THE EDITING SKILL OF TERRY.

M. SCOTT PECK SAID IN "THE ROAD LESS TRAVELED" THAT LIFE IS
DIFFICULT BUT ONCE WE TRANSCEND THE FACT THAT LIFE IS
DIFFICULT, IT NO LONGER MATTERS. THE RESULTS OF OUR
PARENTING HAVE NOT ALWAYS MET OUR EXPECTATIONS, BUT BY
ACCEPTING AND DEALING WITH OUR CHALLENGES, WE HAVE
ACHIEVED A MEASURE OF BALANCE IN OUR LIVES. WE ARE
GRATEFUL TO GOD FOR HELPING US GROW.

Preface

We are writing this book in defense of our memories. Since we have no confidence that our children will pass on our tales accurately or with the proper embellishment, we are recording these memories, as we *want* you to remember them. We hope that they might interest and amuse you, and if you find in these pages some hope or inspiration, we will be doubly blessed. Our children and their offspring are the most important legacies we leave behind, and we hope that our stories might help them to survive and even to enjoy the challenges in their own lives. Learn to laugh, take time to love, be willing to forgive, keep God by your side and pursue your dreams. Enjoy our journey as you live yours.

Chapter One

(Bud)

IN PURSUIT OF A DREAM

One August evening in the summer of 1961, as we were sitting on the front porch of our home in Wheaton, Illinois, I said to Gloria, "I'd like to go to medical school."

"What?" she asked. "Are you crazy?"

Her reaction was not unreasonable. We had eight children at the time, and I was a math and science teacher at Edison Junior High School in Wheaton.

"No, I'm not crazy," I answered. "I'd like to give it a try."

Thus began our great adventure in pursuit of my dream.

Gloria realized that my interest in medicine was not a sudden fantasy. I had spoken of it many times over the years, but until that August evening, I had always dismissed pursuing it. From childhood, I had always wanted to be a doctor, and I had successfully completed my pre-medical studies at DePauw University, in Greencastle, Indiana, 11 years before. However, because my grades were only average, I never applied to medical school. At that time, my fear of rejection overwhelmed my desire to be a doctor. I can still recall when my doctor dream was put on hold, during my junior year at DePauw. My Uncle Howard's brother was dean of Northwestern Medical School in Evanston, Illinois. I arranged a visit with him, expecting to get some encouragement in my pursuit of a medical career and perhaps some help in getting admitted. Instead he questioned my qualifications and suggested I might better pursue some less demanding academic ambition. This, coupled with a vocational interest questionnaire, which suggested I should be a YMCA director, put my doctor-dream on hold for ten years. Therefore, during my senior year at DePauw, I took many psychology courses, suppressed my dream of becoming a doctor, pursued a graduate degree in social work and became a social group worker. After three years in social work, I taught for seven years. It was eleven years after completing my pre-medical studies, when I finally responded again to my dream of becoming a doctor.

A good wife never lets her husband's impulses go unchallenged, so Gloria wanted to find out just how determined I was. She noted how difficult getting into medical school would be and reminded me of our eight kids; observing that if I quit my teaching job, we would have no way to support them. Additionally, we both felt very strongly that Gloria be a stay-at-home mom.

"Where would we live? Better yet, how would we live?" she asked. "We have eight kids! You must be out of your mind! How in the world do you think you're going to medical school with eight kids? I mean, come on, be real! Get a grip!"

"I understand all of that," I responded, "but I have always wanted to be a doctor, and I don't want to discard this dream without at least giving it a try."

Gloria's attitude switched abruptly! She felt that, if she had been able to discourage me, the whole idea would have been doomed from the beginning. However if I held my ground against her, she knew I would make it. Once she settled in her own mind that I was going to pursue a medical career, the idea

of medical school—and all the sacrifices it would require—
seemed exciting to her, and she became a cheerleader for the
idea. She then became a motivator and began to focus on
solutions to our challenges.

"We can do it," she would tell me. "This is going to be
fun." Although the idea had been mine, I began to feel a little
overwhelmed by the reality of what we were about to undertake
and realized that once the decision was made, there was no
turning back. "Fun for her, maybe—TRAUMA for me."

We decided not to tell anyone until our plans were finalized.
The last thing we needed was to have other people telling us
how impossible the whole idea was. It looked impossible enough
without anybody else fueling our anxieties. We had stumbled
on two important keys to success—*Focus on the goal and avoid
negative input.*

The first unknown we had to face was could I even get into
a medical school. We realized how long the odds were—35
years old, eight children and mediocre grades. We could see
that this project would have to be approached on two planes,
the temporal and the spiritual. It would take lots of work on
our part and as much divine intervention as we could get.

We purchased a medical school directory, started a 54-day
Rosary Novena, and I studied for and took the Medical College
Aptitude Test. We poured through the requirements of
institutions all over the Country and sent out exploratory letters
to 25 schools to determine which ones would even consider an
application from me, given my unusual circumstances. We
included information about my age, my grades and our family
because we didn't want to pay the application fee if these
factors were going to automatically eliminate me. I felt
confident that if I could just get to the interview stage, I could
sell myself as a worthy applicant.

We identified six schools that offered hope. Some of these
had well-established reputations, and we thought that they
were secure enough to take a chance on an unconventional

applicant. I applied to Indiana University because I had earned a Masters Degree in Social Work there, and I thought this might make them look more kindly on my application. I applied to the University of Missouri, because they had a relatively new four-year medical school and might have fewer applicants and less rigid admission requirements. The University of Tennessee admitted medical school classes three times a year, so they had more slots to fill, and I applied there. I also sent applications to three Catholic institutions: Loyola in Chicago, Creighton in Omaha and Georgetown in Washington, DC. We were Catholic, and a large family might be viewed as evidence of our adherence to the Church's opposition to birth control!

Meanwhile we were *praying* that I be admitted somewhere. It was rather presumptuous we must admit, but we prayed for a letter of acceptance—signed, sealed and delivered—and maybe some financial aid in the bargain. We hoped that God would bless our efforts, and with that in mind, Gloria didn't worry. *I* did! My faith was tempered with more realistic concern than hers.

The result of all our painstaking research and prayers was amazing. I was accepted on the strength of my application alone at Creighton. (The Jesuits must like large families!) I also received an acceptance from Tennessee, contingent upon an interview and taking an extra course in chemistry. Missouri invited me to be interviewed but cautioned that there were only six openings for out-of-state students in a class of 85. I was also invited to interview at Georgetown. Indiana was the only outright rejection and Loyola never responded. Our prayers had been so completely answered; we had options!

Georgetown was painfully expensive, so we decided I wouldn't even go for that interview. The extra course requirement put Tennessee at the bottom of the list, but it was still a possibility. Therefore, with the Creighton acceptance in hand, I contacted Missouri to get a better idea of my prospects there. Missouri University is located in Columbia, a picturesque college town in the center of the State (and the Country), and eleven years earlier (the same year I finished at DePauw), Gloria had graduated from Stephens College, a two-year all-girls school in the same town. I asked the medical school if I might have my interview during the Christmas break, so I wouldn't have to take time away from my teaching. They agreed, even though they were not planning to interview their out-of-state candidates until January or February.

Because we thought our large family might be a deterrent to my acceptance, Gloria wrote to Grace Curtis, her Senior Hall counselor while at Stephens, and asked her to write a letter to the admissions committee to assure them that she could handle the burden of home responsibilities while I attended school. Grace had become the Dean of Students at Stephens College and was still serving in that capacity in 1961. Never married, she considered the students her family. She was 6 feet tall, very regal in stature, with white hair and sparkling eyes, and although very strict with Stephens' codes of conduct, she was compassionate and had a great sense of humor. Gloria had become very close to Grace during her years at Stephens, and after graduating, had kept in touch via Christmas cards. Grace remembered Gloria well and wrote an enthusiastic letter of endorsement to the medical school concerning Gloria's ability to meet the challenges my schooling would entail.

When we arrived at Missouri for my interview, Dr. Bill Mayer, a new young director of admissions, asked Gloria and me both to meet with the admissions committee. We thought this was routine for married applicants, but found out later that Gloria was the only wife invited. Both of us thought the interview had gone well and felt we had an ally in Dr. Mayer who seemed to take a special interest in us. I was confident that Gloria had impressed the committee, but I knew that my academic credentials were marginal, and the committee gave me no assurances of a favorable decision. We returned home to wait, hope and pray.

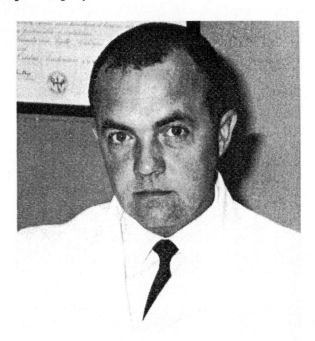

Dr. William Mayer
Dean of Admissions
Missouri Medical School

Since Creighton needed a confirmation by January 15th, we did ask the admissions committee at Missouri if there was any possibility of an early decision from them. Less than two weeks later, they called to say that I was accepted! Now we could finally go public with our plans.

More than a few of our friends and relatives had doubts about our sanity. Gloria's mother dismissed the whole thing out of hand.

"You must not have told them about your eight children."

"They know all about the kids," we told her.

My father was also dubious.

"You can't get accepted," he said flatly.

"I have already been accepted," I replied.

That brought a long silent pause, followed by a question: "How can you afford this? *I* can't afford to send you to medical school."

My dad had been a widower and had remarried after mom died. His new wife, Marika, turned to him and observed astutely, "They didn't ask you, dear." And we never did.

Gloria's mother finally believed us but was deeply troubled about how we would live and doubted I could successfully complete the schooling. Her lack of faith in my ability to successfully complete medical school became apparent when she suggested that Gloria stay in Wheaton with the kids and hold onto the house.

"He may not make it, you know."

"Yes he will," Gloria said confidently, "and I'm certainly going with him."

The reactions of our parents certainly confirmed the wisdom of our not seeking their counsel earlier.

We had devised a plan for supporting the family while I was a student. Gloria would open a home beauty shop when we got to Columbia. This would enable her to be at home with the kids while helping our financial needs. However, this required that she attend 1,000 hours of schooling, in order to obtain a cosmetology license. Gloria enrolled in the Chicago Beauty School in Oak Park twelve months before I was to start medical school.

Financially we hoped to get by on income from the beauty shop, financial aid, loans we might be able to get from the school and whatever money I could earn during my summer breaks. If we could find the right house in Columbia, we hoped to pay our home mortgage by renting rooms to college students. We got this idea from Jim Glassco, a fellow teacher of mine in Wheaton, and his wife, Esther. They had successfully done this with Wheaton College students, and it had enabled them to afford a lovely home of their own. It seemed like a good idea. In Columbia, a major college town, there should be many students looking for off-campus housing.

Gloria started beauty school while I finished my last year of teaching. She had an hour commute by train and bus and put in three 12-hour days per week. We had some day-care help from Bob Porter, a high school boy who lived across the street. Mostly, however, the kids were cared for during the day by Mrs. Eaton, a wonderful woman who shared our conviction that I should pursue my dream. Other than receiving a weekly hairdo from Gloria, Mrs. Eaton refused payment for her childcare services. Our agreement with her was that we would pay her when our house was sold. However, when that time came she refused any money. Gloria insisted that she accept something for all her time. After much coaxing, Mrs. Eaton finally fixed her eyes on an old oriental carpet that was nearly threadbare from years of use and said, "I've always admired that rug. I would like to take that." Mrs. Eaton's generosity was typical of the support and encouragement we received from so many people throughout our struggles. The only way we can ever repay those wonderful people is to try to pass their kindness on to others.

Gloria completed her 1,000 hours in time to take the Illinois State exam and received her license shortly before our move to Missouri. Meanwhile, we had found a house in Columbia that, with some ingenuity, could accommodate our ten-member family, had space for a beauty shop and had two bedrooms on the second floor we could rent out to students. It was a block from the Stephens College campus and close enough to schools, church and shopping that we could get by without a car. A car was a luxury we could not afford. In addition, the neighborhood was zoned for in-home businesses. It seemed like we had found the perfect answer to our prayers, but further challenges soon surfaced.

The first was financial. We secured the house in Missouri with a post-dated check. We had some assets, but they were tied up in real estate. We still owned the small house in Elmhurst, where we had lived prior to moving to Wheaton. If we could sell that property, along with our home in Wheaton, we could come up with enough of a down payment on the Columbia house to keep mortgage payments manageable. However, that meant that we had two homes to sell in three months. It was time for another Novena.

Once more, our prayers were answered. The Elmhurst property was sold in June to the tenants who were renting the house. Now we just had to sell our house in Wheaton, and everything would be set. The Realtor told us we should ask no more than $19,500 if we wanted to sell quickly, but we needed $24,500 (which is what we had invested in it), so we decided to sell it ourselves.

The movers were scheduled to come on August 25th. One week before that date, we had no buyer, only a fraction of the funds we needed for the house in Columbia, nothing to pay the movers, and no income, since I had given up my teaching position. There was no apparent way to go forward with our plans and no going back. Gloria reminded me that we had put it all in God's hands, and assured me it would work out. "Don't worry," she told me. "If we can't sell the house, God will tell us what to do." Pollyanna Gloria was not worried. My prayers, however, were sounding desperate.

Three days before our scheduled move, Mr. Sullivan (who had looked at the house two weeks before) returned, told us he liked the house and offered us our asking price of $24,500. We said, "Yes" on the spot—"Yes! Yes! YES!" Mr. Sullivan was able to push his mortgage through within days. We received our money and headed for Missouri. (In 1999, this same house sold for over $300,000!)

When events like these take place, many people give credit to coincidence or good luck. We prefer to credit the results to God. I continue to marvel at Gloria's unfettered faith without which our project would have foundered many times. She was sure the Lord had blessed our commitment.

Climactic as the sale of the house was, we were to discover that our challenges were really just beginning.

Chapter Two

(Bud)
FIGHTING CITY HALL

The challenges in our lives often produce benefits not appreciated until days, weeks or even years afterwards; and usually we are just relieved to have survived.

Our Family in 1962
as I started Medical School

Our home for four years
in Columbia, Missouri

As we moved into our newly acquired house in Columbia, Gloria prepared to open her home beauty shop. We were zoned for a home enterprise, as long as Gloria didn't hire any employees. No problem there. She couldn't *afford* any employees. The beauty shop met state specifications—its own separate entrance and its own bathroom. Gloria passed her Missouri State Board exam for cosmetology. Everything seemed fine.

There was just one complication: an obscure, largely ignored, city ordinance that restricted the location of *barber and beauty shops* in our zoning classification. Most other home enterprises were allowed. When the owner of the largest downtown beauty shop in Columbia heard about our plans, she immediately contacted the city officials and urged them to enforce this restrictive ordinance. She hired an attorney to make sure our home beauty shop would not be allowed to open.

With absolutely no funds with which to hire a lawyer, we found ourselves embarking on what would become a long and frustrating legal battle. We first informed the Council members that there were numerous home enterprises operating in R-3 neighborhoods. We argued that such neighborhood businesses were a *good* thing, offering convenient service to residents who found it difficult to get downtown. Naturally that point found little resonance with the downtown beauty and barbershop operators. The idea of potential customers being served conveniently somewhere other than downtown was precisely what worried them. One of their arguments to the City Council was that Gloria's shop would drive down real estate values—a contention that was pretty much off the point, but which seemed to strike a chord with some members of the City Council.

We next produced testimony from local residents who said they wanted Gloria's services, didn't feel their property values were at all threatened by the presence of an in-home beauty shop and believed she would be an asset to the neighborhood. We even polled residents of other similar neighborhoods that had in-home barber and beauty shops ("grand fathered" before the ordinance was in place). We went door to door and gathered over 100 signatures on a statement that said they had never found such shops objectionable. The opposition next argued that Gloria's shop would cause traffic congestion. We were on a main thoroughfare, so we counted the number of vehicles going by in front of our house to establish overall traffic usage and periods of peak flow. We demonstrated that, with a maximum of eight possible customers throughout the day, Gloria's activities would increase the number of cars using our street by less than one percent. Additionally, since some of Gloria's customers would walk from their homes in the neighborhood, the traffic impact would be even less. We buttressed our argument with a statement from a city transportation official stating that he had no concerns about increased traffic from a home beauty shop.

The struggle dragged on for *18 months*, creating a distraction, I certainly didn't need during my first year and a half in medical school. Throughout this period Gloria operated on a barter system. She was prohibited from running a business in her home, but nobody could stop her from accepting "gifts" from friends whose hair she styled "gratis". One friend brought milk every day. Others brought different items that helped keep eight children fed and clothed. Moreover, there was the occasional cash *tip*—totaling maybe $50 to $60 per month.

Our economic survival was somewhat creative. Our mortgage and utilities were paid for by rent from our four college girl tenants. We had borrowed some money to put in a kitchenette and a bathroom to go with two furnished bedrooms upstairs. One tenant, Bettina ("Tina") Baker, stayed with us for three years, and she became almost part of the family. She baby-sat for us and helped in many other ways. Tina was a serious student but delightfully warm and friendly and we still maintain contact with her. She is now widely sought as a lecturer on the art of quilting. Her husband, Alan Havig, is a Professor at Stephens College, and they still live in Columbia.

Tina in 1965

We survived through the kind assistance of many people. One Christmas we were "adopted" by a wonderful family. They repaired and repainted old toys and sewed new dresses for old dolls, all for the Vear kids. After the holidays, these people told us it was the best Christmas they'd ever had.

We persevered in our crusade to change the city ordinance on home beauty shops, chipping away at the objections. We sent out a survey letter to Missouri cities with populations of 5,000 or more and found that three-fourths of them permitted in-home beauty shops. However, in spite of all the supporting information we presented, three separate rulings went against us. The zoning board sent a unanimous recommendation to the Council to deny our request. The Council agreed with the zoning board but had some questions, so our request was sent back to the zoning board for clarification. The zoning board returned with the same recommendation. Then there was a tie vote by the city council when one member was absent. This wasn't sufficient to change the ordinance but did keep the issue alive. Our struggles had become a news item in the local press, generating some sympathetic support for the struggling medical student with eight children. Then Dr. Mayer came to our aid once again. He had been instrumental on the admissions committee in my acceptance to medical school and also found scholarships and loans to keep us afloat financially. He hired an attorney to help us with our home beauty shop crusade. Coincidentally the lawyer, Ray Lewis, was someone Gloria had dated briefly when she was a student at Stephens College 12 years earlier.

Some Columbia in-home operators supported us, but our most vocal endorsement came from 82-year-old Fannie Shelton, a retired beautician who was considered the "dean" of Columbia cosmetologists. After her husband died, she supported her family with a home beauty shop, before developing the largest downtown shop in Columbia. She read about our struggle in the local paper and spoke out in support of our request at one of the Council meetings. At that meeting, she turned and scolded the downtown shop owners for their narrow-mindedness and their fear of legitimate competition. The shop owners in attendance were stunned and humbled and said very little after her presentation. Despite her age, Fannie was mentally sharp and well respected among the younger beauticians. Her support was an unexpected blessing.

Ray Lewis made a strong presentation on our behalf. Finally, under all the pressure and publicity we were generating and with a new member appointed to the Council who supported home enterprise, the City Council voted by a margin of one to amend the ordinance and allow Gloria to officially open her home beauty shop.

It had taken 18 months, but we had finally won. Sometimes it does pay to fight City Hall.

Chapter Three

(Bud)

CREATIVE LIVING CONDITIONS

Meanwhile, what was happening to our family? The children were remarkably good sports about the whole thing considering they had been wrenched out of a familiar suburban life with lots of cousins and grandparents nearby and plunged into new surroundings with no close extended family. It wasn't as if they'd been accustomed to living in luxury on my salary as a teacher. I was earning about $5,000 a year, plus whatever I earned painting houses in the summers. We lived frugally, although in Wheaton two or three siblings would share a bedroom; now seven of the children slept down in the basement. It was not a dungeon, but it wasn't "finished" in the manner of today's dry-walled recreation rooms. It was dry and we installed a bathroom and painted the walls and floor, but by 1960s middle-class standards the children's sleeping quarters were, shall we say, unconventional.

The three oldest boys—Steve, Ray and Tony—slept in bunk beds at one end of the basement, enclosed by a long drapery. Baby Rick was in his crib in our bedroom. The four girls—Gay,

Terry, Candi and Pam—slept over a sewer! Before we are reported retroactively for child abuse, please allow me to explain. A storm sewer passed under the house intruding on a portion of the basement. It was enclosed by concrete and created a raised area four feet high and eight feet deep, running the length of the basement. We put mattresses on this large concrete shelf, curtained this space for privacy and stapled recycled bedspreads to the rafters for a "finished" ceiling appearance. It was an odd structural element, but the girls found it a rather unique bedroom. The mattresses also provided the boys (amid loud protests from the girls) a wonderful cushioned wrestling arena.

Since the washer and dryer were also in the basement, one advantage of this sleeping arrangement was that the children's laundry didn't have to be carried very far. The disadvantage? It was impossible to keep the clean and the dirty clothes separated. They all ended up on the floor. In spite of sleeping in such unconventional quarters, the kids *seemed* to get along quite well. On the other hand, if they didn't, we were out of earshot.

Although my schedule at medical school was demanding, I always tried to make it home for supper, and we set Sunday aside for family. On Sundays, after attending Mass together at Sacred Heart Church in the morning, we went for walks when the weather was nice, played board games when it wasn't and Gloria always cooked a nice big dinner. On Sundays during the summer we had cookouts at Stephens Lake (part of Stephens College). I would do the cooking on an outside grill, Gloria would try to relax and the kids would swim in the lake. For a young family struggling to survive, this was a little taste of luxury and the highlight of the week. There was even a nine-hole golf course there with sand greens that we occasionally enjoyed.

To earn spending money—precious little of which was available from us—the kids became entrepreneurs. They collected pop bottles to return to the store for deposits and sold soft drinks at the University of Missouri football games. At holiday time they made articles to sell, such as Christmas trees made from old Readers Digests and wreaths made from tissue paper and metal coat hangers. Some of the kids, without our knowledge, would also sometimes visit the nearby dormitories at Stephens College and the girls would give them treats. The one luxury we sometimes enjoyed was Coca-Cola, which the kids earned by collecting bottle caps. Coca-Cola had a promotion in which they offered a case of Cokes if you turned in a certain number of bottle caps. The kids would retrieve caps from bins under the bottle openers on Coke machines and then turn them in for free Cokes. An extravagant event for us would be a rare family trip to McDonalds.

One enterprise that didn't work out so well was a contract Ray made to clean mortar off old bricks for a penny a brick. There were several thousand bricks, so Ray, age 12, envisioned a big payday. He found however that the job was tedious, time-consuming and grossly under-paid. When it became apparent that Ray wasn't going to finish it himself, Steve, Tony and I helped him complete the job. It was a learning experience in free enterprise. Ray also had a paper route, which required him to collect money each week from his customers. He could keep whatever money was left after he paid his bill, but somehow there was never anything left! Sometimes he didn't even collect enough money to pay his bill, and one week he lost all the money he had collected. (The money he earned from his labor on the bricks was used to pay his paper route bill that week.)

Steve had a little more success with newspapers in Columbia. He had had a newspaper route in Wheaton, but there were no routes available for him when we moved to Columbia. However, he discovered that he could purchase newspapers for 5 cents at the newspaper office and sell them for 10 cents, so he created his own route. He told the storeowners in downtown Columbia that he could hand deliver the paper to them earlier in the day. He assured them that there was no obligation, so if they didn't want it some days, they didn't have to take it. Steve started with ten customers, which earned him a profit of 50 cents a day, and eventually built his route to 30 regular customers. He then found a way to double his profits. He went a little earlier to the newspaper office—before they had finished printing that day's issue—and offered to help them get the papers ready. In gratitude for his help, they gave him his papers *free*, so his profit on sales went from 50% to 100%. The day President Kennedy was shot, Steve sold 100 papers!

Our daily routine rarely varied. We'd get the kids up and off to school, and I would leave for my classes at 7:30, bicycling two miles to campus with my brown-bag lunch. Gloria's days would be spent with beauty shop customers and care of the younger children still at home. I usually came home for supper, spent time with the kids, helped put them to bed and then went back to the library to study until the library closed at 11:00 PM. The children were free from school on Saturdays, but there were customers for Gloria, and plenty of household chores for the rest of us. Sometimes I would take Saturday night off from my studies, but I would be back in the library on Sunday night to prepare for the week ahead, which would always include one or more tests. It would have been pointless to attempt any studying in the house, so the library became my second home. I found I had to study twice as hard as my younger classmates, just to keep up. My father came to visit once (quite unexpectedly), and after dinner and an hour of chatting, I announced, "Well, Dad, it's been great seeing you. I've got to get back to the library." Gloria was very upset with me. "You're father's getting older," she whispered urgently, "This could be the last time you'll ever see him!"

It was a dilemma—but one on which I didn't dwell long. "I have a test," I said, shrugging my shoulders, and I left. A lost hour of study time was too much for me to contemplate. Fortunately, my father understood, and he didn't die for another 20 years.

Chapter Four

(Bud)

FAILURE IS NOT AN OPTION

We had burned all our bridges, and the family's future depended on my becoming a doctor. Not only were we living on a shoestring now, but also we were borrowing money, and there would be debts to pay off. I struggled to keep up with the 22-24 credit hours of class work per semester.

I vividly recall my first day in Gross Anatomy class with Dr. Milton Overholser, a dedicated, no-nonsense, white-haired professor who, though short in stature, was the imposing Head of the Anatomy Department. That first day, with 85 of us sitting expectantly in a theatre-like auditorium, Dr. Overholser asked for a volunteer to describe the trapezius muscle. I had read the first chapter and thought I understood the material, but was stunned when another student recited, from memory, a perfect repetition of the textbook's description of the muscle. When another student repeated this flawless response on another muscle, I began to wonder if I could survive in this environment. My "reasonable knowledge" approach to learning was not going to be adequate for medical school. From the first

I realized I could not absorb everything as quickly as my younger classmates. I studied every spare minute and agonized before every test (which was most of the time). Memorization has never been my forte', and I envied classmates who studied far less but seemed to have total recall at testing time. I tried to compensate by putting in more hours of study, but my most important assets were my dream of becoming a doctor and the unfailing belief and encouragement of my wife. I couldn't afford to fail any subjects because make-up courses were offered during the summer months when I had to earn money to keep food on the table. My grades in medical school were only average, but fortunately I never did fail a course. Academically, it was a very challenging four years for an average student, out of school for 10 years, trying to compete with bright young Phi Beta Kappas.

After two years of classroom study, they started clinical work with patients, and the learning became more meaningful. My communication skills finally became an asset and were called upon often in dealing with patients and instructors. Not to say there weren't some tense moments.

One such moment occurred when we were making rounds on patients with the attending physician on the surgery floor. It was the first week of my surgical rotation, and I had been assigned to change the dressing on a burn patient. I was proud of the thorough job I had done, cleaning the burned area well and removing dead tissue, and I was expecting positive affirmation from the attending physician. Instead he examined the burn site, and, with a look of utter frustration, informed me that I had removed the entire skin graft he had attached a few days before. At that moment I just wanted to disappear, and I'm sure it was also the moment I decided not to become a surgeon. Imagine my relief when I received a passing grade in that rotation.

Another embarrassing episode was the time I was operating the slide project for a noontime lecture by one of our professors, and I fell asleep between slides! It produced an awkward pause in the presentation as the professor waited for the next slide. (In my defense, it was a very boring lecture.)

Daily rounds on patients always produced apprehension, especially on the internal medicine wards with Dr. C. Thorpe Ray, a brilliant clinician who demanded precise information and astute diagnoses. We were each assigned a patient to evaluate and follow, and during rounds Dr. Ray would stop at each patient's room and question us about diagnosis and treatment. He would invariably query me on the one lab test or bit of historical data I hadn't obtained or couldn't remember. Peering at me expectantly through his dark-rimmed glasses, he waited for my response. There was no point in trying to cover up my deficiencies, because I knew further questions from him would quickly expose the gaps in my knowledge. I would usually simply admit my deficiency and hope for the best. My classmates took little pleasure from my struggles because they knew their turn was coming. Salvation usually came when he moved on to someone else's patient. In spite of his intimidating and demanding nature, Dr. Ray was an excellent teacher who taught us to pay attention to details.

Dr. C. Thorpe Ray
Chief of Medicine

When I would share my academic concerns with Gloria, she would listen patiently and then usually respond, "If you would take my advice and relax once in awhile, you would be a lot less stressed." As my faith in the Lord was not as strong as Gloria's, a feeling that my success was dependent on my efforts alone often overwhelmed me. The successful completion of each semester brought me closer to my goal, even though I didn't really feel comfortable until I received my diploma.

Earning money during the first two summers of medical school was critical for our family budget. During those summers, Larry Griffith and I painted houses. Larry was one of the youngest members of our class, married and had a daughter, and we became close friends. Investing in ladders, scaffolds, ladder jacks and brushes, we purchased an old pick-up truck, painted "MEDICAL PAINTERS" on its side and were in business. We dropped advertising brochures at houses that looked like they needed painting and let the doctors at the medical school know we were available. Despite our 14-year age difference, we got along famously. We were both early starters and willing to work long hours. Since we worked on total job bids rather than by the hour, it was to our advantage to finish jobs as quickly as possible. However, we also wanted to have satisfied customers, and word of mouth advertising became our best marketing tool. We kept busy the entire summer, and each of us made about $2,000.

Painting Partners

The next summer we learned some valuable lessons in entrepreneurship. We first learned that hired employees are not as dedicated to a business as the owners. Since we only had 8 weeks of free time from school during the second summer, we decided to hire some young employees to help us paint. Our plan was to line up paint jobs to keep them working through the rest of the summer after we had to return to school. We would line up the work, pay them an hourly wage and make sure our bids on jobs would pay their wages while providing some additional income for us. We thought this was a good way to extend our summer earnings, and we hired four young guys who were looking for summer employment. The first problem we encountered was that we had to pay FICA and unemployment taxes for them, which not only cut into our profits, but also meant that we would be required to do paper work. We never had to worry about this when just the two of us worked as partners. Additionally, their work habits were not reliable, and the quality of their work was not consistent with ours which meant customer complaints we had to correct. The final blow to our entrepreneurial efforts came at the end of the summer. We had a contract to paint a physician's home (one of our professors), and it was a large enough project to keep our crew going for the last month of the summer (when Larry and I would be back in school). Perfect, our plan was going to work—until the whole crew quit! We now had committed to paint a house with no one to paint it. We had no choice but to hire someone else to do it, even though they charged more than we had bid. We actually lost money on the project. We concluded that we were better off when we worked alone.

As I progressed closer to my goal of a medical degree, it was interesting to see how our relatives and friends reacted. Where some had initially been skeptical, they became supportive and our adventure became a popular topic of conversation among people who knew us.

Within the medical school we earned a measure of respect

as well. My academic achievements might not have been stellar, but I became sort of a father figure in the class. Classmates would seek my advice on non-academic topics such as marriage or children. (They never asked me for advice on birth control!) I was also selected to serve on the Honor Council, which dealt with student problems. The other wives admired Gloria for her ingenuity and her unfailing confidence, and they also sought her advice on child rearing and marriage.

The balance in our outlooks was critical to the success of the whole enterprise. I worked like it all depended on me. She believed it all depended on God. Together, we accomplished our goal. In May of 1966, I graduated from the University of Missouri Medical School with my Medical Degree.

Our graduating class had decided not to have a class speaker at our commencement banquet, but I asked the class president to give me the opportunity to say a few words. It was a gamble. The rest of the class was not aware of this request, and I didn't know what their reaction might be. Nevertheless, after four traumatic years of academic pressure, I wanted an opportunity to make a statement. I worked very hard to compose and memorize a short talk that would express my feelings and, hopefully, the feelings of my classmates. I told no one else what I was preparing, not even family members who were coming to the event. In my remarks I commented on the diversity of our class, "From a 23-year-old member of the fairer sex" (it was 1966, remember, when female physicians were still something of a rarity) to myself, "a 40 year old father of nine." I noted that each student would be remembered for some unique accomplishment—in my own case, for having fallen asleep during a noon lecture, when I was running the slide projector. I glanced at Gloria and made note of the "Medical Dames," the wives who had worked so hard and sacrificed so much to earn the degree, "PHT" (Putting Hubby Through). Summarily I spoke of the anxiety shared by all the graduates, as we were about to embark on our careers. "We are sobered by the realization," I told the group, "that in the future, when someone asks for a doctor, they will be asking for us." To my great relief, my classmates responded with applause and best of all when I returned to the table, my father was beaming. It was my most rewarding, medical school moment.

Charles T. Vear, M.D.

I was, indeed, a doctor. Many people had done their part to make it happen, and after four years of struggles and creative management of the family finances, we found ourselves with a total debt of only about $20,000, a modest amount even by the educational costs of that time. We had reached for a dream and with the help of God and others we had achieved it.

July, 1967
Hillsdale, Michigan
Two months
before the twins were born

Chapter Five

(Bud)

CHEAPER BY THE DOZEN

Why would anyone want 12 children? Both Gloria and I had read that humorous account of life in a large family, *Cheaper by the Dozen*, and we were both naively intrigued. Neither of us had grown up in a large family, but, somehow, reading this book impacted both of us deeply and provided a vital link in our relationship and a common dream. Little did we know how prophetic that dream was.

We met in the summer of 1947. Gloria Henderson was between her junior and senior year in high school and was working as a lifeguard at the Wheaton community swimming pool. I had completed my freshman year at DePauw University in Greencastle, Indiana after two years in the Navy, a hitch that had begun in 1944, a year before the end of World War II. I had gone to the pool with a neighbor friend, Mel Chaney, and we were trying to learn how to do a gainer (now called a reverse dive). I considered myself an above average public pool diver, which meant that I could do a variety of dives well enough to impress the girls but not well enough to win any real competitions. However, I had never been able to accomplish a gainer, a benchmark of public pool diving that few would attempt. Although technically not difficult, it requires courage to spring forward off the board and then somersault backwards toward the board. I could never overcome my fear enough to perform a gainer until that day after Gloria demonstrated a gainer from the 3-meter board. This adequately stimulated my "macho" image, and my courage suddenly overcame my fear as this petite and cheerful blonde lifeguard challenged and encouraged us. Both Mel and I learned to do the gainer that day!

Gloria's interest in me was piqued as well, although humility requires that I let her describe her reaction in her own words:

"When I saw this tall, tanned, good looking guy dive into the pool, I knew I wanted to meet him."

Well, what can I say? Her observation was, obviously, very astute.

I asked her out, and we went to O'Henry's, a dance hall 20 miles away that featured a live band. We doubled with Mel and Jean, the girl Mel was dating (who would later become his wife). We had an enjoyable evening, but, as Gloria was still in high school, my younger brother, Dave, had kidded me about robbing the cradle. When Gloria resisted my attempt at a goodnight kiss at the end of the evening, I concluded that my brother was right.

Gloria and I had no further contact until Christmas time *two years later.* In a chance conversation, Louise, Gloria's older sister, happened to mention to me that Gloria had converted to Catholicism. That intrigued me, "cradle-Catholic" that I was, and I called Gloria to ask her why she had joined the Catholic Church. We set a date to go out again and discuss it. However, Gloria came down with a severe case of flu that laid her up for the entire holiday break, and we didn't see each other for another six months. Who knows the timing of things or how relationships flourish? We had been acquainted for three years and had gone out together only once. Yet, we were destined to spend more than 50 years together.

Gloria and I in 1950

I returned to Greencastle to finish my senior year at DePauw, and Gloria went back to Stephens College for the last semester of her two-year degree. We both were dating other people. At DePauw, I "pinned" a very nice young Kappa co-ed, Betsy Veit. "Pinning" was the 1940s equivalent of "going steady." Fraternity men would give their fraternity pins to their sweethearts to wear, and the fraternity brothers and sorority sisters would embellish the occasion with a serenade in front of the co-ed's dormitory. I found it very romantic standing on the porch next to Betsy, listening to my fraternity brothers harmonizing the strains of "The sweetheart of Sigma Chi". The sorority sisters responded with a love song of their own, and the campus was thus informed that we were a steady unit.

Meanwhile at the Iowa State University campus in Ames, Iowa, Gloria was being "pinned" by Johnny Case, her old high school boyfriend. She thought Johnny was a wonderful guy and was thrilled when he offered her his Sigma Nu fraternity pin. She also loved his Catholic family but began to suspect that

Johnny was not a long-term prospect when word got back that he was dating other girls at Iowa State.

When summer came, I saw Gloria for the first time in nearly three years. I told her I wanted her advice about my relationship with Betsy and that I was still curious about why she had become a Catholic. We walked the mile to the swimming pool, swam for a while, and then we strolled leisurely home, giving us a lot of time to talk. As it turned out, Betsy didn't figure prominently in our conversation—nor did Johnny.

Gloria explained how she had begun going to mass with her best friend, Mary Jane Lacy, who was a devout Catholic, and had found it more spiritually comforting than anything she had experienced in Baptist or Methodist churches. She also mentioned that the Catholic tendency toward large families appealed to her, since she wanted to have 12 children.

"I always felt cheated," she said. "I only had one sister."

We had both read *Cheaper by the Dozen*, and I told her that I wanted twelve children, too. We wound up having a lengthy and wide-ranging conversation, and both of us went away with an awakening of new feelings about our relationship. There are moments in life that alter one's path completely. Who can account for why they occur? Someone touches you; some experience impacts you profoundly; something clicks. This was such a moment for us. Both Gloria and I began to sense that we had a lot in common and, perhaps, might have a future together. And we had only had two dates!

During her second year at Stephens, Gloria had made a list of things she thought desirable in a husband. First, he had to be Catholic and attend Mass regularly. Secondly, he had to be taller than her. (This wasn't that much to ask, Gloria being only 5'4") He had to be athletic and like sports, particularly swimming, and he couldn't smoke—she was definite about that. In addition, she didn't want a "party-er." She had another specification as well: "Here's the really shallow part," she recalls. "I thought it would be 'cool' if he was in a fraternity.

When I considered Bud, I realized he met all my qualifications, even the fraternity one; and he said he wanted 12 kids, too."

I had made my own list of qualifications for a mate. Willingness to devote herself to being a wife and mother—implicit in my desire for a large family—was critical, of course. She should be Catholic, attractive, intelligent and cheerful and, of course, she should be in love with me. I also wanted my bride to be a virgin. I admit that in today's society this may sound naïve, but I felt very strongly that sexual intimacy should be reserved for marriage. (I still do.)

A few days after our walk from the pool, I left for my summer job at a Chicago Boys Club camp in Warsaw Indiana. Gloria had intended to send me a birthday card (My birthday was July 5th), but I pre-empted her with a note, thanking her for the lovely time and the gratifying conversation. I also told her I had a third reason I wished to thank her, which I'd reveal when I returned from my summer job.

"That was all very mysterious," Gloria recalls, "but I held my curiosity in check, and we corresponded while Bud was at camp."

Gloria broke up with Johnny that summer, after sending him a "Dear John" letter—which he ignored—and after an unpleasant parting conversation when he showed up at her door.

"I respected Johnny in many ways," Gloria reflects "and I cared quite deeply for his family. But I knew that the commitment for a long-term relationship just wasn't there. It was a hard thing to do, but I knew it was right."

Meanwhile I had gotten my pin back from Betsy. At the end of the summer, the floodgates of our relationship opened and within two weeks after Gloria and I saw each other again, we were talking about marriage! After all, if *I* wanted to have twelve children and *she* wanted to have twelve children, well . . .

Marriage is probably the least logical, most emotional decision people make. Up until that time, in spite of having dated a number of girls—and having been pinned to two of them—I had never really felt ready for marriage. However, at the end of the summer, after spending time with Gloria, marriage became an overpowering desire.

"Bud never promised me a rose garden," Gloria recalls. "He didn't promise me wealth. He didn't promise me trips. You hear all these things about men who promise their wives everything. Bud didn't promise me anything except a lifetime commitment."

Actually, I told Gloria I never expected to make $10,000 a year (this was 1950, remember). Gloria said that none of that mattered.

"Material things aren't important to me," she insisted. "I just want to be a homemaker, and I want a large family."

What mattered to Gloria was that she and I were both Catholic and shared the goal of having a large family. We were both confident that, if the Lord would bless us with children, he would bless us with the means to support them.

Before I went off to graduate school that fall, we had already set our wedding date for the following September. We had been dating for less than a month! I left for Indiana University School of Social Work in Indianapolis to get my Master's Degree, and Gloria took a job at the Produce Reporter Company in Wheaton, a credit-rating service for the fruit and vegetable industry. We saw each other infrequently but nearly every time we did we changed the wedding date. In October we attended my Homecoming at DePauw where my brother, Dave, was a sophomore and on the football team. Our wedding date was still September, but when we saw each other again at Thanksgiving, we moved the date up to June. Our engagement became official at Christmas, when I gave Gloria a diamond ring (after getting the approval of her parents—an old-fashioned custom.) Then I discovered I would not have a break from school in June, and we thought—heck— why not get married in March! We would have gotten married even earlier, but we couldn't have a nuptial Mass during Lent. Fortunately, Easter was early that year. The date was finally firmed up—March 26, the day after Easter.

The reaction of friends and family was not unexpected. "Easter Monday?" Nobody gets married on Monday!" However, the timing proved advantageous. The church was still decorated for Easter, with far more flowers than we could have afforded ourselves. Moreover, the date eliminated a common source of wedding-planning conflict. We had lots of people we wanted to invite, and because we knew many of them wouldn't be able to attend on a Monday, we could afford to invite them all. It worked out well, with no need to cut down the list."

Newlyweds
March 26, 1951

And so began our married life—the life of a graduate student and his bride—getting by on $109 a month from the GI Bill. Such an income didn't allow much in what would now be called, "lifestyle", but the rule for most post-war couples was to set up housekeeping on the proverbial shoestring, find affordable living accommodations and learn to "make do".

I was quite proud of the living arrangement I had secured in Indianapolis before the wedding (unseen by Gloria). The apartment I had found—on the third floor of a building owned by a man named Pandon—wasn't a palace, to be sure. But at least we wouldn't be living in one of the Quonset-hut villages, which were the eyesore of college campuses all across the country.

Mr. Pandon's apartment seemed like a good idea at the time. My future wife was in Wheaton trusting my judgment, and Mr. Pandon appeared the perfect landlord: He was friendly and a Catholic who attended daily mass. The building was located on the north side of Indianapolis at a bustling intersection, with sirens from police and emergency vehicles a daily occurrence. It was a 20-minute bus ride to my school, and there was a food market close by.

Our parents' reactions to what I called "Pandon's Penthouse" were somewhat less enthusiastic. They told me it was a dump and a firetrap! As newlyweds, we thought it was rather quaint, and we were so in love that we were not much concerned about our surroundings. However, it *was* the last home Gloria let me select without her.

To make matters more awkward, when we arrived, our apartment wasn't even ready to move into. Fortunately, my father had given us a gift of two nights lodging at the Claypool Hotel in Indianapolis. He thought we ought to at least spend two nights in a nice hotel. Thanks to Dad, we *did* enjoy a brief two-day honeymoon.

Mr. Pandon let us live in an apartment on the second floor— which was *sort of* finished—while our "penthouse" was being refurbished by an old, black handyman named Henry. Henry was a pleasant fellow who did decent work, but he liked to take a drink *now and then.* And after a few drinks he tended to get sleepy. One day, shortly after we moved in, Henry was drinking while he prepared his lunch and fell asleep with the gas turned up high. We smelled something burning and went to investigate. There was Henry, sound asleep on a mattress on the floor of one of the unfinished first floor apartments, with his lunch burning up on the stove and the flames beginning to leap up the wall. We turned off the gas, put out the fire and revived Henry, who was forever grateful when we promised not to mention anything to Mr. Pandon. Henry couldn't thank us enough. In fact, he made a habit of knocking on the door of our little temporary flat to ask whether we needed anything.

"Are you folks all right?" he'd say. "Anything I can do for you?"

Charming, as it was, Henry's attention often came at the most inappropriate times—which, of course, for newlyweds can be most any time.

"No, Henry," we'd call out. "We're fine. Don't need a thing." We didn't get up to open the door!

About two weeks later we moved upstairs into our third floor "penthouse", which was really just a not-very-large attic room divided into a bedroom, bathroom and kitchen supplemented by a window bay that served as the living—dining area. The bathroom barely had room for the fixtures. The kitchen was no larger and contained a sink with no drain board, a small refrigerator and a two-burner hot plate. Our double bed filled up the bedroom and we could barely put a small couch and a fold-up table in the living-dining area. It cost $65 a month, which sounds cheap now, but at the time was no great bargain. When my father visited, he went out and bought us a rope, so we could escape in case of a fire! We had received an electric roaster as a wedding present and Gloria became very adept at using it. (She even figured out how to bake a cake in it.) But in the beginning, living—and in particular, eating—was pretty sparse. Gloria had not cooked much at home, and our first meal was a kind of chow mien made from a pound of hamburger, a can of mixed vegetables and a can of mushroom soup, all served over Chinese noodles. I looked at this offering and thought, "I may starve". Actually, it was very good, quite economical, and we wound up having it quite often. We served it to guests, and it was interesting to watch their reaction change from "Why did we come for dinner?" to "Can I have seconds."

Gloria was able to supplement our meager income, at least for a short time, by working for Meridian Mutual Insurance Company. However, we wanted twelve children, and we didn't want to postpone getting started. In fact, we were concerned when Gloria wasn't pregnant the first month after we were married. No need to worry; she was pregnant the second month. She worked until November, saving enough money to pay for the doctor. We had medical insurance, but in those days there was a 12-month waiting period for maternity benefits—too long for us. The birth of our first son, Steve, nine and a half months after our wedding, established the principle by which our life as parents would proceed: *Nothing ever happens the way you expect it to happen.* Gloria had read *Childbirth Without Fear,* by Grantly Dick Read, one of the early books on "natural childbirth," and had been lulled into a false sense of complacency. Taking Read's reassuring counsel to heart, and confusing "without fear" with "without pain", Gloria expected a short and painless labor. Twelve hours of womanly suffering taught her otherwise.

Read's approach to childbirth was not without value. For instance, he advised expectant mothers to stay upright and walk around as much as possible during the laboring process so that the baby could progress downward into the birth canal more easily. Unfortunately, Dr. Spahr, Gloria's physician, hadn't read the book and had no understanding of or appreciation for the "Read" method. (Gloria suspected that he thought it meant she should *read* during labor!) She found herself confined to bed with stout side rails in place. Being confined probably made her labor longer, though 12 hours is about average for a first pregnancy.

However, the real drama was in the waiting room downstairs. Typical of those days, before fathers were made part of the birthing experience, I waited for occasional reports on the progress of my wife in the labor unit upstairs. (The most common report was "no change.") Because Gloria was admitted with great confidence that labor and delivery would be a breeze, I was quite calm. I occupied myself by composing what I thought was a clever birth announcement. I indicated the *date of arrival* with the abbreviation "DOA," which produced some embarrassing confusion. Some of our friends who received the announcement couldn't figure out why we would send out cards reporting that poor baby Stephen had been a stillbirth. (They read "DOA" as *dead on arrival!*) The confusion for many wasn't cleared up until the next Christmas when our Christmas picture included Steve.

The hours of Gloria's labor dragged on, and while I was feeling the predictable nervousness of a new father, I had every expectation of a smooth delivery. That confidence was suddenly shattered when one of the other fathers in the waiting room was called aside and informed that his wife had died in childbirth! The very real dangers of this most basic human process suddenly smacked me in the face. I understood then that Gloria was in the middle of something that was all about life and death. It was an awakening for me—another of those truly life-changing moments—and I started pacing the floor in earnest, marking time with the rhythm of my prayers.

Fortunately, Gloria experienced no complications, and Steve, the first of our twelve, was born on January 16, 1952. That's when our life's adventure as a family really began— with all its blessings and challenges.

1952
New Parents

From the vantage point of years—a half century now as we
set down these reflections—we can see that it's not a good thing
to base expectations for your own life on the stories of others. We
both loved *Cheaper by the Dozen,* and it seemed that our life with
twelve children would be as fun-filled as the comic adventures
of the frolicsome Gilbreth clan. But that book was intended to be
humorous, and humor always contains an element of deception.
In our youthful naiveté, we quite naturally assumed we'd be good
parents of a large brood. *Cheaper by the Dozen* made us believe it
would be easy. However, the roots of every family's story lie in
other times and other households. So please allow us to digress,
as we reflect on two very different childhood experiences in a
different age, a very different world . . .

Chapter Six

(Gloria)

GLORIA'S EARLY YEARS IN LOUISIANA

My earliest memories were of sitting on the front swing at Mamo's in Jonesboro, Louisiana. Adonia Jones Carson Bayes was my paternal grandmother. We grandkids called her "Mammoe" but we spelled it "MAMO".

The year was about 1936, and, even though my parents were divorced at the time, Mamo shared her home while mom finished a secretarial school in Shreveport, Louisiana. My mother, Cornelia "Nelia", finished her schooling and obtained a job as a secretary at the Southern Advance Paper Mill in Hodge for $20.00 a week. Until we were able to find another place to live, she commuted to Hodge, about three miles away, on the Nickle-Willi, a bus that cost 5 cents. Every afternoon, I would wait for her to get off the Nickle-Willi, and then I would hop off the swing and run to meet her as fast as my little legs would carry me. This was where my memory started. I was just five . . .

Before there were memories, records and diaries disclose

that my paternal grandfather, Robert Carson, was one of Jonesboro's leading men, a popular and trusted cotton buyer. He had died before I was born. "Mamo" was from the Jones family, one of the leading families of Jonesboro. Her father, Andrew Jones, had been one of the town's founders My mother's father, Walter Lee Bagwell, had been a lawyer who'd served both as Mayor of Oak Grove and as a State Senator, but he also had died before I was born.

Walter Lee Bagwell
State Senator 1926

We enjoyed respect, but we had no money. The Depression capped a series of setbacks, which had begun with the deaths of my two grandfathers. Both their wives were left with little to sustain them. Mamo Carson married again, but very much *down,* both socially and economically. Her second husband, "Pops" Bayes was a widowed barber with five children (Mamo was raising five of her own). Grandma Bagwell was left with many uncollected fees from clients her late husband had been carrying on the honor system ("Pay me, when you can afford it!") It seems that Grandfather had been fond of crisply starched shirts and of projecting a more prosperous and unconcerned image than was warranted by his actual circumstances. When he died from the flu and a ruptured appendix in 1929, the honor of his clients proved as unreliable as their memories of their debts to him, and Grandma was left in tough financial straits.

James Cavitte Carson, my father, had always been something of a hellion. In fact, when he was fourteen, he was so vexing to his parents, that they signed papers saying that he was sixteen, so he could go into the army. At this tender young age, he fought in World War I, an experience that did nothing to temper his pride or impetuousness. He came back from Europe as what today we would call a "stud"—charismatic, likable and very popular with women.

The Bagwells and Carsons had long been friends. My mother, Cornelia, was especially close to Adonia, and she was completely taken with Adonia's dashing son, Cavitte, who returned her interest. Cavitte liked military life and remained in the army after the war. Heading home on leave in the spring of 1927, he announced to his service friends that he intended to marry Cornelia. Mother was eager to accept his proposal, which had an air of urgency about it, since his next leave was a long way off, but she was in the last semester of her senior year at Louisiana Tech. She knew her parents would never hear of her marrying, six weeks from graduation. What to do? A plan was hatched, and a family myth was born.

My mother, 21 at the time, swore to her dying day that my father had kidnapped her while they were out for a drive in his Model T. He refused to take her home without an agreement to marry, she claimed, which put her in a distressing predicament.

In those days, a young girl who stayed out all night risked losing her reputation—no small concern in proper Southern society. She insisted that she accepted his proposal under duress, assuming that once she'd gotten safely home, she could always change her mind. However, Cavitte didn't take her home. Instead, he drove directly to his mother's house, where a minister was waiting to perform the ceremony. Mother never was entirely clear about why Cavitte's mother—or a clergyman, for that matter—would have agreed to participate in such an outrageous abduction. Nevertheless, everyone in the family concurred that, through whatever combination of pressures, my mother became a bride that night.

Mom's parents were devastated, but she told them a terribly romantic and melodramatic story, and she kept them from reprisals when she told them Cavitte had promised he wouldn't interfere with her finishing college, so everything would be fine.

The whole thing was fiction! Only in recent years was I able to extract a disclosure from Aunt Ruth, before she died, that the story had been fabricated with the help of Cavitte's mother. Adonia loved my Mother, and was eager to have her as a daughter-in-law. She also didn't want to miss what she saw as an excellent opportunity for Cornelia to help domesticate her wild son. Mom, apparently, was a willing part of the plan from the very beginning.

If there's something to be learned from this incident, it might be that a commitment based on a deception is not very stable. The marriage quickly went sour. The first crisis was Daddy's insistence that his bride must come with him to Fort McPhearson, Georgia. He was in charge of an ROTC training program at Georgia Tech in Atlanta, and he wouldn't hear of his new wife living apart from him for the six weeks it would take for her to graduate. Despite tears and pleading, mother went—and never graduated.

Their life at Fort McPhearson went downhill from there. A

daughter, Hazel Loraine, was born in 1928 and died within 24 hours. When my sister, Louise, was born healthy the next year, and I followed in 1931, it seemed like mom and dad had a chance for a normal family life. However, my father never made the adjustment from the life of a bachelor soldier to the life of a family man. Mother always said, "Your Daddy wasn't immoral, he was *amoral*". He just didn't accept his responsibilities as a husband and father. His gambling and carousing, and his insistence that my mother wait on his card playing buddies— who were forever hanging out at our house—all *that* was bad enough; but the proverbial straw that broke the camel's back, was when he spent all the grocery money, one week, on fireworks for the Fourth of July. Mother decided to leave him, but it wasn't until two months later, that she packed up my sister and me (I was only nine months old at the time) and went home to live with her mother, Grandma Bagwell, in Oak Grove. Mom left us with Grandma Bagwell while she went to Lake Village, Arkansas, where she could obtain a divorce in just six weeks.

When Daddy heard about her plans, he took a leave from the service and threatened to stop the divorce unless Mom agreed to let him take us. She agreed, I guess, because she had no other options at the time. Louise and I lived with Daddy and his mother, Mamo, in Jonesboro until he returned to his base and signed up for a tour in the Philippines.

After the divorce from Cavitte was final, Grandma Bagwell encouraged Mom to marry Herbie, a local boy, who had been in pursuit of "Nelia" for years. Grandma thought he would be the answer to Mother's problems. The marriage to Herbie was sudden and ended abruptly. It soon became apparent that this new son-in-law was not the solution Grandma had hoped for. In fact, he added to Grandma's burdens. Herbie couldn't get a job, so he helped "Pops" Mouser. Grandma had already given a room to "Pops", a pipe smoking, craggy old man, who did some work for Grandma and sharpened lawn mowers for just twenty-five cents in the workshop behind the rooming house. Herbie enjoyed Grandma's generosity but she wanted him to leave.

Herbie had heard that work was to be found in factories in Detroit and that Detroit had food lines for the unemployed. He wanted Mom to go with him, but she refused. Her diary reveals that she felt she had made a terrible mistake to marry Herbie, that she still loved Cavitte and she was missing Louise and me. She told Herbie that she did not love him any more. Herbie wept, but left for Detroit. She made another trip to Lake Village for her second divorce, to close that brief chapter in her life.

Shortly after mom's divorce from Herbie, Daddy returned to his base and was shipped to the Philippines. Mamo wired Mom to come get us in Jonesboro. NOW! Mamo was a very loving person, but she was prone to yelling, and I suspect we were driving her up the wall. In addition to us, Mamo had three teen-agers living at home, which would be more than enough to unnerve most parents.

In 1933, few people had cars, but Uncle Grady had a Model T convertible with a rumble seat. He took Mom to Jonesboro to get us. It was cold, but they bundled us up in the rumble seat and we returned to Oak Grove. However, our stay there was brief. Mom realized she needed to learn new skills, in order to support us, and she convinced Mamo that it would be good for us all to live with her. Mamo really liked my mother and was hoping for reconciliation with her son. Therefore, we moved back with Mamo in Jonesboro, and Mom began secretarial school. This is when my own memory begins.

Mom learned shorthand and typing, a necessity for a secretary in those days, and in 1936 she began working at the Southern Advance Paper Mill in Hodge. This is also when she obtained her nickname, *"Kit"*. Her new boss did not like the name Cornelia, and he asked if she was any kin to Kit Carson (1809-1868), a frontier scout, Indian agent, and Brigadier General in the southwest during the Civil War. (His activities helped settle the American West.) She denied any relationship, but her boss insisted the name fit her, and she was known as "Kit" Carson until she became "Kit" Henderson, after marrying my adoptive father.

My Dad, Cavitte, was due to come home from the Philippines, and mom wanted to move from Mamo's, before he arrived. Since she worked at the Mill, she was eligible to rent one of the little square four-room houses, on 1st Street in Hodge, that were owned by the mill. Most of the Mill employees lived in them, and they cost only $20.00 a month. At that time, the mill owned every house and business in Hodge. Our new home was small, but there were screen porches across the front and back of the house, and this home sheltered seven family members.

Louise & I
In Hodge, LA
1935

Mother, being the oldest of five siblings, made the plans. Grandma Bagwell, a widow then, known by most as "M.G.", had moved from Oak Grove to take care of us while Mom worked. My Uncle Grady, the oldest son, and his wife, Laurene, agreed to look after M.G.'s rooming house in Oak Grove. Aunt Edy, the middle daughter, agreed to move in with us, after getting a job at the Southern Advance Service Station for $18.00 a week. Uncle Mason, the youngest son, was the valedictorian of his high school class in Oak Grove and had a scholarship to Louisiana Tech, located in Ruston, a 20-mile commute from Hodge, so he lived with us. Aunt Ruth, the youngest of the siblings, was also tops in her junior class in Oak Grove and did not want to move, but Mom insisted Ruth leave her friends behind and move to Hodge. She still graduated as the valedictorian of Jonesboro high school (Hodge had no High School) at 16 years of age. Mom insisted that Ruth forgo her college scholarship and get a job at the Mill for just $16.00 a week. Understandably, Ruth was not happy, but in 1939, with help from "Uncle" Harry Moseley, Grandma Bagwell's first cousin, Ruth was able to attend College of the Ozarks and graduate in 1942. During that time, Mom and her siblings managed to pay the bills.

How did we all fit in such a small house? We used two rooms for bedrooms. In the front bedroom, Louise, Mom and I slept in a double bed. In the back bedroom, Grandma slept in a single bed, and Edith & Ruth slept in a double bed. On the back screen porch, Mason had the coolest area in the summer and the coldest in the winter,

Hodge was a nice place to be a child. We saw a lot of our aunts and uncles, and there was a public swimming pool only a block from our house, where I learned to swim before I was old enough to go to school. There were tennis courts, where we tried to play tennis and learned to ride our new bicycles. In Hodge we had lots of friends.

My very best friend, Jenny Beth Bennett, lived across the street. She was a year younger than I, so I started school a year before she did. The grade school was only two blocks from our house, so Louise and I always ran home for lunch, and just as quickly as I could gobble my lunch, I would dash across the street to play with Jenny Beth. We played *"house"*. We had an on-going *building* project. We would use piles of pine needles to make walls for our *pretend* rooms in our *pretend* house. We stuffed pine needles in "toe-sacks" (burlap bags), and these became chairs. Our dishes were pie tins, glasses were tin cans, and sometimes Mrs. Bennett would let us use some of her old silverware. With our active imaginations, we wrote new scripts daily. One day, Jenny Beth was the *daddy*, and I was the *mama*, and the next day we would switch.

Our dolls were the children, and we were very stern with them.

"No, you can't stay up, Mamma is tired."
"No, you can't have candy; it'll rot your teeth out."
No you can't go play; you have to clean your room."

One day, we had such a good play*time* going that I forgot to return to school. When Mrs. Bennett realized that "Stink Pot" (her name for Jenny Beth since diaper days), had not come in the house to pester her, she came out and found us having a marvelous time playing house. Mrs. Bennett asked me, "Gloria, why aren't you in school?" "Oh", I lied earnestly, "I am so good in school that Miss Carter said I don't have to come back this afternoon!" She believed me! Jenny Beth had an older sister, Clotielle, a year older than Louise. She and Louise hated it when I tried to tag along with them, so they did not bother to let me know, when they returned to school after lunch. They were delighted to let me keep playing, so I wouldn't be walking back with them.

Jenny Beth and I were still playing house when they returned from school, and we were so deeply engrossed in our make-believe, that I hadn't thought about the consequences of my actions. Clotielle felt it her responsibility to inform me. I believed every thing Clotielle said. After all, she was in fourth grade! "Gloria", she said, "when you lie and play hooky, the school can expel you, and then you will be stupid all your life!" This was my first month in school, and I did not know what "hooky" was, but I knew it must be real bad. I did know that I had not exactly told the truth to Mrs. Bennett. I was scared. I begged Louise and Clotielle not to tell Grandma Bagwell, who was watching us while Mama worked. They agreed to do something, *if* I agreed to do every thing they said. I think Louise was afraid *she* would get in trouble, if Grandma found out about my playing hooky, since she was supposed to be watching me.

They developed a plan, Clotielle wrote a note.

> *Dear Miss Carter,*
> *Please excuse Gloria from School yesterday afternoon, she was sick.*
> *Mrs. Carson*

I couldn't read yet, so they read the note to me in secret and told me to put it in my schoolbook and give it to Miss Carter the next day. I listened carefully and asked, "Why did you say I was sick, and why did you sign *"Mrs. Carson"? You* wrote the note." After that comment, Clotielle realized just how naïve I was and understood that my transgression had truly been an innocent mistake.

It was my first lesson in forgery, and the last time I ever skipped school in Louisiana. First grade was hard for me. Miss Carter was a very strict old maid teacher and she liked silence in the classroom. I did not know how to keep my mouth shut, so I received a "C" in conduct at every grading period. I didn't learn to talk well enough for most people to understand me until first grade, but, once I did, I never wanted to shut up. When some of our children and grandchildren were slow in developing their verbal skills, I didn't worry. I knew it must be heredity!

The summer of 1939, mother had the opportunity to get a much better paying civil service job in Chicago. This opportunity was orchestrated by my future adoptive father, Clark Henderson, a consulting engineer—a chemist and water-filtration specialist—from Chicago, who had been on assignment to the paper mill in Hodge. He and Mama had become acquainted on his business trips to Hodge. Their plan was for Mama to move north to work in Chicago as a secretary with the War Department, and, when she could find a suitable house, she would bring us up there. Louise and I were to move back to the boarding house in Oak Grove with our Grandma Bagwell, just for that summer, and Mama moved to Chicago.

Grandma Bagwell

While Grandma had been living with us in Hodge, life in her boarding house in Oak Grove, under the supervision of her son, Grady, had taken on a suspicious coloration. A number of dubious characters—and worse—unwed couples—had frequented the place, and it was getting an unsavory reputation. Uncle Grady was a talented artist—a wood carver, sign painter and cabinetmaker—but his creative skills far exceeded his managerial ability. Grandma reclaimed her boarding house and banished her creative son to his workshop out back.

It was summer, and Louise and I assumed we'd be returning to Hodge for school in the fall. However, things didn't work out that way. In late August of 1939, we were told that we were not going back to Hodge, but we were going to stay, for *"awhile"*, with Grandma Bagwell. We were very sad because most of our friends were in Hodge, and our mom was going to be gone for at least a year. Then in September, we received word that our dad, Cavitte Carson, still in the army, was killed in an explosion in California. Even though we had had little contact with him, Louise and I were devastated that we had lost our father for good.

The living arrangements at the boarding house were somewhat primitive. Grandma had a corner of the dining room partitioned off with fiberboard panels positioned about eighteen inches from the floor, which, I guess, was to allow for more ventilation. This created an area about five feet wide by eight feet long. In this small area, she put one twin bed and a small dresser. Louise and I shared both, which resulted in some lively arguments between us every night over where the middle of the bed was, and who was on whose side. We got a real room the next year with a double bed, but the arguments over bed space continued. In the third year, twin beds replaced the double, and we had our own *space*. The arguments almost ceased, but our room would be commandeered to accommodate one more roomer when the rooming house was at capacity. I loved those nights because then we could sleep with Grandma.

That *summer* with Grandma lasted from June 1939 to June 1944! I attended third through seventh grade; and Louise, fifth through ninth grade in Oak Grove. Grandma was an independent and resourceful person. She'd had two years of college, and it seemed like she could do anything. She was a "handyman" at a time when the concept of "Do it yourself" was not common for men, and certainly not for women. Grandma was in motion all the time. She ran the rooming house and expected our help, since she could not afford outside help. She put on trousers and did the plumbing, the wiring and all other maintenance tasks. She also tended her large garden and a small orchard we had on the grounds. I remember watching her attach burlap to the end of a long pole, soak it in kerosene, light it on fire and burn out the webworms that infested her pecan, peach, fig, pear and apple trees.

Grandma had a very limited income. Bagwell House had six rental rooms, with three of the rooms having two double beds. There was a bathroom at each end of the hall. Grandma charged seventy-five cents per night per bed, so if the patrons used both of the beds, they would pay $1.50. Thus, on nights all rooms were filled, the total income was $6.75. Unfortunately, we weren't always filled to capacity.

Mom wasn't able to send much money to help, but she vowed, someday, to take care of her Mother. Grandma would never have considered taking any sort of charity or public relief. "We may not have much," she would tell Louise and me, "but we're not poor. Poor is how you see yourself." Grandma certainly did not see herself as poor. In fact, she frequently gave things to other people, including meals for the hobos that came through town.

Grandma considered her family *special*. "We are not common. Hadn't our grandfather been the Mayor and a State Senator!" She was forever correcting our English. We never said, "Ain't", and we were to consider ourselves apart from the people who did. She would often remind us, "You reflect on your family." (A saying I would later use with my own children.) She was very careful about whom she allowed us to play with. Grandma hardly ever allowed us to spend the night with a friend.

She wasn't above letting us wear the made-over clothes Mamo Bayes (Carson) provided. Mamo was a superb seamstress. She would create beautiful clothes for us out of remnants and flour sacks. In those days flour came in 50# cloth sacks that were printed with different designs. Grandma tried to get the same design several times. She made dresses with matching bloomers from the flour sacks. I hated them! I wanted real silk panties. She could also take a man's suit apart, turn the fabric inside out and make the best-looking woman's suit you ever saw.

In Grandma Bagwell, I had a daily example of a person who met life head on. She had her frustrations, of course; like the summer when she was trying to carry a couch up the stairs to the second floor in the rooming house by herself. She had removed the cushions, hoisted the couch up on her head and started up the stairs. When she reached the top, the front end of the couch hit the wall, knocking her backwards, and she came tumbling down with the couch on top of her. We thought she had broken her back. Fortunately, Uncle Grady was home to help lift the couch off Grandma, and we called the doctor. The doctor came to the house to check her and determined that no bones were broken. Since there wasn't a hospital in Oak Grove, the doctor told Grandma to stay in bed at home until she got better. After several weeks in bed, she was still in great pain, so she was sent to the mineral baths in Hot Springs, Arkansas. While Grandma was gone, Aunt Ruth came to help at the boarding house, during her summer break from college. The mineral baths must have helped, because by the end of the summer Grandma returned and took over the Bagwell Boarding House once again.

Ruth returned to college, but her presence in the Boarding House had made that summer my best summer ever in Oak Grove. Ruth had made a game out of cleaning the house, changing the roomer's bed linens, washing the dishes and raking the yard. Ruth even let Louise and I cook—teaching us fractions at the same time. Louise did not share my opinion of the summer. Louise loved to read and the above activities interfered with her reading time. Louise thought I was the dumbest ever.

"Don't you see, she is just getting you to do all her work?" she would tell me, but I learned a lot that summer, including not to wear plaid shirts with flowered skirts. Later, Ruth wrote a poem about me for one of her classes.

> *I'm Gloria, aged nine and going on ten,*
> *I'm a blue-eyed blond, complete with a grin . . . .*

I think I grinned all summer. I forget the rest of the poem, but I still remember that she made me feel very special.

Grandma worked hard, and she was exasperated when she was limited by her sex and her height. (She was only 4'11") I frequently heard her say, *"I wish I were a man!"* She probably would have been at the forefront of the "equal rights for women" movement, had she been born a few decades later. She certainly was a survivor.

Those years in Oak Grove were about adjustment, acceptance and responsibility. It was probably the best preparation for life, I could have had. Grandma let us know she loved us; that life was not always easy; and, while we had very little money, we were not poor. I learned about the consequences of my actions. I never remember her telling us when to go to bed or when to take a bath, but after her wakeup call each morning, if we dallied, we had to run to school, because she had no car to drive us. She expected us to keep a clean room and make our beds as soon as we got up. She also expected us to get good grades, but I don't remember Grandma ever checking to see if our homework was done. I *do* remember Grandma letting me stay up until 4 AM to get a semester project done when I was only in 5th grade. The project, of course, had been assigned at the beginning of the school year.

Louise and I chose to attend church and Sunday school at

the Baptist Church, located only a block away, but Grandma rarely attended. She usually said she was too busy keeping up with the home repairs. We were never subjected to any type of conflict in the house, other than our own sibling rivalry. Back talk, sassiness, and disrespect were not allowed, and there was only one head of the household. Grandma!

For those five-years, we saw mother at Christmas when she came south, and in the summers of 1940 and 1942, we visited her in Chicago. She planned to marry Clark Henderson, even though he was 24 years older than Mom was. They were first married May 24, 1940, but then Clark found out his first wife had never gotten the divorce in 1920 when they had separated. So, after he obtained a divorce, they were remarried on November 26, 1943.

Mom's contact with Louise and me, during that time was mainly through letters. I recently found some of our letters that Mom had saved. Sibling rivalry was obviously alive and well.

Louise wrote, *"Don't get Gloria's diary as pretty as mine or I'll be jealous (you know what that spells I hope. Jealous)."*

My letter, written about the same time, said, *"Mama pretty please get my diary prettyer than Louise and she will have to go jellous will you."* My letter also included a request for overshoes. *"My shoes are 2's. Up in front before my toes is 3 inches."* Not long afterward, Mother sent a pair of black, goatskin, lace-up shoes that looked like they should be worn by a Nun. She bought them at a second hand store in Chicago. They were very comfortable, but I was so embarrassed to wear them that I walked to school through the tall grass along the side of the road, so no one would see them and I walked home the same way. I refused to wear them again.

The letters also had some interesting remarks about our conditions at the time. In a letter to Mom, Louise wrote, *"What kind of Christmas presents do you intend to get us I don't know but include in mine a good pair of gloshes. I don't know what sice but my shoes ar sice 5 ½ I think. Don't get us any underwear or night clothes or I will scream but one dress we need at least 1 good school dress. We have lots of dresses, but they are old and most have a hole in the upper part but I just put a sweeter on and go on so it isn't notisble but I would like 1 good school dress. Don't say any thing about patching. It dose not good and besides I am growing to big for lots of them they burst out under the sleves. Gloria says to get her some to and not to give mine to her. For Thanksgiving, we had bread and syrup. Grandma says Sunday week Edith and Cousin Harry and Coz Attalie are coming and we will have our dinner then. Grandma is painting the kitchen now and trying to get things in shape. There has only been two roomers in the house this week grandma say. But I rather enjoy hot biscuit and syrup."*

Our letters also contained some melancholy comments to our mother. At the end of my letter I wrote, *"Mama I do wish you could come home for Xmas, but the only way to show my love is to write you letters. Mama I love you more than the world can tell."* And Louise wrote, *"When do you think you will get to come home? I miss you and I want you to come home Really I do."*

Though I missed my mother, I consciously cultivated a bright outlook. In fourth grade, I started reading the *Pollyanna* books. Pollyanna always had something to be glad about, and that naïve positivism called out to me, even at a young age. I would reflect on my situation—on all the moving around, the long absences of my mother and all the uncertainty and hubbub of my family life—and then focus on those things for which I felt grateful *"I'm glad I have a coat,"* I'd say to myself, *or "I'm glad I have a bed."* And that was reassuring. Just recently, I re-read *Pollyanna,* and it stirred my emotions to the point of tears.

I took piano lessons from a lady named Mrs. Copeland, who had a daughter named Juanita. Juanita was much older than I was. She was in high school and was an excellent student. She was also something of an acrobat. I idolized Juanita, but what I most admired about her was her wonderful smile. It was big. It lit up her face. It was the first thing you noticed about her, and the thing you most remembered. I was in fourth grade, and I can recall asking Juanita why she smiled all the time. Her answer struck me deeply. "No matter what you look like," she said, "if you smile, you're beautiful." I don't know if Juanita had discovered that truth for herself, or it someone had passed it on to her, but she understood one of the most basic secrets of what today we would call having a "positive self-image." It occurred to me, later, while looking at myself in the mirror, that I really *did* look better when I was smiling. It even made me *feel* better. So that night—before prayers—I resolved that I was going to smile more. This probably was responsible for the nickname, "Sunni", that I acquired in college.

Mom wrote often, and on her Christmas visit in 1943, she had a special surprise. She told us she had married Clark, and that we would be joining them in June at the end of school. Years later, after mother died, I was reading her journal and found that mother and Clark had initially *pledged* themselves to each other prior to their first marriage in 1940, so they were actually married *three* times. Three times is a charm, I guess, because their marriage lasted 29 years!

Chapter Seven

(Gloria)

GLORIA IN SUBURBIA

Finally, in 1944, Mama was prepared to bring us north, and Clark finally agreed that we were old enough. Mama had been reluctant to make her daughters live in the big city, so she and Clark had saved $2294.47 to make the down payment on an $8,500, 100 year old, five-bedroom house in Wheaton, Illinois. Wheaton was a small suburb twenty-five miles west of Chicago, with a population of 7,000. No one had lived in the house for three years. The yard was waist high in weeds, and there was dried kitty poop on every hardwood floor in the house. However, Mama had a dream of bringing her daughters to a home in the suburbs, and her dream was coming true. Louise and I were very excited. We drove up from Oak Grove with Aunt Edy and arrived at our new home at 1:30 PM on Sunday June 4, 1944. (I found these details in Mama's diary.) Grandma waited in Oak Grove for the moving van to arrive. Actually, the moving van did not arrive until June 19, when Mayflower moved 14,300 pounds of furnishings from Oak Grove to Wheaton at a cost of $861.66. (The diary again) Mama did not realize there would be so much, and she had to borrow $300 from Edy to finish paying the movers. We were thrilled! There was lots of work to do: floors to sand and refinish, weeds to pull and windows to wash, but this was fun, and we were with our mother again on a fulltime basis. The nights were cool—a pleasant change from summers in the South. We camped out on the floors, waiting for the furniture to arrive and discovered that hardwood floors are HARD. Grandma and Uncle Mason finally arrived with the furniture on June 26, 1944.

319 N. Cross St.   Clark & Mama
In Wheaton, Illinois

My life was transformed! One day I was living in a boarding house in rural Louisiana, and the next day I was a Northern, middle-class, suburban teenager.

How do you get acquainted in a new town in the summer time? The lady at Allmart Realty suggested Mom get a season pass for the family to the public outdoor swimming pool. What a blessing. My first day at the pool, I met Eileen Lacey, and she introduced me to her younger sister, Mary Jane. Mary Jane was my age and became my new best friend. We both loved swimming, and we spent many hours at the pool together.

At age thirteen, I had a mother, a father, and a real home. I even had *my own room*. I could have friends over, which was never possible in the boarding house. My ongoing responsibility at home was to keep my room neat, and Louise and I got an allowance of $5 a week for doing the weekly cleaning. What a change! In Louisiana, Grandma had no money to pay us, but we'd been cleaning, doing the wash, making the guest's beds (with proper corners, which Grandma would inspect closely) and emptying slop jars. All of that was behind me. I was in heaven.

One dark cloud appeared over our lives just a few months after we made our move north. Grandma Bagwell had come to help take care of us in our new home, and she obtained a job working at the main post office in downtown Chicago during the Christmas season. She was thrilled at the opportunity because she liked to earn her own way. The post office asked her to stay on a couple weeks more after the holidays, and she was heading for her night-shift job one evening, when a tragic accident occurred. She had to cross the Northwestern Railroad tracks to catch her train. A train from town was coming into the station, and she decided to go around the rear of it when it passed and cross the adjacent tracks to catch her train into town. When the train passed, she stepped out, not realizing that another train was coming from the opposite direction. She was struck and killed instantly. We were all stunned—I especially. I was 14, and the woman who had raised me and provided such a strong foundation for my life was gone. It was the final closing of that chapter of my old life.

My new father, Clark Travis Henderson, was a fascinating man. He was a genius, with a photographic memory—a chemical engineer who also held an electrical engineering license. He was an inventor, and he was a wonderful storyteller. He claimed that he had read the Merck Manual (the handbook for physicians) and had passed the licensing exam for physicians in Canada. I could never be sure if that were true, but knowing him, it was certainly possible. He was the primary developer of Bromicide, a chemical treatment for swimming pools that could also be used to cure "athlete's feet".

Clark could have been a wealthy man. He normally made seventy-five dollars a day consulting—good money at the time. I can recall him talking about one assignment where he earned seventy-five dollars per hour. Therefore, we had a comfortable life in Wheaton. My new father provided well for our family; eventually putting both Louise and me through Stephens College, a two year private girl's school in Columbia, Missouri.

However, academics didn't go so well for me in school—at least not at first. If I had stayed in Oak Grove, I would have entered 8th grade, which was the first year of high school there. You graduated after the 11th grade in Oak Grove. In Wheaton you graduated after the 12th grade. Louise had finished 9th grade and would have been starting her junior year in Oak Grove. Therefore, she enrolled as a junior in Wheaton (the 11th grade), thus skipping a grade. I decided, quite on my own, that I too would skip a grade. I didn't want to fall any further behind my sister in school, so I took advantage of some uncertainty about my status and enrolled as a freshman in high school. I had been a straight A student since 4th grade, but by skipping, I missed taking 8th grade English and Math, and the studies were a lot tougher in the Wheaton schools. I found myself enrolled in Latin, Algebra and English courses I was not prepared for and dropped from my customary A's to C's and even a D in English my first quarter. I was devastated! I cried and cried.

Fortunately my parents understood. "You're just getting adjusted," they encouraged me. "Don't worry about it. You didn't realize how different the schools would be." Eventually, I sharpened my study skills and did better. I did make the honor roll by the end of high school, but it took me all four years.

Meanwhile Louise was reborn. She made a new beginning with our move to Wheaton. No one knew what a pain she'd been in Oak Grove. She became a dream sister. She was suddenly the charming Southern girl with the delightful magnolia accent who attracted boys like flies. As the new girl in town, she won the lead in the junior play. This, combined with my poor grades, briefly put my nose out of joint.

However, Pollyanna was alive and well. I adjusted to my changed circumstances and felt blessed to finally have a normal family life. I was perplexed hearing my new friends quarreling with their parents and grumbling about the rules they had to follow. I related well with Mary Jane because I never heard her complain about her parents and my relationship with Mama was great. Mama turned out to be a great Mom, despite her years away from Louise and me. I knew where I stood with her, and I was smart enough not to argue.

Mama allowed us to have a party every week if we paid for the soft drinks and popcorn with our allowance, cleaned the house before and after the party, made sure the guest were gone by midnight and had ABSOLUTELY no alcohol or smoking. I loved it. I usually had a party at least once a month that frequently ended with a slumber party for the girls after the guys left.

There were about 8 to 10 girls in the group I hung out with. I was on the outer circle of this group, but they loved the fact that my mother was always home and allowed us to gather there on weekends. Mama was also very out-spoken and eager to share books and articles on proper behavior. My friends were constantly asked by her, "Have you read this?" If they hadn't, she was happy to share it with them. I think she was trying to make up for those lost years of parenting. Many of the girls had been friends with each other since grade school, so I was a newcomer, but they were all very nice to me. My best friend was Mary Jane Lacey, who seemed to be the best friend of many people.

Mary Jane helped educate me in the ways of the North. We both tried out for cheerleading at the end of our freshman, sophomore and junior years of high school. We would practice, practice, practice, and I would be sore from all the stunts we tried. Mama would laugh at us laughing. We would giggle at everything. Every year Mary Jane was selected to be a cheerleader and every year I was not. It was a great disappointment to me and I cried, but I survived. Other people encouraged me by telling me I was really better than some of the girls selected.

I did get elected to the Student Council, and was eager to work on a lot of committees. Whenever volunteers were needed, I was usually the first to raise my hand. Senior Class Nite was a big event each year for the seniors. However, in my senior year it precipitated a challenge to my integrity that I still remember. Everybody in the senior class could be in the show, but every person or group had to get their own act together. Our group of girls decided to do a "can-can" routine and because we did not have an even number of girls, we invited another girl to join us who didn't normally hang out with us. A few days before the event, I was called to the principal's office. Since I was involved in the preparations for Senior Class Nite, I had no apprehensions as I bounded into the office with a big smile on my face. The office people weren't smiling! I became concerned when I was taken into the principal's office and the door was shut. Although this happened 54 years ago, I can still remember being confronted with, "If you confess, we will not press any changes against you."

"What are you talking about?" I asked, completely baffled.

"Don't deny it because we have proof that you did it."

I turned to Mr. Burger, the principal (who, I thought liked and trusted me) and pleaded for an explanation. Mr. Burger said, "I'm really very disappointed, Gloria, that you would do something like this, but your handwriting is the only one that is even close." He handed me a note with printing on it that read, "Can't you see you are not wanted in our class night dance. Why don't you drop out, or are you just too dumb?"

I was the only one of our group that had taken Mechanical Drawing, and the note was lettered in the style taught in that class. Therefore, their conclusion was that it had to have been sent by me.

The note had been stuck into the locker of Joan Hoffman (the sheriff's daughter), the girl we had invited to join our routine. What a cruel act. By whom? I knew it was not me. I could also not believe that anyone else in our group would have done it because we needed Joan for our routine. The administration didn't believe me, so to prove my innocence; I offered to take a lie-detector test. The school officials agreed to set one up.

My parents were furious about the accusation and expressed their concerns to the administration. Thankfully my parents believed me, but I was so nervous, I failed the lie-detector test! (I understand why lie-detector test results are not admissible as evidence in courts of law.)

I don't know what went on behind closed doors, but a few days later the matter was dropped, Senior Class Nite went on with Joan in our dance routine, and we all tried to make her feel welcome. The mystery was never solved. Possibly it was just a prank but I am so thankful that I had earned my parents trust. There are few things so devastating as not to be trusted—a point we often stressed with our own kids. It takes years to develop trust and just a few moments to lose it.

Mothers' one idiosyncrasy was the way she managed the household budget. I don't know if it was a reaction to our newfound affluence, after years of pinching and stretching, but my mother developed a very good credit profile. With every remodeling, she would re-mortgage the house so the bills could be paid on time, but she never had any cash. Mother tithed with the belief that the Lord would take care of her. And the Lord did.

Wheaton was a community of contrasts. On the one hand, it was a typical, suburban bedroom community with nice homes and good schools. At the same time, it was an active center of Christian fervor, with numerous evangelical movements centered around Wheaton College and several major Christian publishing houses which had headquarters in town. (Wheaton

College was the alma mater of evangelists like Billy Sunday and Billy Graham.) In the 1940s, the proselytizing was very aggressive. It seemed like every week someone would come up to you on the street, hand you a tract, and ask, "Have you found Jesus?" (The favorite teenager response was, "Is he lost again?")

Most people in Wheaton, however, practiced their religion in typical, middle-class moderation. Jim Lane, who attended the College Church and later Wheaton College, was our class president, and after graduating from college, he went on to become vice president of the Chase Manhattan Bank. He is a wonderful example of someone achieving success without compromising his values.

I never questioned *my* faith. I had accepted the Lord and was baptized at twelve in Louisiana. I attended Sunday school and church regularly at the Baptist Church, and I went to all the revivals that came to town. I often admonished my worldlier sister for dancing or going to movies on Sundays. "You'll be sorry, when the Lord comes," I'd warn her.

However, in Wheaton, I attended the Methodist church, and I encountered a different spiritual climate. The congregation seemed to lead decent Christian lives and didn't condemn smoking, dancing, playing cards or going to movies on Sunday. Could Louise have been right? Just what *was* so bad about dancing and going to movies on Sunday? Even more disconcerting, Clark, my new father enjoyed the occasional drink—*hard liquor*. I could see he wasn't a drunkard or an immoral person, and he had even offered *me* a taste. He said that he'd rather I satisfy my curiosity at home, rather than sneaking drinks on the outside. It was the beginning of a time of deep questioning on the "doctrines" of the Baptist church.

My best friend, Mary Jane Lacey, was Catholic, and, out of curiosity, I asked her once if I could attend Mass with her. I found the experience surprisingly moving. This was a style of worship unlike any church service I had ever seen. There were candles and incense, and the priest spoke in Latin (it was the forties, years before the liturgical changes of the Second Vatican Council). I wanted to be a part of this. To help me appreciate the Mass, I was given a St. Joseph Daily Missal. On the left page was the Latin and on the right page was English. It took me quite a while to learn how to use it, but after I did, when I entered any Catholic church, I felt a familiar presence of the Lord. There was an aura. It was a sense of reverence, holiness and sacredness. Even before Mass began, there was silence. There was none of the casual chitchat that went on before the minister arrived in the protestant churches. Before Mass, some parishioners would be on their knees praying. There was something special. I felt the Lord's hug and I wanted to belong. I began attending Mass regularly with Mary Jane.

I also dated a very nice Catholic boy from a wonderful family, and through them I learned even more about Catholicism. I discovered that the Church took a very balanced stand on wearing make-up, dancing, playing cards and going to movies on Sunday. These practices were not considered immoral. There were clear moral lines, to be sure, but even the Protestant Churches held those. The key was moderation and developing a controlling conscience. You didn't need to live in fear. If you obeyed the Commandments and were honest with yourself, you wouldn't have to worry about going to hell. I found the Catholic view refreshingly upbeat.

I began to sense an actual *call* to the Church, and I took formal instruction in the Catholic faith during my first year at Stephens College at Sacred Heart Church. I lived in Oakcrest Hall my first year at Stephens, and one of my dorm mates was Pat Laxdal from Eugene, Oregon who was also dating a Catholic. During that fall of 1948, she and I would walk over to the rectory each week and Father Flood would go over a part of the catechism for just the two of us. The issue of birth control— and the Church's firm opposition to it—came up in the discussions, and I saw absolutely no conflict with my views. I had already decided I wanted twelve children. Finally, on

Saturday April 16, 1949, I was baptized a Catholic at Sacred Heart and the very next day, Easter Sunday, I received my first Holy Communion during the 10 AM Mass. It was a scary feeling of surrender to the Lord's will, and I wondered if I was really worthy to receive the body and blood of the Lord? I felt loved and protected by Christ, and I wanted to always keep that feeling. I loved starting my day with early Mass. I was blessed to have the opportunity to attend Mass almost every day for the next two years because, during the summer, I could attend an early morning Mass at St. Michaels in Wheaton.

I tackled college life with gusto. I waited tables in the campus dinning hall my second year at Stephens, and I always preferred the early shift, because I got up early to go to daily Mass. Girls dragging into breakfast would see me and with more than a touch of irritation in their voices, ask, "How can you be so *happy* in the morning?" It was fun.

All my friends at college had nicknames, and I wanted one too. My last name was "Henderson", since Clark had legally adopted Louise and me in 1945, but "Henderson" didn't seem to have very much nickname potential. I didn't want to be called "Sonny," which was a boy's name, and certainly not "Henny". Someone observed that I was always sunny and suggested the nickname, "Sunni". From that point on, my signature was "Sunni" plus a little smiley face. This was years before the smiley face became a popular sticker. When anyone phones and asks for *Sunni*, I know it is a Stephens College friend.

With my conversion to Catholicism, I began to have a deeper awareness of God in my life. It wasn't a feeling that I'd been changed—that I hadn't had God in my life before and now I did. Not at all, because I knew I'd been as much of a believer when I was a Baptist as I was now that I was a Catholic, but I felt a new confidence that God would guide me and protect me and give me strength, no matter what I might have to deal with. It was a confidence, which would be tested often, but at the time I couldn't have known how. The challenges of helping my husband achieve his dream, of raising a dozen children, and of charting my faith journey through generation gaps and other struggles, lay ahead.

Chapter Eight

(Bud)

FATHER KNOWS BEST

My childhood experience was worlds apart from Gloria's. I was born in 1926, the second of four boys, in Lockport, New York. Judd, the firstborn, was three years older than I, and my parents had lost their second child, Rosemary, in infancy a year before I arrived. In Lockport, Dad was teaching and coaching high school football, a career he had started at Marino City and Albion High Schools in Michigan after graduating from Michigan State University (then called Michigan Agricultural College) with a degree in Animal Husbandry. He had been born in Chicago in 1896, the oldest child of Taylor and Rosa Vear. Taylor was one of four brothers who immigrated to the United States from England in 1875. Taylor and Rosa had one other child, a daughter, Elizabeth ("Babe"), four years younger than my father. Taylor died of cancer when Dad was only ten years old, so I never knew my grandfather. Apparently Dad didn't know him very well either, because he remarked one time that he couldn't ever remember his father talking to him. His father left early in the morning and worked until late at night in order to make a decent living. This was in the days before government welfare programs, so hard work was necessary for survival, and the job consumed most of the waking hours of his day.

Dad's mother I remember well. Left with two children to raise by herself, she never let the fact that she was a woman restrict her activities. Although she performed the usual household chores and braided oval rugs out of rags, she much preferred to work outside in the yard. Even though she lived in a residential neighborhood in Beverly, on the south side of Chicago, she raised chickens in her back yard, and she tried to teach me how to chop off their heads and pluck their feathers. While she accomplished the killing with one accurate and decisive blow with the hatchet, it usually took me several tries. (I didn't want to hurt the chicken!) Actually, my approach only extended the chicken's suffering. Grandma Vear was a throwback to the Pioneer women of Colonial days, and one day, when I was still in grade school, I made the mistake of listing "Indian" as part of my genetic ancestry. Someone in the family had made the comment that Grandma worked like an Indian, and I thought it would be neat to list that in my heritage. Grandma was not amused, and she assured me emphatically that she was *not* part Indian!

Dad lost his job in Lockport during the start of the Great Depression and returned to Chicago with his family to live with his mother in her large home in Beverly. Jobs were scarce, and he worked for a while in the nearby Chicago Bridge & Iron Steel Mill at $24.60 per week to keep food on the table. In 1928 he landed a job with Swift & Company, a meatpacking firm headquartered on Chicago's south side, from which he would retire 40 years later. Swift sent him back to the northeast for training in sales, and, for a short time we lived in a cottage in the mountains of Rutland, Vermont. I was probably four or five at the time and one of my earliest memories is begging to sleep on the screened porch during thunderstorms. I'm not sure what the psychological significance of this is, but I think it has a hereditary component. Many years later my father stood at the back door of his farmhouse in Marengo, Illinois watching a tornado pass through his back yard!

We lived in Rutland only a short time; then Dad became a regional director for Swift, and we moved to East Orange, New Jersey. My only memories there include a wonderful attic with all kinds of "treasures" and a garden that we planted and left behind before the crops were harvested. (Perhaps this explains why my gardens always end up with overripe tomatoes still on the vine.) I must have started my formal education in East Orange, but I remember nothing about school there. Swift moved Dad back to Chicago in 1932 when I was in second grade and we rented a two-story stucco home in Wheaton, a suburb of 7,000, 25 miles west of Chicago. Dad was one of the many men, living in Wheaton, who commuted to Chicago. He never liked to be called a salesman, but he traveled a lot, calling on hotels and restaurants to make sure they were happy with Swift's meat products. I would call that "sales", but Dad preferred the term "public relations".

Dad

Even though we lived in town, many of my early memories

of Wheaton relate to animals. "King" was a large, friendly collie we had, and, when Dad brought a goat home from the stockyards for a pet, we called him "Smokey" and created our own backyard hunting adventure. King became a mountain lion, stalking the goat around our large back yard, and we, in turn, would stalk King and "capture" him before he could catch the goat. Smokey and King acted out their adversarial roles well, even though they were great friends. Smokey was a frisky, friendly goat that was not above a bit of mischief. One time, as mother was bending over, he butted her from behind and sent her sprawling. He also would chew on anything he could reach, including the metal light fixture on my bicycle, which he reduced to a twisted, useless jumble of tin.

Smokey finally succumbed to too much human kindness. During an unusually cold winter, while Dad was out of town, we decided to put the goat in our unheated, unfinished basement to keep him out of the bitter cold. When Dad called, and we told him what we had done, he assured us that goats can tolerate the cold just fine and insisted that we put Smokey back out in the garage. Unfortunately, Smokey had become acclimated to the warmer basement, and the next morning we found him frozen to death on the floor of the unheated garage. Dad felt terrible, and we had a tearful burial service in the backyard for our beloved goat—and our backyard mountain lion adventures ended.

We had canaries and other dogs, but our most unusual pets were alligators! Dad sometimes had to travel to Florida, and from one of these trips he brought home a couple of 12-inch alligators. (Fortunately, they grow very slowly!) Dad built a small cement pond for them in the back yard, and this was fine during the warm summer months. In the winter, however, we brought them inside and turned them loose in the house. This resulted in some startling encounters for visitors. We would be having a quiet conversation in the living room when an alligator would suddenly appear from under a chair. When our visitors recovered from their initial shock, we tried to reassure them that the creatures were harmless. This was not always sufficient to keep them from leaving early. I'm sure, they carried some wild tales to their friends, but we simply thought we had some unique pets, and we delighted in showing them to our friends (or *frightening* them, when appropriate). The alligators liked the warmth of the radiators, so, when one disappeared (this happened often), we could usually find him under one of the hot water radiators. We offered them hamburger meat, but they didn't eat much, required little care and were quite clean.

Others did not always share our perception of our pets. One summer night, when the alligators were in the outside pond, it rained and the pond overflowed. One of the alligators disappeared, and, three days later, a lady six blocks away reported to the police that there was a DRAGON in her front yard! The police heroically "captured" the creature and returned him to us. Only in a small town would police know the owners of strange pets. The alligator had apparently fallen into the storm sewer in front of our house, enjoyed a nice swim, and had exited the sewer in front of the lady's house. Sometime later, after another rainstorm, the alligators disappeared for good. They are probably quite large by now!

Dad should have lived on a farm, but the first home he bought for $7000 was a large, six bedroom white frame house, surrounded by a big porch in a nice old residential neighborhood only a few blocks from downtown Wheaton. During World War II, to help compensate for the strict rationing that was in effect, Dad fenced in a part of the backyard, built a chicken coop and brought home 100 chicks. (Shades of his mother!) Meat and eggs were both rationed at the time, so this greatly enhanced our food supply. Zoning restrictions were either not in place or were not enforced because "victory gardens" were common sights in city backyards.

After the war, Dad converted the chicken house to a stall for two thoroughbred racehorses he had purchased. (Remember, this was right in the middle of a residential neighborhood!) Thoroughbred racing was a favorite hobby of Dad's, and he often went to Arlington Race Track in Chicago to wager on the horses. He enjoyed the challenge of gambling and played poker with his friends every Friday night, but I don't remember the family ever suffering from his losses. I was not aware of any success he had with racehorses he owned, until recently when I found several pictures of his horses in the winners circle. While the horses were housed in our back yard, we all were involved in their care. During the cold winter months, Mom would make warm "mush" for us to take out to them, and it was our job to keep the stalls clean. That onerous task eliminated any desire I might have had to own a horse.

The horses occasionally escaped from their enclosure and wandered around the neighborhood, so Dad wisely (and perhaps with entreaties from the neighbors) decided to board the horses at a stable out in the country. The horses needed to be exercised, and one day Dad decided I should be the rider. It was a disaster! I was about 12 at the time and, not only was I not skilled in riding, but this high-strung, half-ton animal, which quickly recognized my fear, also intimidated me. Dad helped me into the saddle and led the horse around a very small exercise track. Then he let go of the lead rope and I was on my own. Or, rather, the horse was on his own! Suddenly he started galloping toward a fence at the end of the enclosure. The horse stopped suddenly in front of the fence, but I didn't! After picking myself up on the other side, I quickly convinced my father that I was much too big to be a jockey.

Although Dad's job often took him out of town on business trips, that job also shielded our family from most of the jolts, which the Depression had brought. We lived a comfortable middle-class life at a time when many families were living on the edge. I don't think any of us boys realized, at the time, how fortunate we were. In spite of all his travel, Dad was still a strong presence in the household. We seldom intentionally disobeyed him, and when he was going to be gone for a few days and left us with chores to do, we would scramble (usually at the last minute) to get them done before he returned. Of course, he always found something we had neglected or hadn't completed to his satisfaction, so we seldom achieved his full approval. In those days, school counselors and government social agencies did not undermine or question parental authority. We knew what was expected of us, and we understood the consequences of not living up to expectations. Obedience was the norm, not the exception.

John (3), David (8), Bud (13), Judd (16)
1939 in Wheaton, IL

While Dad was the authority figure in our home, mother was a full-time, stay-at-home mom who involved herself intensely in our lives. It was Mom, who hovered over us at our studies, counseled us through our formative years, explained the birds and bees, and took us camping.

Boy, could she camp! Mom went everywhere with us, and

each summer we went traveling or camping for a month or more. John, our youngest brother, 10 years younger than I, came on the scene too late for most of these summer excursions, and he was generally left behind with mother's Auntie Fitzpatrick. So, most of our trips involved only my older brother, Judd (3 years older), my younger brother, Dave (5 years younger), and myself. We'd depart with our old Gilkey pop-up trailer hitched on the back of our 1934 Buick. The camper was an early model of the fold down trailers of today. It allowed good rearview mirror visibility on the road, a place where supplies could be stored inside, and when we arrived at a campground, we would unfold it to create a double bed on each side with a small area for cooking in between. It was certainly not elegant, but campsites were a dollar or less a night, so it was an inexpensive way to travel. The first trip I can recall was to Mammoth Cave, Kentucky, and I remember my fascination with the stalagmites, stalactites and subterranean lakes as we hiked through the vast network of underground caves. This was followed by trips that were more extensive.

When I look back on those summer excursions from the perspective of a parent, I'm awed by my mother's courage and spirit of adventure. It must have been difficult for her, without Dad, but she never made it appear so. She made our summer vacations special, and we saw much of the Country at a time when cross-country family trips were uncommon. Money was very limited, and I can remember our stops at Western Union offices (no ATMs then!) so Mom could pick up money that Dad would wire ahead. If the money hadn't yet arrived, we would find the least expensive campsite and stay there until it did.

One year we traveled to the East Coast to watch paper money rolling off the presses at the Mint in Philadelphia. We walked up the steps of the Washington Monument and the Lincoln Memorial, spent a day at the Smithsonian Institute and viewed New York Harbor from the lamp of the Statue of Liberty. The next summer we camped our way across eastern Canada. We drove down the world's narrowest street in Quebec City, and I can still remember poor children reaching through our car windows from their doorways asking for money as we passed. The following summer we pulled a small upright trailer 6000 miles on a long journey to the West Coast. From the Black Hills of South Dakota, to the bears of Yellowstone National Park, from the majesty of the Grand Canyon to the Golden Gate Bridge, mom exposed us to most of the tourist attractions west of the Mississippi. On this trip Dad actually joined us for a couple of days in the Black Hills; the only time I can remember him being with us on a summer vacation trip.

Mother did not seem to have the slightest concern about being a lone woman on the road with three sons, and that was before interstate highways, rest stops and camping resorts. She did all the driving, (Judd was still too young), and she was not intimidated by people or circumstances. Once, during our Canadian trip, we were headed out to the Gaspe' Peninsula in Quebec, and when we stopped for gas, the attendant asked, "Lady, where are you going? You can't take those kids out there by yourself. There aren't many gas stations or restaurants, and everyone speaks French."

She just answered, "Why not?" And she did! We enjoyed bakery goods purchased at roadside stands, traveled the road along the St. Lawrence River and, fortunately, completed the trip without any major mishaps.

Strong as she was, Mom was also warm and infinitely maternal. She understood the importance of teaching us some of life's important lessons. Her camping routine was relaxed but very organized and when we arrived at a campground, our first task, before we went off to explore the area or meet our new neighbors, was to set up camp. We each took our turn at cooking, washing dishes, gathering firewood and cleaning up the campsite. She was insistent that the campsites look better when we left than when we arrived. She made friends easily with other campers even though we might be at a place for only a night or two. She made camping fun, but she also helped us realize that everyone had to contribute his fair share. "Positive Affirmation" was a technique she used long before it was promoted in self-help books. She *expected* us to do the right thing. She raised us using a *common sense* approach, which is so *uncommon* today. We were reminded often that *we* were responsible for our own behavior, and she wasn't at all sympathetic with any attempt to blame others for our transgressions.

This didn't mean that we always used good judgment. On the Quebec trip, Judd and I decided to go climbing up the face of a cliff along the St. Lawrence River. We left David at the bottom to watch us, and to run for help if we got in trouble. We reached a six-inch, natural ledge about 80 feet up and couldn't find any more footholds to climb the remaining 30 feet to the top. We also learned a lesson in mountain climbing. It is easier to climb *up* a mountain than it is to climb back down. What to do? There are some occasions in my life when I would like to re-wind the clock to undo a crisis I have created for myself. This was one of those times. Large boulders awaited us below if we fell, and the ledge on which we were standing was broken away in spots. We perched there, flattened against the wall, clutching a small tree to keep from falling backward and considered our options. We had to threaten David with his life to keep him from running to tell mother about our predicament. She would not have been happy. There was a clump of trees about 40 feet off to one side, and we decided trying to reach these trees was our best option. Judd suggested I go first! He told me he wanted to watch me, so he could offer help if I needed it; but I suspect I was really the experimental guinea pig. I surveyed the rocks below, determined that I probably would not survive a fall, said a quick prayer, tried to control my fear and then slowly inched my way along the ledge until I was close enough to jump and grab a tree. Judd followed and also made it successfully. When we both got safely down to the bottom of the cliff, we breathed a sigh of relief and decided it was better not to share this adventure with Mom just yet. No need to worry her, we reasoned, but, more importantly, we were concerned about the consequences. We did finally tell her, later in the trip (when David wasn't around), and we made it sound exciting and heroic. And, of course, we assured her that we were *never* frightened and always in control.

The summer we spent six weeks traveling to the West Coast produced two more life-threatening experiences. The first occurred when the Buick's engine stalled on a steep, curving mountain road. Mom tried to get it started again, to no avail, and both car and trailer began inching backward toward a perilously sharp and deep drop-off. Mom put on the emergency brake, but it couldn't hold the combined weight of the car and trailer against the incline. She quickly told us to get out of the car, and struggled with the foot brake to keep from rolling back over the edge. We scurried around trying to find stones to block the wheels, while Mom pressed on the brake pedal so hard, her leg began to shake. All we could find were chunks of clay, which were of little help, and the car and trailer moved closer and closer to the edge. Our main concern then was whether mom could get out of the car before it went over the embankment.

Just then, a bus came up the hill. The driver saw our plight and pulled up behind the trailer to keep us from rolling any further. With the help of other motorists, who stopped to volunteer, we were able to maneuver the trailer back against the cliff wall on the side of the road away from the drop off. This timely help saved us, but without Mom's initial efforts, we would surely have lost car and trailer.

Later, on that same trip, we were just starting to descend

from the peak of a high summit, called "Camel's Hump", when one strut of our V-shaped trailer hitch broke. The trailer started to lean, pulling the car toward a steep drop off on the left side of the road. Just before we reached the edge, the other strut snapped. Our car suddenly jerked the opposite way, and the trailer flipped over on its side. Fortunately no car was close behind us. We flagged down several motorists who stopped to help us tip the trailer back up on its wheels and push it off to the side of the road. We had just restocked with provisions, and when we opened the door of the trailer we were faced with a three-foot layer of bedding, dishes, clothes and groceries. I can remember standing there and wondering what we were going to do. But mom arranged for the trailer to be towed into a small town at the bottom of the mountain, and we went to see a Shirley Temple movie while the hitch was being repaired.

In my early teen years we spent summers at Van Riper campgrounds on Lake Michigamme in Michigan's Upper Peninsula. (My pleasant memories of those summers were one of the reasons I later decided to set up my medical practice in Michigan.) I learned to dance on a cement floor to music from a jukebox in an open-air pavilion. People of all ages would assemble there in the evenings for dancing and conversation. The campers would join with the "locals" from nearby Champion and Beacon to two-step, jitterbug, and polka and circle the pavilion doing the schottische (a Scottish round dance). The Schottische was the first dance I learned (One two three hop, one two three hop, skip, skip, skip) and was a great way to meet girls (a primary objective in my early pubescent years). With my failing memory, it is, perhaps, notable that I still remember the names of Dorothy Virta and Rose Pascoe from those days more than half a century ago. They were both "locals" and helped initiate me to the joys of kissing.

I also formed a friendship with Bruce McLain during

those summers and we exchanged Christmas cards for 54 years. He died in 1994, just a month before I planned to visit him in California. After 54 years of corresponding through the mail, I had waited one month too long! I was devastated, but this experience taught me one of life's important lessons. *If a relationship is important, pursue it today.* I have reached that stage in life when memories become more important and the opportunities to rekindle them less abundant.

Mom approached everything in life with confidence and an independent spirit. A good example of that spirit was her attitude toward education. My brothers and I all attended public school—much to the chagrin of Father Epstein, our parish priest at Saint Michaels in Wheaton. He regularly admonished Mom for not enrolling us in the parochial school. Mother would respond, "You pick any four kids from your Catholic school, and I'll match my boys with them." She made no apologies and, except for one brief time, none of us attended the Catholic school. I was briefly enrolled at Saint Michael's grade school but was very unhappy and didn't last two weeks. I convinced mom that the kids that went there were from the wrong side of the tracks and would be a bad influence on me. Surprisingly, she agreed and transferred me to Longfellow School, one of four public schools in town just a couple blocks from our house. At Longfellow I completed my elementary education, met Barbara Grove, my grade school sweetheart, was introduced to theatre and sports and looked forward to fire drills when we would slide down a spiraling large metal tube to exit the building from the second floor. I enjoyed my years at Longfellow and discovered I was good in math and had no artistic ability. A junior high addition was added to the Longfellow building, so I actually continued my education in that school until I entered high school.

Mom

Mom was outspoken about her beliefs and believed in getting involved in community activities. She ran, as an independent, for the Wheaton Public School Board, and I think she was the first woman and the first Catholic ever to be elected. I didn't think too much of it at the time, but it took on greater significance when, many years later, I ran for a school board position in Hillsdale and finished dead last. Mother was involved in numerous other civic organizations, as well, and was what today we would call a "people person". She had no class-consciousness, and, when she died, the garbage man, the mail carrier, Catholics, Protestants, neighbors and members of the Country Club, attended her funeral, and many commented, "She was my best friend".

I was very close to my mother, and I marveled at her practical wisdom—like tending the punch bowl at our holiday open houses. For many years these were very popular annual events held at our large home on the Saturday between Christmas and New Years, and they always attracted large numbers of our friends and classmates. The times were staggered, so that the youngest group came first and the oldest last. Mom's duty at the punchbowl served two purposes. She not only had an opportunity to meet and talk to everyone, but her presence also made it very difficult for anyone to "spike" the punch. Ginger ale and orange sherbet was the beverage mixture of choice every year, and, even in our college years, alcohol was never served at these events. We occasionally found an empty liquor bottle discarded under a bed or a chair, but if someone was exhibiting inebriated behavior, Dad would simply instruct us to ask him or her to leave. I don't recall that we ever had much of a problem with obnoxious behavior, and, after our graduations from high school, these events became great annual opportunities for everyone to find out what everyone else was doing.

Mother dealt with our budding masculinity in a very straightforward way. There was no talk about "safe sex" or birth control. She reminded us often that it was *our* responsibility to control our youthful passions and not take advantage of our dates. For me, her "wait until marriage" message had a tremendous impact on my dating behavior. Sometimes, at home, the subject of boy-girl relationships would come up, and Dad would leave the room and say, "Talk to your mother." Dad's one bit of sex education to me was given as I was leaving on my honeymoon. He took me aside and, in a quiet, confidential tone, advised me, "Son, take it easy". I'm still not sure what that meant, but I think it was his vague effort at marriage advice.

Mom loved to converse. By 9 am each weekday she had seen Dad off to work, straightened the house, washed a load of laundry, hung it on the clothesline to dry, fixed our breakfast, gotten us off to school and was ready to talk with her friends in person or by phone. I suppose her morning conversations were that era's equivalent of today's TV soap operas for stay-at-home moms.

With all of Dad's travel, he didn't get involved in many community activities. His work schedule precluded his taking part in our extended summer camping excursions, but he didn't like camping anyway, so this was no great sacrifice on his part.

What he did like was sports. My father loved *all* sports. He exposed us to football, basketball, baseball, hockey, track, rodeos and Golden Gloves amateur boxing. He was a loyal fan of the Blackhawks, White Sox and Bears—to all of whose games he took us several times each season. I watched the Chicago Bears when they dominated pro football as the "Monsters of the Midway." One year they annihilated the Washington Redskins 73-0 in the national championship game! (The equivalent of today's Super Bowl), and I was properly impressed that Dad was on a speaking basis with the legendary Bear's coach, George Halas. When I later started playing football in college, Dad arranged for me to spend a few days at the Bears' training camp in Rensselaer, Indiana. That experience yielded some useful tips on how to play the game, but it also dispelled any dreams I might have had about playing professional football. I thought I was a better-than-average small-college football player, but, at 195 pounds, I was the smallest guy in the Bears' camp! Fortunately I didn't have to scrimmage with the team. It was intimidating enough just holding the blocking dummies while they ran their plays.

Dad never forced us to compete in athletics, but it was obvious he wanted us to. Fortunately, I shared his interest in sports and competed in some sport every season starting in fifth grade. Football, basketball and track filled my after-school hours, but in junior high (middle school now); everything but my feet stopped growing. I was slow of foot, not very big and never achieved much success in high school sports. I did manage to earn letters in three sports as a senior, but, in truth, some of the better athletes in our class were a little older and had been drafted into service before their senior year. (World War II was in full swing.) Because of this, I became the starting center on the football team and earned letters in basketball and track. Probably my most significant high school athletic accomplishment was simply *qualifying* to run on our *sprint* relay team in the final track meet of my senior year.

The other interest I shared with Dad was live theatre. He had been involved with dramatics in college and with the USO during World War I and, at one time, actually considered seeking a career on the stage. He was personally acquainted with some professional performers through his work with Swift & Co. He took the family backstage once at the Blackstone Theater in Chicago to meet Sydney Blackmer, who later played some leading roles in the movies. Dad had been in a play with Sydney some years before, and I was impressed! Dad also knew people associated with Ringling Brothers, Barnum & Bailey Circus. What a thrill it was when, at ten years of age, I shared lunch under the Big Top at a table with a group of real circus performers.

The first professional live theatre production I attended was "Harvey," which Dad took me to see at Chicago's Schubert Theatre. I was entranced by the classic tale of a lovable lunatic and his invisible, six-foot rabbit friend. I decided that stage productions were great fun. But later, when Dad suggested we go to a musical comedy, I had my doubts. Never having experienced a musical production, I assumed I would be bored by operatic arias sung in a foreign language. With little enthusiasm, I agreed to go, but when we saw "South Pacific", I was hooked on live theatre for good.

While Dad decided not to make acting his career, he did get up on stage now and then. He was well respected as a Director in the Wheaton Drama Club. Bruce Barton, who later went into professional theatre, sent a beautiful and touching letter, which was read at Dad's memorial service, in which he described the thrill of getting Dad's modest approval early in his acting career. Except for coaching a local semi-pro football team for a while, the Wheaton Drama Club was the only community activity I can remember Dad being involved in while we were growing up.

Like my father, I became more than just a theatergoer. Being a small part of a high school variety show—singing an eminently forgettable little number called "Never Hit Your Grandma with a Shovel"—convinced me that I liked to perform. Acting provided an opportunity to assume a different personality for a short time and to receive recognition in the form of laughter and applause. Acting continues to fascinate me. It is an exciting challenge, whether in small bit parts with few lines (I once played the "Mute" in "Fantastics" and had *no* lines.); or in more major roles, such as "Tevye" in "Fiddler on the Roof". It also helped me to be more comfortable in front of a classroom when I was teaching and more confident when talking to a group of people at meetings.

One of my most memorable moments in community theatre occurred after I became a Family Physician in Hillsdale. I had a small part as one of the cowboys in "Oklahoma," and had very few lines; but during a rather solemn scene, when Judd, the villain, falls on his own knife, my line, as I bent over Judd, was, "Let's get this man to a doctor." This always produced laughs from the hometown audience, who knew me, but during our last performance I embellished the line by calling out, "Let's get this man to a *real* doctor!" I had warned the cast ahead of time that I was going to enhance my line, but the resulting explosion of audience laughter forced the other cast members to turn their backs to the audience to regain their composure. "Bit" parts can be *so* rewarding.

Not only did my father pass his lifelong avocation on to me, but also this interest in live theatre has continued down through the generations to some of his grandchildren and great-grandchildren. In amateur theatre, your reward is the approval and response you receive from others. Dad understood this and one time, at the age of 78, he drove six hours to Hillsdale to watch a community theatre production of "Oklahoma" which

Gloria was directing. He had seen this show many times, and his wife, Marika, thought he was foolish to make the trip, but he came because he knew how important it was to Gloria. His approval of her production was one of the greatest compliments she could receive.

On Dad's 91st birthday, I made a surprise visit to his winter home in Sun City, Arizona. Mother had died many years before, and he had married Marika, who was with him for the last 25 years of his life. She probably extended his active life at least 10 years. Marika ushered Gloria and sister-in-law, Barb, into another room and left Dad and me alone to converse. We spent two hours talking and reminiscing about his life, and it was, unquestionably, the most meaningful conversation I'd ever had with my father. When we finished, I realized with astonishment that we hadn't once mentioned sports or theatre. Dad died two months later on March 26, 1987, and I shall always cherish that last conversation. I only wish that I had had the wisdom to record it.

With the economic security provided by father's work and my mother's spirited participation in our lives, my brothers and I had the kind of childhood that's associated more with the more prosperous '50s than with the Depression-laden Thirties. If ours could be described as "The Greatest Generation" (as Tom Brokaw did), then much of the justification for this recognition was the strength and unity of families coming out of the depression and into the challenges of World War II. "Father knows best" was the overriding mantra of many families in the thirties and forties. It certainly was for mine.

Chapter Nine

(Bud)
ANCHORS AWEIGH

In 1944, just 10 days after graduating from high school, I enlisted in the Navy. With World War II raging on two fronts, serving in some branch of the military service after you turned 18 was not an option—it was a requirement. However, patriotism was very high at that time, so serving in the military was considered more of a privilege than a requirement. Unlike the draft dodging of a later era, a 4-F classification (unfit for military service) during World War II was not a sought-after label. If you didn't enlist voluntarily, you were drafted, usually by the Army. I decided that flying an airplane was more glamorous than marching, so I filled out an application to enlist in the Naval Air Force. My older brother, Judd, was a fighter pilot in the Army Air Force, and pilots were held in high esteem. I applied for the Navy program because I thought my chance of acceptance was more promising. Dad knew Harry Kippke, the recruiting officer in charge of the Chicago office, and I thought this might be of help. Harry had been a football coach and athletic director at the University of Michigan, so, was quite well known, and I think Dad had met him while he was a student at the University of Illinois. My hopes were quickly shattered! One of the first questions posed by the interviewer was, "Have you ever been dizzy?" Trying to be impeccably honest, and having ridden on roller coasters and merry-go-rounds, I answered "yes", and he immediately rejected me. Dad called Harry and convinced him that I had no more dizzy spells than anyone else (which was true), and they let me return to complete the evaluation. I promptly flunked the eye exam!

Since I couldn't be a glamorous pilot, I decided that sailing on a ship was also better than marching, so I joined the Navy. I went to Great Lakes Naval Training Center, north of Chicago, for 12 weeks of Boot Camp, and, unlike many of my contemporaries, I actually enjoyed the regimentation of Boot Camp. They certainly fed me well. I finished Boot Camp two and a half inches taller and 25 pounds heavier than when I started! However, I was somewhat humbled when the Company Commander said that I was 1/16th of a step behind everyone else and wouldn't let me participate in the marching competition. Who ever heard of sailors marching, anyway!

Because of my interest in medicine, I applied for the Medical Corps after Boot Camp, but to my great disappointment the Navy sent me to radio school. I spent 20 weeks in Madison, Wisconsin, an idyllic location, on the campus of the University of Wisconsin, nestled between Lakes Mendota and Menona. I learned how to copy and send Morse code while in Madison, but their attempts to teach me how radios worked were mostly unsuccessful. However, in the infinite wisdom of the military, I was *promoted* to 12 more weeks of advanced radio schooling back at Great Lakes. In a class of 32, I ranked 31st! It was certainly my low point in academic achievement. The Navy *rewarded* me again by sending me for 6 more weeks of advanced radio schooling in Washington, D.C. All this training was supposed to equip me to both repair and operate radios. However, in spite of all the schooling, I remained oblivious to how radios worked, so, it's a sobering observation of military preparedness that they actually passed me.

While I was in Washington, the war ended in the Pacific (V-J Day) after the atom bombs were dropped on Hiroshima and Nagasaki. There was a big celebration in our nation's capital, which, for some reason, I chose not to attend. I certainly missed a golden opportunity to get kissed by lots of girls because servicemen were treated as heroes and the streets were filled with pretty girls, in sweaters and skirts, kissing any man in uniform.

Although the war had officially ended, my service career had not. I boarded a ship for Hawaii and spent a couple of enjoyable weeks there, awaiting further orders. To prevent boredom, the Navy even provided free golf lessons for us sailors at a beautiful seaside course. These were my first and last golf lessons, which is certainly why I don't play better golf now. We also found a nice secluded swimming beach, which the servicemen enjoyed until one day when I thought I would be lunch for a shark! I swam out about 100 yards from shore, climbed on a large piece of driftwood and was floating leisurely toward shore. Suddenly, I heard someone shouting, "SHARK, SHARK," and, when I looked up, all the rest of the swimmers were lined up on the shore, yelling frantically to get my attention and pointing to the water out beyond me. I looked around to see two fins, about 50 yards further out, slowly cutting through the water toward me. For a brief moment I thought of staying on the driftwood, but it wasn't large enough to get my whole body out of the water, and I had this awful vision of the shark removing some of my dangling parts. I scrambled off the driftwood and started spinning my arms like propellers as I frantically headed for shore. I'm sure I shattered the world 100-yard freestyle record that day, but, fortunately, the "shark" did not chase me. The fins continued to move toward the shore, but when they got close enough, we realized it was not a shark at all. It was a large ray-fish (the "fins" were the tips of the ray's wings), and it actually came almost all the way to the shore, before turning and going back out to sea. We didn't swim at that beach again!

Finally, my orders put me aboard a Navy transport ship for a lonely three-week voyage across the Pacific to China. When I boarded, I knew no one else on the ship; and for the first time in my life, I couldn't seem to make any new friendships. Most of the other sailors had boarded with men they knew, so they had their own circles of friends. At one point, I tried playing poker with a group of street-wise sailors from New York City, but I found we had little in common, so I pursued that only briefly. After that, I spent a lot of time writing letters and standing at the rail of the ship watching the ocean. There is something mesmerizing about the deep blue of the ocean and the white foam rolling out from the bow of the ship as it cuts through the ocean swells. We sometimes washed our clothes by tying them to a long piece of rope and dragging them along in the ocean. The saltwater really bleached our white sailor hats, but clothing was lost if it wasn't tied securely enough.

I did learn to be an altar server during the voyage and helped at the daily Masses, which were held on the deck of the ship, but most of the time, I had little to occupy my long days. I became seasick only once, when they put me to work painting below deck in the bow of the ship, but I don't ever recall missing a meal. The navy chow was good, for the most part, and there were only three items I wouldn't eat. One was, of all things, baked navy beans, which I still don't like. The other two items were chili and stew, which I enjoy now.

We finally reached our destination in Tsingtao, China, a coastal city about 200 miles north of Shanghai. I spent the next year assigned to the Port Directors unit there, a small radio shack located on the end of a wide pier. China had been our ally during the war with Japan and our armed forces were there to protect against any further aggression by the Japanese. The Port Director post was staffed by 5 radiomen and 5 signalmen. Our commanding officer was an Ensign, whose hobby was transmitting on a Ham Radio. Occasionally he was able to contact people in the United States, and, on one occasion, I talked with my parents from half way around the World.

Navy buddies in Tsingtao, China
1946
Jack Marrs, Tom Josephson, Me
T. Washolus, Dick Weigel, Joe Crespo

Our assignment at the Port Directors was to direct the movement of vessels into and out of the harbor. Fortunately, we used a voice circuit to communicate with the ships, which meant I didn't have to copy or decipher Morse code messages. I hadn't copied code for nine months. I was never asked to repair a radio, but on one occasion, I demonstrated my communication incompetence. I was covering the night watch for one of the signalmen, who sent Morse code messages, with a spotlight, to incoming and outgoing vessels. Usually they received no messages at night, so I felt comfortable taking that shift. While I had learned to use the Morse code with a radio key, I had not been taught how to transmit with a spotlight. That night, several spotlight signals came from ships in the harbor. My attempts at answering with my light were pathetic. For all I know, some of those ships may still be sailing around in Tsingtao harbor waiting for instructions. They surely didn't get any clear messages from me. It was a good thing the war was over!

My duty was easy during my year in Tsingtao (now called "Quindao"). There were five radiomen, so we would each work an eight-hour shift and then be off duty for the next four shifts (32 hours). This gave us a lot of free time to explore the city, but we did have to be cautious. Although the Chinese Nationalists were our allies, the Communists were in the hills around Tsingtao with plans to take over the city, and occasionally we would hear gunfire. We were issued rifles. Fortunately, we never had to use them, because my ability to use a gun was no better than my ability to fix a radio.

Postwar China was a revelation to me. Though Tsingtao had not suffered much damage during the war, sanitation was non-existent. There were no sewers, and the smell was strong enough to cause my eyes to burn. The "honey carts" would go up and down the streets, collecting human waste to be used as fertilizer. Swarms of flies bussed around the meat hanging in the open markets, and houses built along the rivers had privies over the water. The carp in the rivers would eat the waste that fell, and the local people would eat the carp. It was two weeks before I could adapt to the odor and venture forth into the city. I ate little of the native food. It was disturbing to my middle-class American sensibilities. Some of the servicemen were more adventurous and ate at the local restaurants, but, when I wanted food ashore, I visited the Red Cross canteen. It was about the only place, in town, to meet American civilians and to find reliable food. We ate most of our meals on board one of the U.S. Navy ships docked in the harbor.

When we first arrived in Tsingtao, we lived aboard the USS Ringness, the ship that brought us across the Pacific; but after a few weeks, with some "requisitioned" lumber, four of us built our own two-room dwelling on the end of the pier near the radio shack. Elmer Burns, an entrepreneurial member of our group, had, somehow, located some plywood and 2 x 4's and had talked someone into letting him have them. We didn't ask Elmer where, or how, he had gotten it, but we used it to build our home away from home. Although our little cabin would certainly not pass any building inspections, it served us well, the roof didn't leak, and it afforded us a measure of privacy. We hired an 18-year-old Chinese youth, Liu Cho Fu, as our houseboy. He kept our place clean. In addition to giving him a small wage, we would bring leftover food from the ship's mess hall for him to take back to his family. I'm sure it was probably the best food they ate. Liu was very reliable and eager to learn English. Consequently, we learned very little Chinese. He really wanted to go back with us to the U.S., but we weren't able to arrange this. I have often wondered what became of him.

During my time in Tsingtao, I attended Mass at the Catholic Cathedral in the city. These services provided a certain sense of familiarity. Catholic worship was much more "catholic", or *universal,* in the days before Vatican II. Every Sunday the same readings would be shared in every Catholic Church in the world, and they would be read in Latin. Like most Catholics, I didn't understand Latin, but sitting there, following along in my missal, I enjoyed the sameness of the Mass. A religious event of some historic importance occurred while I was in Tsingtao: the installation of the first Chinese Cardinal, Bishop Thomas Tien Keng-hsin, who was a priest at the Cathedral I attended in Tsingtao.

My one foray outside Tsingtao was to an inter-service track meet held in Shanghai. I had been a very average high jumper and half-miler in high school. However, I kept myself in shape while in China by running a couple miles along the pier each day, so, when they announced that there would be a track meet in Tsingtao, with the winners going to Shanghai, I entered. As I stood at the starting line for the half-mile, I glanced to my right, and there stood Robert Stupay, an American serviceman, whom I had raced against back home. Robert had been our conference champion in the half-mile when he ran for Naperville, a rival town seven miles from my hometown of Wheaton. And here we were, two years later, racing each other again on a track halfway around the world. Although Robert beat me in the race, I was a lot closer to him at the finish than I had been in high school, and we both qualified for the meet in Shanghai and enjoyed seeing the sights there together.

Shanghai was much different from Tsingtao. It was (and still is) one of China's largest, and most westernized cities. Neither Robert nor I accomplished much in the track meet, but the commanding officer told us, at the outset, that we were there primarily to get a break from our regular duties, so we should enjoy ourselves. We did.

In China I was introduced to rickshaws, whore houses, poverty and rice paddies. The rickshaw drivers seemed to be able to run forever, pulling their rickshaw-taxis, with little evidence of fatigue and receiving very little money for their efforts. I thought they would probably make great marathon runners, but was told, by someone, that they had short life spans, seldom living beyond the age of 35. One of their side businesses was soliciting customers for the prostitutes in town. (Houses of prostitution proliferate wherever servicemen are found.) Their English was limited, but they quickly learned enough to proposition the American sailors & marines. While the rickshaw drivers were transporting you, they would whisper in solicitous tones, "Nice *clean* girl, Joe? *Family* girl, Joe?"

My service buddies and I were rather innocent and naïve, but one day we decided to have a "look see". The rickshaw driver was more than willing to take us to see his "girls" in a "house" in downtown Tsingtao. We paid the girls a little bit, had our "look see", and left with our innocence tarnished but still intact. One of our group wanted to avail himself of more of their services, but we dragged him out with us. That was my first and last exposure to prostitutes.

The poverty in Tsingtao was unlike anything I had ever been exposed to back in the United States. Hunger was a constant companion for many of the Chinese, and I can still remember watching Chinese "Gooks" (men, women and children, dressed in black rags) forage through the ship's garbage cans on the pier, looking for edible food. They would sit on the pier and eagerly eat the stew, chili or baked beans they had salvaged. While our leftovers were probably better, and more nourishing, than what they normally ate, the idea of eating garbage was unsettling, if not downright nauseating.

When I flew the 200 miles from Tsingtao to Shanghai for the track meet, I had a chance to view the myriads of rice fields that dominated the landscape. There were many workers in these fields, tending or harvesting the rice, and I saw no machinery. There were very few roads of any kind, and the dwellings were little more than shacks. I was struck by the vastness of these rice paddies and wondered at the time how such a Country could be governed. Communication was difficult and travel routes primitive at best. This vast land, with its masses of people and its primitive transportation and communication, was fertile for the Communist take-over that was soon to follow our departure in 1946.

After 12 months in China, I finally had enough points to return home. Points were awarded for months in service plus extra points for time overseas, and the more points you had, the sooner you were discharged. When my point total was high enough, I boarded a ship and headed for home. After crossing the Pacific Ocean and passing through the Panama Canal, we were discharged at the Navy base in Norfolk, Virginia. I had been out of the Country for more than a year. It was good to get home.

My return to civilian life was somewhat bittersweet. While overseas, I had corresponded with Mildred Kearnan, a charming Irish girl I had met at a roller skating rink in Chicago when I was in radio school at Great Lakes. Our relationship could not be described as a fiery romance, but it was nice to receive occasional perfume-scented letters from a girl back home when you're half a world away. Before I left China, I used most of my savings to buy eight yards of beautiful, royal blue silk fabric, which I envisioned being turned into an elegant gown. I gave the silk to Mildred on my return, but shortly thereafter, she broke up with me, so I never did see the elegant silk gown. Mildred said she was thinking of entering a convent to become a nun. I don't know if losing your girl to the Church is worse than losing out to another guy, but it certainly makes rebuttal more difficult. As it turned out, she didn't become a nun. (In fact, she eventually married and had ten kids of her own!) My experience of losing my girlfriend while overseas was certainly not unique. At least Mildred waited for me to return home. Many servicemen received "Dear John" letters while they were still overseas fighting a war. These letters were devastating to the morale of our fighting men.

My service career had ended. I had grown physically, but, more importantly, I had met, and learned to get along with, a cross section of Americans. The experiences in China had exposed me to a different culture and had certainly given me a new respect for the USA.

Chapter Ten

(Bud)

JOE COLLEGE

I was discharged from the Navy on August 6, 1946, just in time to be accepted by DePauw University for the fall semester. The GI Bill provided scholarship money for ex-servicemen who wanted to pursue a college education, so the number of college applications and the maturity of the students increased dramatically. DePauw was a small (2000 students) Liberal Arts college in Greencastle, Indiana with a strong pre-med curriculum, and I was eager to get started on my quest to become a doctor. I remember traveling to Greencastle on the Monon train, a steam powered antique, the last week of August two weeks before classes began, so I could try out for the football team. DePauw was a Division III school that offered no athletic scholarships, so I thought, with my increased size and maturity, I might have a chance to make the team. I met some of the other football hopefuls during the train ride, but was surprised, and somewhat concerned, to find that Warny Guild, a high school teammate and friend since grade school, was going to DePauw and would also be trying out for the team. Warny was bigger and better than I in high school, and had been an all-conference center in our junior year. Since I also played center, I spent most of the games that year sitting on the bench. However, he was drafted into service before his senior year, and because of his absence, I had a chance to play regularly in my final year of high school. But what a difference in two years! He hadn't grown much in service, so when we arrived at DePauw, I was heavier and taller than he was. The memory of playing behind Warny was still there, however, so I decided to go out for end instead of center. This proved to be a wise decision because I earned four football letters as an offensive and defensive end. (Most football players played both ways in those days.) The recognition this gave me on campus was an asset on a campus with 2000 other students. I certainly had merited no recognition as an athlete in high school. College football was much more enjoyable, partly because I played more; but also I finally realized that football was more than just banging heads with people. I developed skills and techniques that compensated for my deficiencies in strength and speed. My accomplishments on the field may not have merited me any All-American honors, but one time I was flattered to be introduced by an opponent's announcer as the Leon Hart of small colleges. Leon Hart was a Heisman Trophy winning end from Notre Dame. While the comparison had little validity, it was nice to be introduced with such high praise. I remember making very few tackles in that game, because they refused to run any plays around my end.

My football career at DePauw did have a couple of memorable moments. One was catching a touchdown pass in front of my father who was walking by the end zone, arriving late for a game. Another was catching a touchdown pass and blocking a punt for a safety, to account for all our points in an 8-0 victory over Wabash, our bitterest rival, in our annual battle for the "Monon Bell". (This was our small-college equivalent of the annual Harvard—Yale rivalry.) That was the only time we beat Wabash during the four years I played at DePauw. My younger brother, Dave, doesn't razz me about this losing record because he was on the DePauw team for four years when DePauw didn't register *any* victories over Wabash.

I did play JV and Varsity basketball my sophomore and junior years at DePauw, but I was one of the "Black Five," the bottom five on the 12-man roster, and we only entered the game when it was hopelessly lost or we had a safe lead. However, I did have an interesting experience in my junior year when I started at center during our opening game against Indiana University. I think our coach started me because he wanted a football player on the floor. My task was to guard the All-Big Ten center from the year before. He was five inches taller and 25 lbs. heavier than I, so I was certainly not going to out-jump or out-muscle him. Instead, I decided to try to rattle him with constant chatter. It worked! He had a very bad night. Since a victory by little DePauw over Indiana was not really a possibility (We were just a warm-up game for them.), I continued to taunt him, and, when he became angry and threatened me, I just stood next to the referee. I was fortunate to escape with my life. We were only five points behind at the half and ended up losing by 20 points, certainly a moral victory for us. A few weeks later, I suffered a severe ankle sprain in practice, and that ended my college basketball career.

Joining a fraternity turned out to be a much more positive experience than I had anticipated. When I first came to DePauw, I had no intention of joining a fraternity. I understood they were exclusive, snobbish clubs with strange customs and bizarre initiation rituals. However, with about 75% of the men on campus in fraternities, it soon became apparent that the Greek societies dominated campus activities. I decided I was going to miss a lot of college life if I remained Independent, so the second semester I pledged Sigma Chi. My choice of fraternities was not because of their most famous fraternity song, "The Sweetheart of Sigma Chi". It was because of my friends from Wheaton, Warny Guild and Bart Anson (another high school classmate and close friend). They had already joined Sigma Chi, and so had Glen Shoptaugh, my roommate in off-campus housing. Glen was a very bright pre-med student and I thought by joining his fraternity I might acquire some of his intelligence. (It didn't work!).

Living in a fraternity house with 45 fraternity brothers taught me how to get along with a diversity of personalities, how to handle some challenging interactions and how to tolerate some bizarre initiation rituals. I can still remember crawling downstairs, on hands and knees, to the basement to put out a fire with mouthfuls of water sucked up from a bucket with bread and other soggy food floating on the surface. I also remember searching, in the dark, for a ping-pong ball buried in the coal bin—in the nude! However, although some fraternity antics were nonsensical, my membership did afford opportunities for leadership that would not have been available to me as an independent. For instance, in my senior year, I was elected as pledge trainer for the Sigma Chi pledge class, which included my younger brother, Dave.

My time at DePauw was marked by a few athletic achievements, probably more leadership recognition than I deserved and many academic struggles. I worked hard to earn B's in most courses and in the pre-med sciences I struggled to get C's. The few A's I got were, unfortunately, in courses that weren't my major. I was not a good test taker because I had difficulty with memorization (which would also be a handicap in med school, years later). I did best in math, where the emphasis is on figuring things out, rather than on recalling retained facts. I almost didn't graduate with my class! The last semester I took a course in Abnormal Psychology, and the professor, Dr. Warren Middleton, was notorious for giving difficult tests and low grades. Phi Beta Kappa's would get C's in his classes. I needed to get a passing grade to complete my credits for graduation, and I was happy and relieved to finish with a D. Surprisingly, I felt that Dr. Middleton was one of the best teachers I encountered at DePauw. I just didn't do well on his tests, which required accurate recall of everything, including footnotes.

In order to offset living expenses, I waited tables at the Kappa Alpha Theta sorority house. This was the Alpha Chapter of the very first national sorority, and their house was a white pilloried southern mansion built on a hill. For three years, I helped serve lunches and formal dinners for the Thetas. (During my senior year, I switched to doing breakfast chores at the Kappa Kappa Gamma sorority house, so I could enjoy the fellowship of supper in my own fraternity house.) Waiting tables for the Thetas was a pleasant way to work my way through college. Dinner, each night was very formal, and we waiters wore white shirts, ties and white jackets, while the co-eds wore dresses. The housemother, "Ma" Kircher, was an elegant and imposing woman who insisted on the decorum and manners that would be appropriate in a fine restaurant. Sorority girls were sometimes maligned as wealthy snobs, but I found them to be delightful and friendly. I also became well acquainted with the kitchen workers, most of whom were black—or, as we said in those days, "colored" (this was long before the term "African-American" came to prominence). It was broadening for a suburban white boy to work closely with a whole category of human beings with whom I'd had very little contact prior to college. I found these folks gracious and warm. Ada ran the Theta kitchen and Roxie was a fixture at the Kappa House. Both were lots of fun, with great senses of humor, but they also made it very clear that they were in charge in their kitchens. One of the things that struck me most vividly was how upbeat the black workers at DePauw could be, even as they endured their marginalized, late-1940's, pre-Civil Rights-era discrimination or coped with significant personal hardships.

One of the most memorable persons I met at DePauw was

Pat Buckner, the general handyman at the Theta House (though in the less-than-sensitive parlance of the time, he was referred to as the "houseboy"). Pat was one of the most courageous people I've ever known. He was going blind, but he was working to put his son, Pat, Jr., through DePauw. In fact, the younger Pat was a classmate of mine, and we played together on a championship intramural basketball team in our freshman year. His father, in his early years, had often suffered bigoted ridicule and persecution because of the color of his skin, and yet, instead of becoming bitter, he had adopted a cheerful and optimistic attitude toward people and toward life. He was one of the most generous and grateful people I have ever met, and he and I had many interesting conversations. In spite of his lack of formal education, Pat had wisdom, built from life experiences, that was profound.

Pat Buckner with some of his Thetas

Pat wrote poetry, and he was often asked by the Thetas to share his compositions with them and their guests. Just recently,

34 years after his death, a tribute to Pat appeared in the DePauw
Alumni magazine. It included the following poem.

A PRAYER FOR DEPAUW

Written by Pat Buckner for the Theta Class of 1942

*Within the vined brick walls
Of her quiet simple halls,
O God, may ancient wisdom ever rest.*

*May truths of each past age
Be her great heritage
And understanding ever be her quest*

*Yet may she feed young souls
With more than lengthy scrolls
And hypotheses by theorist decreed.*

*May her environment
The high challenge present
Of nobleness in every thought and deed.*

*May DePauw's altar fire
Cause her students to aspire
Their selfless service to all mankind give;*

*That each a live coal take
When leaving thence—and make
This world a saner place in which to live.*

All five of Pat's children attended college and Pat, Jr.
graduated with me in 1950 and later became a professor at the
University of Houston. Failing eyesight forced Pat to bid the

Theta sisters farewell in 1962. Crediting his self-education and convocations at DePauw as having "made a minister out of a houseman," his time at DePauw enabled him to take to the pulpit of a small Baptist church near Greencastle.

Pat died in 1966 at the age of 59 and wrote his own epitaph:

Although no flag for me is flung
At home or in foreign land
If I must die unknown, unsung,
Then let me die a man.

I finished at DePauw with an overall grade point average of 2.47 (B-C), so it surprised me when I was tapped for Gold Key, a coveted honorary based on scholarship, leadership and citizenship. I was one of 14 members of my class to be selected, and I think I set a new low for scholarship. (Blessedly, they didn't publish our grade-point averages). I've always suspected that one of the reasons I was nominated was that I called other students by name. I studied the college yearbook and made a concerted effort, to learn the names of people I commonly encountered on campus. I had stumbled onto one of life's valuable pearls. People like the sound of their own names. The more you use them, the more status you give them, and the more respect they have for you. (Today I often can't remember the names of good friends.)

After completing my BA degree at DePauw and shelving my dream to become a doctor, I entered the Indiana University School of Social Work in Indianapolis to pursue a Master's Degree in Social Work. Bart Anson, my classmate and close friend from high school and college, was enrolling there, so I decided to enroll with him. Social work was just achieving graduate status at the time, and the course at Indianapolis was a brand new two-year program. Since I thought I would enjoy working with kids, I selected the Group Work division. I had saved two years of my GI Bill eligibility for medical school, so, since I wasn't going to medical school, I decided to use it for my Master Degree in Social Work.

However, during the summer of 1950, before graduate school started, there were other things on my mind. I worked that summer at Camp Winona, a boys' camp in northern Indiana that was affiliated with the Chicago Boys Clubs. (I didn't realize at the time that the Boys Clubs would be my first employer after I received my Master's degree.) However, more importantly, that summer marked the beginning of my whirlwind courtship of Gloria.

Graduate school was quite different from DePauw. Overall, I found the course work boring and repetitious, and, of course, there were no sports teams or fraternities. There *was* one course, called "Health and Disease", which I did find interesting. It fanned the embers of my old dream of becoming a doctor, and at times made me wonder if I had made the right decision not to apply to medical school.

Chapter Eleven

(Bud)

EARLY MARRIAGE AND
THE INNER CITY

The combination of youthful idealism and early marriage combined to help diminish the realities of our early living conditions. This helped us survive without a welfare mentality. Owning a home, not unusual for newlyweds today, was a distant dream for most young couples after World War II. However, when classmates, friends and neighbors are sharing similar struggles, the hardships are more tolerable. We had moved out of "Pandon's Penthouse" and were living in half of a one story duplex in Indianapolis by the time our first child, Steve, came on the scene. Our accommodations were still snug but somewhat nicer and cheaper too. The rent was only $40 per month, and it was reassuring not to have to bring our new baby home to a third floor firetrap. That satisfaction was short lived. After my graduation from Indiana University School of Social Work in May of 1952, I took my first job in Chicago, and we found ourselves in marginal quarters once again.

I was employed by the Lincoln Boys Club on the near north side of Chicago. The pay was minimal (less than $300/month), but they promised an additional benefit—a place to live for minimal rent. And what a place it was! It was the second floor flat in a small, dingy, deteriorating frame building owned by the Boys Club, and it was located behind another two-flat in a neighborhood in which many buildings were being razed. The floor in our kitchen was not sturdy enough to support a standard sized refrigerator, so the Boys Club loaned us a smaller one. Our hot water supply presented an additional challenge. When we wanted hot water, we had to light the tiny water heater, and if we forgot to turn it off when we finished, hot water and steam would come out of *both* taps, and the hot water tank would be in danger of exploding. The building was actually condemned and slated for demolition, and the neighborhood was crawling with rats displaced from other buildings that had been leveled already. We frequently chased these critters off the garbage can on the landing just outside the front door. Although the Boys Club *only* charged us $20 a month, a building inspector of today would never have issued an occupancy permit.

1720 ½ N. Vine St.
Chicago, IL—1952

Fortunately, our residency at 1720 ½ N. Vine St. was temporary. Five months later we moved into another club-owned property, at 1663 N. Orchard, a neat three story brick building with twelve apartments and a big, fenced-in, grassy backyard—a rarity in the city. Mostly German immigrants populated the building. It was perfectly kept up, and each week one of the housewives on each floor would take turns scrubbing the hallway and stairs. Gloria thought this was cleaning overkill, but she took her turn in the rotation.

I was the Boys Group Director at the Lincoln Boys Club, an affiliate of the Chicago Boys Club organization near North Avenue and Halsted, and my task was to organize activities at the club that, hopefully, would turn neighborhood *gangs* into *groups*. I enjoyed the challenge, and Gloria and I were exposed to urban life, quite different from our lives in suburbia. We found that a city is really a blend of multiple neighborhoods located right next to each other. Each neighborhood develops its own personality, usually based on the predominant ethnicity there. The Boys Club was located in an interesting neighborhood, from a social work perspective. Youthful gangs would organize and their attempts to defend their *turf* would often produce ugly conflicts with outsiders. The neighborhood was undergoing a population transition with a colorful mix of nationalities—African-Americans, Italians, Hispanics, Orientals and Hungarian "Gypsies", along with the original Germans. With a Master's Degree and a salary of $3,450 a year, I attempted to develop activities that would bring the gangs together peacefully. I was not always successful, but I was young, ambitious and idealistic, and the challenge was stimulating. I felt I could make a difference, although my limited accomplishments certainly fell far short of my dreams.

I did learn a little about big city politics while we lived in Chicago. While I was there, there was a Mayoral election in which Democratic Mayor Richard Daley was running for re-election against Robert Merriman, a very capable Republican. Since I was a loyal Republican, I decided to do a little campaigning in the neighborhood on behalf of Merriman. After

I started to go door to door with campaign literature, an older man from our neighborhood visited me. He was the B*lock Captain* in Daley's very powerful political machine. He tried to talk me out of campaigning, but I told him that I thought it was time for a change and continued my efforts in support of Merriman. I received no threats, but became a little more knowledgeable about how efficiently the political machine was organized down to the grass roots level. The City was divided into precincts and each precinct was broken down into neighborhoods and then into blocks with someone in charge at each level. At election time, campaigning was just a matter of activating this team of supporters and a political party could effectively reach each voter on a very personal level. Daley's political machine was very efficient and my efforts had little impact on the election because Daley won re-election easily. My learning process wasn't finished, however. Shortly thereafter I had occasion to contact Paddy Bauler's office about something we needed done for the Boys Club. Paddy was a powerful precinct Committeeman for Mayor Daley, and he kept tight reins on his precinct, in which the Boys Club was located. I was concerned that there might be some negative repercussions from him because I had campaigned for Merriman, but there were none; and our request was taken care of promptly. I finally understood the value of the "machine". While there certainly are abuses and occasional corruption, it *is* a very efficient way to run a large city. The city is divided into manageable-sized precincts, and the needs and complaints in each precinct can be dealt with much more quickly. I don't know how else you could effectively manage the affairs and needs of the hundreds of thousands of people in a big urban population. And Daley had a very effective organization.

Shortly after I started working at the Club, I also received a lesson in working with inner city youngsters. I had driven a group of nine and ten-year-old boys in the Club bus to a nearby arena to watch a professional wrestling match. I told them that they were to return with me on the bus. Unbeknownst to me, two of the boys saw this trip as an opportunity for freedom from supervision and had no intention of going back on the bus. After the matches finished, instead of getting on the bus, they took off running. I spotted them and chased in pursuit. I finally caught up to one of them, and, seeing his friend was caught, the other boy also returned. They both went back to the bus, with appropriate admonishment from me. The real surprise came the next day when I was life guarding in the Club swimming pool. The boy I had caught came swimming and stuck very close to me. I surmised that the attention he received from me the previous day, even though it was disciplinary in nature, was probably more attention than he normally received at home from his father. It made me realize how important the Boys Club was for some of the kids in that neighborhood

I was associated with other young, energetic, idealistic social group workers. Mal Shanower, the Club Director, was our mentor, with many years of experience and a dedicated commitment to the Boys Club. He screened our program ideas, kept close tabs on the budget and dealt with complaints from the public. He was not much of a fundraiser, but he utilized volunteers very effectively. We had a tight budget and low salaries, but there was never any doubt about his commitment to serving the needs of the youth. Mal eventually became part of the Chicago Boys Club administrative staff downtown before his retirement. He set a strong example of commitment and ethical behavior.

Fred Lickerman joined the Lincoln Boys Club staff as Program Director at the same time that I arrived. He was younger and didn't have a Masters Degree, but as Program Director, he supervised me. Although I was initially disappointed that my advanced degree hadn't entitled me to fill the Program Director's job, it turned out to be the right choice. Fred had wonderful ideas, was committed to the program and had good leadership skills. He remained with the Chicago Boys Club for many years and moved up the corporate ladder to become overall Director of the citywide organization. In later years, he became an International spokesman for the Boys Club movement. He and I, along with Shig Murao, a teacher and part-time Boys Club employee, spent many hours over pizza discussing our work, and at one time we talked seriously about developing a Boys Town-like facility in the Chicago area, where troubled children could live—away from the unhealthy environment in their own homes. The idea never progressed beyond weekend camp outings at the Boys Club camp in Indiana, but it kept us focused on improving the program. We concluded that a separate facility would not help young people as much as working with them in their own environment. (By a strange coincidence, the Boys Club Camp on Lake Winona, near Warsaw, Indiana, was where I had worked during the summer that Gloria and I began our romance.)

My job at the Lincoln Boys Club posed new challenges each day, but it also produced some surprising results. One weekend we took two competing teenage gangs, the "Trojans" and the "Diablos", camping together. For most of these boys, it was their first camping experience, and we had planned many outside activities to keep them occupied and out of trouble. It rained the entire weekend! This presented a challenge. What do we do to prevent boredom and mischief for two and a half days in a rainy wilderness setting? Fortunately, we did have the benefit of sleeping cabins, and we decided to tap into their competitive instincts by inventing all kinds of indoor contests, such as volleyball over the bunks and indoor tug of war. We survived the weekend, the teens had fun and stayed out of trouble, and, surprisingly, no one complained about the weather. Actually, our success was in part related to the fact that the boys were in unfamiliar surroundings, and they found the dark woods somewhat intimidating. None of them admitted to being frightened, of course, but their bravado was much diminished. When they returned to the neighborhood, their greatly embellished "survival" stories gave them hero status with friends who had not been with them.

Sue Samuels was the Girls Group Director at the Club (Yes, there *were* girls at the Boys Club!), but her short stature was deceiving. She was a very strong presence, and the girls (and boys) learned very quickly not to challenge her. Even the rest of the staff learned to tread lightly on her turf. She ran a wonderful program, including weekly dances at the Club with help from Paula Cheney, an attractive, mild mannered young woman who was a part-time staff member. Neither Sue nor Paula was married, so they devoted many hours supervising activities at the Club.

My father wasn't so sure I had chosen the right profession after he visited me one summer weekend. A group of older teens had assembled in front of the Boys Club, preparing to *rumble* with a gang from a nearby neighborhood. I had been unsuccessful in my attempts to dissuade them, so Dad decided to exert *his* authority, and went across the street to confront them. He always commanded obedient respect in his family and among his sons' friends, but he had no impact on the Boys Club teens. In fact, they ignored him! When he came back across the street from his failed intervention, his gruff comment to me was, "Why don't you get another job!"

Sometimes parents could pose a challenge—and even a threat! In those days, you could still count on some parental support and backup for your authority, but parents could also be protective and defensive when their child got in trouble. It wasn't all smooth sailing. One day an 8-year-old boy got into a fight and used foul language at the Club, so I told him I was going to talk to his mother. The boy ran home ahead of me and made up some story about what the *mean* Boys Club worker had done to him. As I was walking toward his house, I saw this large, angry black woman coming toward me, brandishing a baseball bat. I was tempted to turn and go back to the Boys Club, but I didn't want to back down on what I had told her son. As soon as she was within earshot, I shared my side of the story and was able to calm her down before she reached me. I then suggested that she go and talk to the mother of the other child. I was hoping the two parents could resolve the conflict more amicably, but this didn't happen. I watched a shouting match between the two mothers, one on the ground shouting up and the other in the window of her second floor flat, shouting down. I decided the mothers were no more controlled or rational than their sons.

Another time, Mal Shanower and Fred Lickerman came to rescue me when I went to talk to some "Gypsy" parents. We had just completed a basketball tournament at the Club, and the Trojans, a talented team of Italians, had won the tournament by beating the Dukes, a team of Hungarians. The Hungarians were referred to as "Gypsies" in the neighborhood, which, I suspect, was not considered a complimentary label. In my dealings with them, I found them to be very agreeable as long as things were going their way, but they could be very combative if things went against them. Fifteen-year-old Louis "Greeny" Polo was the intimidating leader of the Dukes. In fact, during the game, when he started dribbling the basketball toward the opponent's basket, everyone got out of his way. He scored lots of points, but his supporting cast was less talented, and the team less organized, so the Trojans had won. The next thing I knew, Greeny was gathering his teammates in the hallway outside the gym to even the score in an after-game "rumble". I succeeded in aborting this plan by telling Greeny I was going to talk with his parents, and I headed to his house by myself without knowing what response I might receive. I had never met his parents, but found them very receptive and supportive, and we had a nice conversation. I liked their son and told them that I felt he had a lot of potential if we could redirect some of his energy into positive channels. Greeny showed up as I was leaving and acted quite repentive and concerned about the consequences from his father. As I was leaving, Mal and Fred showed up, fearing that I might be in danger, and they were prepared to rescue me. I assured them that everything was fine, and in my naiveté, wondered why they were so concerned. "Greeny", who was a natural leader with good athletic ability, did treat me with more respect after that. I have often wondered what became of him. I have attended a couple Boys Club reunions in recent years and have had a chance to renew acquaintances after 47 years with some of the young people I had worked with. Even though the Lincoln Boys Club no longer exists, many of the former members returned for the reunion, and most of them (at least the ones that returned) have done quite well, with families of their own and fond memories of their Boys Club days. None of them, however, had any information on "Greeny".

Chapter Twelve

(Gloria)

HEALTH CHALLENGES AND ADJUSTMENTS

Supporting a growing family on a small salary was challenging for Bud. He had just started working at the Boy's Club in July and, in those days; health insurance would not cover preexisting pregnancies. I was already pregnant with our second child, and I was determined to have this baby with the *Grantly Dick Read Method*. Mama's O.B. /Gyn, Dr. Harold Miller, with his office on Michigan Avenue in Chicago, supported this method. He agreed to take me as a patient and to only charge $100.00 for pre-natal care and delivery. Dr. Miller's surgical nurse of many years, Margaret Gamper, had developed her own system of teaching expectant mothers via the "Read" method and called it *The Gamper Method*. I attended eight classes, and was well prepared when David Ray was born on February 27, 1953 in Chicago's Frank Cuneo Hospital. Dads still could not go into the delivery rooms in 1953, but this time I knew what to expect. I was able to walk around during the contractions and Bud was able to stay with me until I was ready to deliver. This labor was a great experience. Number two on the way to a dozen.

Steve & Ray: Jan, 1954

That August, Bud and I wanted to drive south to visit my relatives. It would be our first real vacation, something like a honeymoon we'd never had, but we had no car and little money. I think Mama wanted to help make up for those *lost years* when we were separated, so she said we could use her Nash Rambler Station Wagon and we could leave the babies with her.

We took a pup tent, packed food in a cooler, and headed south. Although I had lived in Louisiana until I was thirteen, I had never been to Baton Rouge or New Orleans, so I was looking forward to visiting those cities in addition to re-connecting to my southern roots. We stayed in our pup tent and sleeping bags at Kentucky Lake in Kentucky, but we enjoyed sleeping in a real bed at Ruth & "T" King's in Conway, Arkansas. This was our first *relative* stop, and Bud met their three kids, Kaye, Mary Jane and Dick. Ruth, mama's youngest sister, and "T" had always been very special for me, and, when I was ten, I had been a "witness" at their wedding. Aunt Edy drove from Norman, Oklahoma to see us while we were there, and Uncle Grady and Aunt Laurine came up from Mountain Home, Arkansas. This was the "Bagwell" side of the family—three of Mama's four siblings. A couple of days into the trip, Bud was tiring more quickly and had no appetite, but since Southern hospitality includes bountiful offerings of food, he struggled to eat enough to be polite.

Next on the itinerary were Mamo Bayes and the Carson/ Bayes relatives, and I had to remind Bud just where they fit into the family tree. Great aunts, from the Jones side (Mamo's first cousins), uncles, cousins, second cousins once removed, etc. assembled at Mamo's (my paternal grandmother) to check out my new husband. Every one wanted us to visit them, but since our time was limited, most everybody within seventy miles came to the big Sunday Potluck that Mamo had planned in Jonesboro. There was more southern food than Bud had ever wanted to see, and the relatives confirmed some of the wild stories I had told Bud about my relatives—which Bud had thought were just Southern fables. In spite of Bud's lack of energy and appetite, we had an enjoyable visit.

We did get down to New Orleans for a brief bit of sight seeing, but didn't enjoy the luxury of a hotel. In fact we pitched our pup tent on a grassy area in front of the airport for the one night we were there and woke the next morning to find out that some escaped criminals had come to the airport during the night to make their get-away. Fortunately they didn't bother us. They probably figured we didn't have much to steal.

When we returned home, Bud went to see Dr. Dan Jamison, his old family doctor in Wheaton. Doc Jamison could not figure out what was wrong, so he suggested Bud go to the Hines Veterans Hospital in Chicago for further evaluation. Dr. Kellogg, the physician who checked Bud at the VA Hospital, had just finished a rotation at a TB sanitarium, and he arrived at the diagnosis quickly. Lab tests confirmed that Bud had *Tuberculosis!*

I was called and told to come right in. When I arrived, Bud was very somber. I had been grateful that, with the Korean War going on, he was not in Korea, but now my fear was that he might have cancer. That was what I feared the most. I let my fear run away with me. "Oh no", I thought, "He has cancer and is going to die . . . . I'm going to be a widow with three little kids to take care of . . . I wonder how long he has to live?"

The nurse stopped me at the door saying, "Mrs. Vear, You have to put on this gown before you go into the room and please remain away from his bed."

"What is so bad that I can't even kiss my husband?" I asked the nurse.

"Your husband will tell you." she replied, helping me slide my arms into the visitor's gown.

I stepped into the room, expecting the very worst.

"I have some bad news," Bud said in a solemn voice.

"What is it?" I asked tearfully.

"I have tuberculosis!"

"Is *that all*?" I broke into a big smile and heaved a sigh of relief.

Bud was perplexed at my response,—but it lifted his spirits too. He hadn't known of my fears. I could cope with anything as long as I didn't lose Bud. He would be safe in the hospital, and I was confident he would get well. I prayed that God would give me the strength to cope with the months ahead.

Bud was quickly transferred to the V.A. TB sanitarium (Downey Hospital) in North Chicago and put in isolation for six weeks. TB is a contagious disease and it was endemic in inner city Chicago. He probably contracted the disease at the Boys Club. People, living in these areas from childhood, develop antibodies to protect them later. I had spent the first 13 years of my life in Louisiana where I was exposed to TB many times. My TB test would always come up positive when I lived in the south, but after I moved north the tests were always negative. The health professionals had no explanations as to how this could happen. Even after Bud was infected, my test remained negative. On the other hand, Bud was raised in the suburbs, with minimal exposure, and had no such immunity. The fatigue from his long hours of work at the Club had further reduced his resistance to the disease.

Bud spent the next fifteen months in the hospital! I sublet our apartment to Fred Lickerman, one of Bud's colleagues at the Boys Club, and I moved to Wheaton. I spent six months with my Mom and six months with Bud's Mom. The last three months before his hospital release, I returned to our apartment in Chicago with our three kids.

Life has a way of closing doors while opening windows. Bud's hospitalization happened to be at a time when drugs for the treatment of tuberculosis were being tested, and the Veterans at Downey Hospital were part of the test group. Research focused on three drugs; INH (Isonicotinic Acid Hydrazide), Streptomycin and PAS (Para-amino-salicylic acid), and Bud was in the group that received Streptomycin and INH. By the luck of the draw, INH proved to be the first effective cure for tuberculosis. In fact, it was so effective that within just a few years most of the TB Sanitariums were closed.

His symptoms disappeared, and he was pretty much back to normal after six weeks, but with the reliability of the treatment options still uncertain, the hospital required six months of negative tests before pronouncing anyone cured. Once a week cultures were done to see if the infection was still active. The cultures took several weeks before they could be evaluated, so there was always at least a month's delay between the test and the results. Caution was warranted because of the contagious nature of the disease, the lack of any proven cure and the life-threatening potential of the illness. In the early days before there was a true cure, one of the treatment approaches was to send TB patients to a warm, dry climate, like Arizona, in hopes that rest, and the climate change would promote recovery. Some people got better, but many did not. Other treatments were more extreme. Mechanical collapse of the diseased lung was promoted, in order to allow the lung to heal. The two methods of accomplishing this were pneumothorax (injecting air under the pleural cavity once a month to collapse the infected lung) and thorocoplasty (removing 6 to 8 ribs on the infected side to mechanically collapse the chest cavity.) Neither of the approaches was really a cure, but they did sometimes provide the patient with additional years of life. Both options, of course, restricted the lung capacity, and the second option left the patient with a deformed chest. There were patients at Downey Hospital, who had undergone one of these treatments, and Bud was not anxious to join their ranks.

He wasn't required by law to remain at the Sanitarium once his symptoms disappeared, but he was concerned about the possibility of infecting us. I assured him I could manage, and he decided to remain in the hospital and wait for his six months of negative tests.

After six weeks, isolation ended, his energy level returned to normal and he was free to move around the hospital grounds with no responsibilities and lots of time. Actually, except for being away from his family, his months in the hospital were almost like a vacation. The hospital and the nearby service clubs offered many different activities, and he took advantage of most of them. He took a writing course, entered limerick contests, participated in a Great Books group, learned to knit scarves and hats, made hand tooled leather billfolds, belts and purses and even wove place mats on a small loom. All of our Christmas gifts for two years were handmade by Bud. He also was involved in the politics of the hospital as a member of the Patient Council, a small representative group of patients who brought patient concerns and suggestions to the hospital administration. He even played golf! There was an 18 hole-putting course on the grounds, and each week a service club from Waukegan would sponsor a tournament. Actually, his experience at Downey Hospital was more like living at a resort, with meals furnished, but he didn't get much exercise, so his weight ballooned to 230 lbs. (His normal weight was 195.)

Meanwhile, I had lots of emotional support from our families. I was able to attend daily mass, and in Wheaton I had many friends. Neither family expected me to pay any of the expenses while living with them, and the Veterans Administration was paying for all of Bud's medical expenses. We were blessed. The boys provided many antics I could report to Bud. I wrote daily and if Bud had kept my letters, I could have written a book on the hilarious things the kids did. I could laugh the next day, but when they occurred, some things weren't so funny. I couldn't keep *his* letters because he was very lonely and the letters were X-Rated.

Thanks to Mama, who let me use her car, I was able to visit Bud every Sunday. Bud came home for a short visit at Christmas 1953 and made a surprise appearance at the hospital when Gay, our first daughter, was born March 30th, 1954. He was due to be discharged in June, but one of his tests came back positive, and we still wonder if it could have been a mistake. Could specimens have gotten mixed up? This produced another difficult decision. It would require six more months of negative tests before the doctors would consider him free of the disease, and the hospital was closing. Since they had found a cure for tuberculosis, the V.A. had started closing most of their TB facilities. All the patients remaining in Bud's hospital were being transferred to a V.A. Hospital in Madison, Wisconsin, which would isolate him even further from his family. He went to Dr. Kratzner, the hospital's surgeon and medical director, and asked if there were any other alternatives. Dr. Kratzner offered Bud the option of surgery to remove the lobe of his lung that had been infected, and he said that he could be discharged as soon as he recovered from the surgery. Bud quickly agreed, and in August of 1954, Dr. Kratzner removed the middle lobe of Bud's right lung.

Before the surgery, Bud created an awkward situation in the family. He told me not to tell *anyone* ahead of time that he was going to have major surgery. Bud had always been very close to his mother, and I could not understand this request; but I agreed until I started to think about what would happen to my relationship with the family if something happened to him. The day before the surgery, I confronted him and convinced him that it was not the right thing to do. I don't remember if Bud or I called his Mom to let her know about the surgery, but for a long time his mother blamed me for not wanting her to know. It took a long time to get over that misunderstanding.

Bud's surgery was the next to the last one performed at Downey, before it closed, and, by his own admission, his "macho" image was seriously compromised. He was a terrible patient. He refused to breathe deeply or to cough after the surgery because it *hurt*, and the first couple of nights he was sure he was going to die. I was witness to his behavior, and, I thought, "It's a good thing he doesn't have to go through childbirth."

Actually, the surgery went well, and, since he was young and in good health otherwise, his recovery was quick. There was, however, one final, painful post-operative ordeal. Bud recounts the experience . . .

"I had two large drainage tubes still in my chest cavity, held in place with sutures, and I can remember vividly my post-op visit to Dr. Kratzner about a week after surgery. He was sitting down as I stood in front of him, and he asked how I was doing. He was checking the tubes, when all of a sudden— *Bam-m!*—With one swift motion he yanked them both out. I had never felt pain like that in my life. It was so severe, I couldn't breathe. I couldn't even swear at him. I tried to yell, but not a sound came out. I practically collapsed in front of him, but he just smiled and said, 'Well, they're out!'". Dr.

Kratzner was a no-nonsense doctor—a man's doctor, and Bud liked him and respected his surgical skills. Bud's memories of him, however, are embellished by this final post-op experience.

There was another physician at Downey Hospital who impacted Bud, though fortunately in a less painful way. Dr. Thomas Worobec was part of the medical staff at the Downey VA Hospital when Bud arrived. He grew up in Ukraine, a Soviet satellite in southeastern Europe which was scourged by imperialism and ruled by dictators after World War I. In 1919 the Communists were overrunning Eastern Ukraine and 20-year-old Thomas joined the Ukrainian Resistance Army for Independence. He was captured and sent to a Communist prison in Moscow. Conditions in the prison were deplorable, and, in four months, 700 of the 1200 prisoners perished from typhus or starvation. Thomas was afflicted with typhus and, during his life and death struggle with this disease as he watched his friends suffer and die, he promised to serve mankind through a medical career if he survived. His mother died in a flu epidemic during his imprisonment. Thomas *did* survive. He was finally released from prison and went on to receive his medical degree in 1928 from Charles University in Prague. He specialized in the study of tuberculosis and internal medicine, and, at the age of 31, he was one of the founders of the Ukrainian Hygienic Association, which educated the public on the control of tuberculosis. During World War II, he continued his medical career during occupations by the Nazis and the Communists. In 1948, Dr. Worobec moved to the U.S., and, shortly thereafter, became a staff physician at an Indian Hospital in Oklahoma. Less than two years later, he was named Superintendent of that Hospital. He came to Downey Hospital shortly before Bud arrived, and, his life was the basis of a paper Bud wrote as a part of the writer's course he took while in the hospital. A fascinating, but friendly survivor of severe challenges, Dr. Worobec helped keep Bud's dream of a medical career alive, even though Bud didn't pursue that goal for another seven years.

In 1995 Bud and I were reading "Compassionate Capitalism", a book by Rich DeVos, one of the founders of the Amway Corporation, and he talked about the "mentors" in our lives. Bud realized that Dr. Worobec was one of his "mentors", so 42 years after his last contact with Dr. Worobec at the VA Hospital, Bud contacted his wife, Sophia, and his son, Thomas, by phone to express a long overdue appreciation for the impact Dr. Worobec had on his life. Dr. Worobec, himself, had died some years before.

The fifteen months of hospitalization passed quickly; and in December 1954 we were reunited in our old apartment on Orchard. It seems strange to say, but during that period I was really thinking how lucky I was. I knew where my husband was, and I knew he was going to get well. Many husbands were in Korea at that time, and there were a lot who didn't come home. I counted my blessings. I knew Bud wouldn't be drafted. We have often thought about all of the help we have had, and we will forever be indebted to friends and family for their support during this long separation while Bud was in the hospital. If you can bless people by being willing to accept their help, then we blessed many people during those challenging fifteen months.

Chapter Thirteen

(Bud)

A NEW PROFESSION, A NEW CRISIS, A NEW HOME

I left the hospital in December of 1954 and returned to the Boys Club on a part-time basis. The limited schedule worked out well, since it gave me time to become reacquainted with Steve and Ray, who hadn't been permitted to visit during my 15-month hospitalization. Also, I had a new daughter, Gay, who hadn't known me at all. It took a while before she was willing to accept her "new" father.

Ray, Gay & Steve

By the time I was back to a full-time work routine I found myself reconsidering my future at the Boys Club. While I enjoyed working with kids, I was bothered by the lack of work parameters. It was one of those *no-end* jobs. I finished one day, and it went right into the next. There were always more things I could do, more activities I could run, and more children I could counsel. There was no end to the needs, and I felt overwhelmed.

I decided it was time for a change. However, a change to *what?* I thought, briefly, about my medical dream, but dismissed this as far too impractical. I began to consider teaching as an alternative. I wrote to the Illinois State Department of Education to find out what would be required for me to become certified. They responded that with a Master's Degree and my experience at the Boys Club, all I would need was credit for one course in the U.S. Constitution. This was a new requirement for all teachers, so I found the course I needed and enrolled at Pestalozzi Froebel, a community college in downtown Chicago. It could have been tedious and boring, but it turned out to be one of the most interesting courses I ever took. A Socialist taught the class! I can't recall his name, but I remember he was an avid supporter of Norman Thomas, the perpetual Socialist Presidential candidate. At the first session, he told us, "I know most of you are teachers, here just to fulfill a requirement, but there is no way we're going to spend ten weeks talking about the Constitution. We're going to talk about current events." He assured us that in the last couple of sessions he would provide us with all the information we needed to pass the test on the Constitution.

It was 1956, the year of Dwight Eisenhower's second presidential race against Adlai Stephenson. Our teacher didn't like either of the major party candidates for President or Vice President, so we had some lively political and philosophical discussions. Though most of us in the class didn't agree with his political views, he made the course very stimulating.

After successfully completing this course, I received my teacher certification, and I may be one of the few teachers ever certified who never took an education course and never did student teaching. They apparently accepted my social work fieldwork as my practice teaching, but I don't know how I avoided the education courses. I didn't ask any further questions!

I was able to find a middle school Science-Math teaching job at Elm School in Elmwood Park, a school district on the far west side of Chicago, and Gloria and I looked forward to a more structured schedule which would provide a positive change in our family life. However, a new challenge was just ahead.

On August 23, 1955, just before I started teaching, Gloria (8 months pregnant) and I were planning to attend a party celebrating my parents' 33rd wedding anniversary at the Black Orchid Restaurant on the near north side of Chicago. Steve—then three and a half—was ill with a high fever and a stiff neck. He also was acting lethargic and couldn't move his left arm. We called the doctor, who told us to take Steve to the hospital immediately. He suspected Steve might have polio! Polio was much in the news at the time, and the Salk vaccine was still in development. With no car at the time, we asked our neighbors across the hall for a ride, but they refused because of their fear of contracting the disease, so we called a cab.

When we arrived at the Michael Reese Children's Hospital on the south side of Chicago, Steve was examined, a spinal tap confirmed the diagnosis of polio, and he was immediately hospitalized. We weren't even permitted to kiss our tearful son goodbye before he was placed in isolation.

We already had a baby-sitter for Ray & Gay, and since there was little we could do for Steve, we decided to go to the anniversary celebration. When we arrived, my father scolded us for being late, but the scolding came to an embarrassed halt when he found out what had detained us. Our news, not surprisingly, subdued the party.

Gloria, Ray, Gay and I all received gamma globulin—one

hefty injection in the buttocks for each of us—with the dosage determined by our weights. It proved too late for Gay, and about a week later, our 18-month-old daughter could no longer walk. She spent a week in the hospital, but the gamma globulin apparently kept her infection mild, and she recovered quickly without any residual paralysis. Steve was hospitalized for about two weeks and he was left with partial paralysis of his left arm. We gave him daily exercise treatments to try to strengthen the muscles in that arm, and he also had several surgeries to redirect some muscles so he could use the left arm and hand more effectively, but they never did return to normal use. (To his credit, Steve has never used this as an excuse to avoid any activity, and he has successfully done everything from swimming and canoeing to home building and auto mechanics.) Many died from polio that year and survivors often spent years in iron lungs because they couldn't breathe on their own. We feel fortunate that our children were spared more serious consequences.

On September 28, 1955, our fourth child, Tony, was born and I began my second career. I found teaching to be challenging and stimulating, and I enjoyed the more structured schedule. I learned early the importance of planning. The principal at my school was very strict about lesson plan preparation, and he required teachers to turn in their lesson plans for the next week before they left school each Friday. This forced me to be prepared before I walked into the classroom on Monday morning, and I learned, early on, that students would quickly take over the class if a teacher wasn't adequately prepared. I taught science and math to seventh and eighth graders, and I visited each of the lower grade classes once a month with my rolling science lab to introduce the younger students to science. It provided an opportunity to observe the other classrooms and to make my own assessment of different teaching skills and techniques. One of the most memorable teachers in that school was Mildred Kehoe. Millie was an imposing woman, in both stature and reputation. (When she walked into the teacher's lounge, the other teachers stopped talking!) She taught 5th and 6th grades (in alternate years), and, although I never heard her raise her voice, students in her classroom were well behaved even when she was out of the room. As a first year teacher, with no practice teaching, I was struggling to control my students. Much of my time was spent on discipline rather than teaching. I tried all kinds of penalties for the offenders (names on the blackboard, after-school detention, escorting recalcitrant students out of the room, and loud threats of dire consequences if they didn't pay attention.) None of these methods had much effect. One day I asked Millie how she maintained such wonderful control in her classroom without ever raising her voice. She smiled and said, "You should have heard me my first two years. I shouted at the kids all the time and had no control. Give yourself time." I had great respect for Millie, and her words of encouragement at that time meant a great deal to me. She was right. In my third year I felt I had control of my classes and truly began teaching. I suspect this is about average for classroom teachers. Some may arrive sooner, some later and some never.

Teachers, I truly believe, have a unique opportunity to impact people's lives. Most adults will name at least one teacher if they are asked to name the five most influential people in their lives. My hope is that my seven years as a teacher entitled me to appear on at least one such list.

I am still in Christmas card contact with one of my Elm School students, Cathy (Valeska) Davis. Cathy was an outstanding student, as well as a wonderful human being. She attended DePauw University, my alma mater at the same time I was attending medical school at Missouri University. Before she enrolled, we were still living in Wheaton, and I attended a DePauw recruitment dinner in Chicago. Cathy was there with her parents and I hoped that my degree from DePauw might have had some influence on her decision to go there. She and her husband, Bronson, send fascinating Christmas letters, which we always look forward to reading, and we have visited them several times through the years. However, a special treat awaited me, when I returned recently for my 50th class reunion at DePauw. I was surprised and thrilled to see Cathy and Bronson (who returned for his 35th class reunion) receive an Outstanding Alumni Award for contributions they have made to DePauw since their graduation. They are special people.

In December of 1955, we purchased our first house with the help of a friend and volunteer at the Boys Club, who loaned us $3,000 for the down payment. We moved from our two bedroom apartment at 1663 N. Orchard to a four-bedroom Cape Cod house located on an unpaved road in Elmhurst, a suburb 15 miles west of Chicago. The price was $16,500, which for us was a huge sum, and I worked weekends as Director of the York High School Youth Center in Elmhurst to supplement my teaching income.

Our first house
Elmhurst, Illinois

Our Elmwood Park years saw further expansion of the family with two more daughters: Terry, born March 17, 1957 and Candi, born on February 23, 1958, which meant that Gloria was pregnant most of the time. I enjoyed teaching at Elm School, and the commuting distance was about the same as when we lived in Chicago. However, my weekend work at the Youth Center started hitting some snags.

It was a classic dilemma of a well-intended organization—and of social service in general—to meet the needs of clients while keeping the supporters happy. The Center's mission was helping young people, but the young people most in need of help can often present a threat (real or perceived) to the organization that has help to offer. Many larger, more prestigious and better-endowed institutions have failed to solve this puzzle.

Having worked in inner city Chicago, I had worked with young people from less fortunate backgrounds, and I encouraged some of the more rebellious kids in Elmhurst to become involved in the Center's programs. My inclusion of these problem youngsters was not always appreciated. Some parents—and particularly some Board members—felt very uncomfortable having such kids at the Center because of the worrisome influence they might have on their own teenagers.

We moved to Wheaton in December of 1958, but I had planned to continue working at the Youth Center in Elmhurst because we needed the extra income. The Center was struggling financially at that time, and I offered to reduce my hours and my salary to help the Board balance the Center's budget. Our move to Wheaton and my offer to work at reduced pay was interpreted by the Youth Center Board as a lack of commitment to the Youth Center, and I was dismissed. I'm sure an additional factor was that I had not spent enough time developing a better relationship with the Board members. I had spent most of my time working with the teens, and I think the Board members didn't feel that I had kept them well enough informed about what was going on.

With an additional mortgage payment to make (we had been unable to sell the Elmhurst house and were renting it out), the loss of my extra income from the Youth Center put additional stress on our finances. We also had added our seventh child with the arrival of Pam, on May 8th, 1959. Moreover, I had never before been fired from a job, and to be released from a job, for which I was academically well qualified, was especially ego-deflating.

Better news was on the horizon, however, when I was offered a teaching job in the Wheaton school district, to start in September, 1959. The home we had purchased the previous December, at 427 N. West St. in Wheaton, was the same house where I had spent my childhood. It was a big, two story, six bedroom home, with a large porch wrapped around three sides, and it was located on an attractive corner lot within walking distance of schools, downtown shopping, a public swimming pool and Saint Michael's Catholic Church. My father had sold the house several years before. The man who bought it discovered, too late, that his wife did not like the house or the town. He had been trying to sell the house for over a year, and it was sitting empty. We made an offer of $21,000 (He was asking $26,000.), and he refused. A few months later, the house was still not sold, and, after re-evaluating our finances and the fact that the house needed new wiring and plumbing, we felt we could not offer more than $19,000. He accepted! It was the best real estate purchase we ever made, but, with us, it was naiveté rather than shrewdness. It was a wonderful home for a large family, and we enjoyed our four years there.

Our home in Wheaton, IL

In Wheaton I continued to enjoy the challenge of classroom teaching as a seventh and eight grade science teacher at Edison Junior High, but it was becoming more and more of a challenge trying to stretch my modest teacher's salary to meet the needs of our growing family.

Our family in 1959

Our large home became a home for others as well. Gloria usually originated the idea, and then, in her visionary way, would convince me that it would work out fine.

The summer of 1959, following our move to Wheaton, Gloria's sister, Louise, and her family came to stay with us while her husband, Arnie, a college Physics Professor, pursued a summer job at Argonne National Laboratories, twenty miles from Wheaton. They had three children, Jeff (8), Sandy (6) and Gary (4), and Louise was very organized. She not only established a workable routine, but, while she was there, she stripped off all the paint and refinished all the woodwork in the living room! In spite of the additional number in the household, the summer went quite smoothly— except for the fire the kids set under the front porch! (See Chapter 15.)

In September of 1959, an important chapter in my life closed with the sudden and unexpected death of my mother, at the age of 61. She had broken her ankle in a fall down the stairs in her country home a few weeks before and a few days later had a pulmonary embolus (blood clot to the lungs) and nearly died. Dad, who had been traveling on a business trip when she broke her ankle, came home and spent some very meaningful time with her, talking about things they hadn't discussed in years. Dad had purchased the farm five years before he retired from Swift & Company, and, while he was still traveling a lot, Mom was left alone on the farm, away from the many friends she had made in Wheaton. She tried hard to adjust and to make new friends, but I think she was very unhappy living in the country away from the social interactions she had enjoyed so much in Wheaton. I think her hospitalization was a wake-up call for Dad that he needed to give her more attention. However, after a few days Mom was doing better, so Dad left on another business trip, and, while he was away, Mother suffered another pulmonary embolus and died. The woman who had nurtured and advised me was gone. She died just a few years before I began my pursuit of a medical degree. I know she would have encouraged me on the journey toward my dream.

In September, shortly after Louise and her family left, Jim and Russ Newhouse came to live with us, so they could attend Saint Francis, the new Catholic High School in Wheaton. In August, there had been an appeal in our church bulletin for temporary housing for these two boys while their new home in Wheaton was being completed. Their parents wanted them to start the school year at Saint Francis, so they wouldn't have to transfer schools later in the school year, and the parents and boys came by for an interview to see if ours would be an appropriate temporary home. Our own kids must not have been home because we passed their inspection. Jim, 15, & Russ, 14, lived with us for several months, and they provided us with our first experience raising teenagers. Considering what came later with our own children, they were easy. Their father was a pilot for American Airlines and both of them later became commercial pilots.

We added another Vear with the arrival of Rick on November 1st, 1960. That made eight. The following year on July 5th, my thirty-fifth birthday, Gloria had a miscarriage after a severe episode of acute rheumatoid arthritis. She did not know she was pregnant, and the doctor prescribed cortisone to relieve her excruciating pain. The cortisone may have caused the miscarriage—or possibly, it was related to our experience with a Cuban family . . . .

In April of 1961, the year before we left Wheaton for medical school, we hosted a Cuban refugee family, the Aguilars. We were members of a Christian Family Movement (CFM) couples group in our church, and the group decided to offer help for a refugee family escaping Castro's Cuba after the Bay of Pigs takeover. We had the largest house, so we volunteered to house them, while the other couples contributed money for food and other necessities, and they would also help the husband, an engineer, find a job. We expected that this would take no more than six weeks. It took six *months!* Their lifestyle didn't mesh with ours, and it was during their stay that Gloria had her arthritis attack—possibly stress-related. The Aguilar's concept of time was very casual. They never rose before 10 or 11 and were in the habit of having their big meal at noon. They had servants in Cuba, so neither of them could cook, and housekeeping was a skill they never needed to develop. We gave them an upstairs bedroom, with an attached sunroom and a bathroom, to use. Gloria suddenly had more laundry and more housecleaning to do. *Our* big meal was in the evening, and, for a while, we tried to convert them to our routine. Often at 5:30 p.m., as they were preparing to go for a walk, we would tell them that dinner would be ready at 6. They would promise to be back, and then, about 7:30, they would stroll in, without apology, and act surprised that we were upset. The husband was also frequently late for job interviews that had been set up by another CFM member. Time schedules just didn't mean the same for them as they did for us. Their children, ages two and four, were extremely rambunctious and would be given bottles of heavily sweetened milk to keep them in bed later in the morning. No parental discipline was ever apparent, so their kids had lots more freedom than ours did; a fact pointed out to us often by our own children.

We finally decided to let them fix their own meal at noon and not worry about sitting down with us in the evening. Since neither of them could cook, Mrs. Aguilar would simply throw a whole chicken and a beef roast in a pot of boiling water at a time when we felt either kind of meat to be a luxury. I'm sure their time with us did nothing to improve international relations, and we were delighted, and relieved, when they finally moved out on their own. It was a long tense six months.

Our time in Wheaton would end with the decision to follow my irrepressible dream of being a doctor, but while we lived there, we were quite happy. Wheaton was a nice place to raise children. (After all, *we* were raised there!) I had enjoyed my teaching, and we had reached the two-thirds mark toward the goal inspired by our reading of *Cheaper By The Dozen*. But even with eight kids, we still didn't fully understand what our fascination with that book had set in motion. If we had been a bit more perceptive, we might have seen in those years the seeds of future challenges for us with our growing family.

Chapter Fourteen

(Bud)

LOW BUDGET VACATIONS

How do large families vacation? Two week Cruises in the Caribbean? Sunbathing on the Hawaiian Islands? Luxurious travel in motor homes? Not really. For us it was tent camping in State campgrounds, canoeing in rented canoes on Michigan rivers, or traveling with a rented fold-down camper on a budget of $10 a day! Financial frugality and family togetherness were the primary criteria for our vacation excursions, and we survived large doses of both.

Before medical school, when the children were young, and we were struggling to remain financially solvent on a social work and then a teaching salary, we didn't take any lengthy family vacations. In the summer, we would go to a park for a picnic on a Sunday afternoon, a nature walk in a forest preserve nearby or a swim at the public pool. On rare occasions, we would visit the Zoo, or travel into Chicago to enjoy the Aquarium, the Planetarium or the Museum of Science and Industry. We found inexpensive activities the whole family could enjoy. In the winter, we would bundle the kids up in snowsuits (a monumental task in itself) and spend the day at a sledding hill before warming up at home with hot chocolate and marshmallows.

Since I taught Science in middle school for seven years, our walks in the meadow or woods, or our evening views of the stars, became teaching opportunities, and some of our children can probably still identify Trilliums and May Apples in the spring and the Big Dipper and Orion the Hunter in the nighttime sky.

About the only time we would be gone for more than a day, was Thanksgiving, when we would load the kids in the car and drive a couple of hours to join with the Vear clan at Dad's farm in Marengo or, later, at my brother, Dave's, house in LaGrange. Those were always fun times, with spirited competition in football, croquet, ping-pong, pool and horseshoes and of course a huge turkey with all the trimmings. The winners' names in ping-pong and pool were recorded on traveling trophies that the winners kept until the next year's competition. Modesty does *not* prevent me from reporting that most of the names on these trophies were from the Bud Vear family! After my older brother, Judd, broke his collarbone in one of the family Thanksgiving football games, we turned the football heroics over to the younger generations.

When I was growing up, summer touring and camping with mom and my two weeks each summer at Phantom Lake YMCA Camp in Wisconsin produced some of my most memorable childhood experiences. Therefore, it is not surprising that camping our way to Colorado was our initial extended vacation with our own family. I had just completed my third year of medical school in Columbia, Missouri, and we had purchased a used Ford station wagon with a bank loan that required us to pay only $25/month until I graduated from medical school. We rented a fold-down camper and headed west with nine children, a supply of food, a credit card for gas purchases and $120 for all other expenses during the 12 days we would be gone. We played the alphabet game while traveling, suffered through frequent arguments over the seating arrangements (everyone wanted a window), stopped occasionally to enjoy free public playgrounds and parks and looked for $1.50/night campsites after we had traveled three or four hundred miles. Dinner was prepared over a Coleman stove, while the kids explored the surroundings and met our new temporary neighbors. Campers are friendly and relaxed, so it was easy to strike up conversations. The kids would return with reports of, "You should see this cool guy (or sharp girl) I met" or "You should see *their* trailer." Sometimes the kids would beg us to stay in a campsite for another day because of an instant friend they had acquired, but traveling to Colorado and back in twelve days, didn't allow us that luxury.

Our sleeping arrangements were challenging. After our evening meal, we would prepare wall-to-wall beds in the camper and the two older boys would sleep in the back of the station wagon. If you were sleeping in the trailer and had to go to the bathroom in the middle of the night, you had to climb over the other slumbering bodies to get out. Unfortunately, some of the younger children didn't make the effort; so wet beds were a much-too-frequent occurrence. A feeling of a helpless "Oh not again!" envelops you when the moisture creeps over to your side of the bed.

One night was particularly memorable, but the humor of the episode was not apparent until much later. We had traveled farther than usual that day in an effort to reach Pike's Peak, so when we pulled into a campsite part way up the mountain, it was already dark. We were all tired, hungry and irritable, we couldn't find our flashlight, and the lantern didn't work. A couple of the kids became nauseated from something they had eaten earlier in the day, so we fed the rest of them in the dark and made up the beds for the night. During the night, two of the kids each wet their beds twice, two others were sick to their stomachs, and some animal made off with all of our meat from the cooler, which we had placed outside the trailer. We were not a happy, cheerful family the next morning.

Fortunately, Glen and Joey Shoptaugh came to our rescue. Glen had been a fraternity brother of mine at DePauw and was a Pediatrician at the Air Force Academy in nearby Colorado Springs. He and his wife, Joey, and their eight children welcomed us to their hillside home for the day. They grilled hamburgers and steaks, buoyed up our spirits and gave us a lantern to use when we returned to our campsite. They certainly blessed our lives that day. Not only did they soothe our appetites, but our kids had a great time playing with the Shoptaugh kids, and our sanity was restored.

If family vacations are supposed to bring families closer together, this trip certainly accomplished that. It kept us in very close proximity most of the time! We drove over 600 miles the last day so we wouldn't have to spend another night in the camper!

A week after we returned from our trip west, we took the family for a long weekend with some of Gloria's relatives in a housekeeping cabin at Buffalo River State Park in Arkansas. It was a peaceful experience after our trip west, and we decided that staying in one place had definite advantages over daily travel with a carload of active "Are we there yet?" children.

We had one unusual experience during the trip to Arkansas that, I suspect, still stirs nightmares in some of the children. One evening at dusk, while I was driving, I noticed *hundreds* of small creatures crawling across the road. I suddenly realized they were tarantula spiders! I awakened my slumbering family to view this spectacle and received drowsy comments questioning the credibility of my observations. Finally, I stopped the car and suggested they open the back door and look more closely. The door remained open only briefly, there were screams as my observations were confirmed, and the whole family was quickly wide-awake! They urged me to keep the car moving before the tarantulas found their way in! I thought this must be a common seasonal occurrence in that part of the country, but, not according to the people I talked to. Apparently, we had encountered an unusual tarantula migration that most people in the area had never seen. Although this event occurred over 30 years ago, I suspect that some of our children still have vivid memories of it. I certainly do.

Regular family vacations really started after we moved to Hillsdale to start my medical practice. We still didn't have much money, and I couldn't afford to be away from the office for very long, but we tried to get away for a couple long weekends each summer. When our children were asked recently to relate their childhood memories; camping, canoeing and our two trips west were the items mentioned most often.

When Steve was 16, I decided to try canoeing. Michigan abounds with wonderful rivers on which you can paddle, or just float, downstream for many hours and camp in the woods along the shore. Steve and I spent a weekend paddling 100 miles down the Per'e Marquette River to its mouth on the shore of Lake Michigan. Each night we pitched our tent, gathered firewood, cooked our supper and enjoyed s'mores around the campfire. It turned out to be a great bonding experience. Each summer after that, I repeated this trip, on different rivers, with one of our children when they became teenagers. Camping in the wilderness, away from siblings, TV's, radios, indoor plumbing and electric lights, certainly produces bonding memories. I always made sure we had ample food, including junk food (a rare item in our household). I picked a different river for each child, so his or her experiences would be unique. We canoed the Au Sable, Manistee, Pere Marquette, Pine, Rifle, Sturgeon and Pigeon Rivers, but the Two Hearted River in the Upper Peninsula produced one of the more memorable experiences. I canoed this with Candi.

The river wound through a very remote, densely wooded area on the southern border of Lake Superior. It was beautiful, but wild and desolate, and we didn't see another canoe all day. As we neared the end of the river, a storm came up, the sky darkened, rain began to fall and thunder rumbled like an approaching locomotive. We feared we were about to be enveloped by a tornado, so we quickly beached the canoe and dove for cover among the scraggly bushes along the river. Along that section of the river, there were no large trees to grab onto. We knew the bushes would offer little protection in a tornado, so we resorted to prayer. While the rumble continued, the sky started to clear, the rain stopped and birds were flying without apparent concern. We convinced ourselves that tornadoes were unlikely in the Upper Peninsula, and that birds probably didn't fly in them, so we got back in the canoe and paddled quickly to the mouth of the river. Only then did we discover the source of the loud rumble. It was the sound of the surf crashing on the shore of Lake Superior. After recovering from our unnecessary anxiety, we fixed supper and prepared our campsite. There was a rustic park there at the mouth of the river where we had pitched our tent and parked our car before the people from the canoe livery transported us back to our starting point on the river to start our canoe journey. After supper, with renewed courage, we took a spooky drive down a very narrow one-lane trail—more a path than a road—with trees brushing both sides of the car. Candy was convinced there were monsters or wild animals lurking in the woods, but we never saw either, and the road ended at a beautiful Bay, which emptied into Lake Superior. We survived the night and collected some beautiful stones from the shore of Lake Superior before departing the next morning. Candy has expressed no desire to return to Ernest Hemingway's Two Hearted River!

Probably the canoe trips our kids remember most are the ones they took with their cousins from LaGrange, Illinois. My brother, Dave, and his wife, Barb, had eight children who pretty much matched ages with ours, and we took many weekend canoe trips with them. To quote the kids, "It was a blast!" The cousins paired off with two in each canoe and gender separations in the tents. Often, the canoes became battle stations, with competition and overturned canoes inevitable. Perishable supplies were always carried in the adult canoes, which usually protected us from attack. On one memorable occasion, Tony and Brad, the two oldest male cousins on the trip, boasted loudly about their superior canoeing skills and raced ahead of their siblings in the other canoes with taunts of "you're a bunch of wimps". However, they were soon humbled by the river. As the rest of us rounded the first bend in the river, Tony and Brad were seen floundering in the water under a tree with their canoe overturned. Sibling laughter descended on the pair as the younger cousins passed by, and for a short time we didn't hear any more boasting from those two.

Our kids and their cousins were all excellent swimmers and good canoeists, but paddling through white water rapids in the rivers without tipping over is a challenge, and unplanned plunges into the cool water were common. Two of the most challenging rivers in Michigan were the Pigeon and the Sturgeon, located in the northeast corner of the Lower Peninsula just south of the Mackinac Bridge. I canoed down these rivers with Rick, one of our more adventuresome children, and we struggled to stay afloat while traversing wild turbulence and tricky bends in the rapidly flowing rivers. We managed to remain upright on the Sturgeon, and were feeling over confident when we flipped over while rounding a bend of the Pigeon. I was taking movies at the time, and the camera went to the bottom of the river. Rick dove for it and, miraculously, retrieved it. When the film was developed, there was actually some underwater footage!

My bonding weekend canoe adventures changed to whitewater rafting with the youngest four children. The Youghiogheny (Yough) River in the southwest corner of Pennsylvania provided the whitewater and the thrills for Lisa, Mike, Kevin and Kelly, and there is no adequate way to describe the excitement and exhilaration of challenging a turbulent river in a rubber raft. The challenge is enhanced when you are thrown out of the raft and are at the mercy of the cascading current as it carries you downstream between and over huge rocks! Our usual routine was to go down the river with a guided group on Saturday, so we could learn how to safely navigate the rapids, camp out Saturday night and rent rafts on Sunday to go down by ourselves. The challenge, of course, was to complete the wild four to six hour journey without being expelled from the raft. I don't recall that any of the four accomplished this, although Mike would have succeeded had he not been forced to rescue his father from the water after I had fallen out in the middle of a major rapids. There is a feeling of total helplessness, when you are adrift in whitewater rapids, because your swimming ability is completely nullified! Fortunately, the life jacket (which you had better be wearing when you go rafting) pops you to the surface, and the current carries you past the protruding rocks. So long as you keep your feet downstream and up off the bottom, you are relatively safe. It was somewhat comforting when the canoe livery assured us that no one had ever perished on a *guided* raft trip on the Yough. They gave us no such assurance about an un-guided trip. As a "macho" father, I felt it appropriate to expose my children to *some* peril! Fortunately, neither the kids nor I incurred any serious injuries.

Gloria was not so fortunate. She courageously exposed herself to the rigors and excitement of whitewater rafting one weekend. Mike and Kevin were on a Hillsdale College football team that was playing a game in Slippery Rock, Pennsylvania (Yes, there really is a Slippery Rock College!), and we decided to go to the game and then drive the short distance down to Ohiopyle to go rafting on the Yough. To her credit, Gloria, while not athletic, is usually willing to try most anything; and she, of course, had heard my intriguing tales about the thrills of whitewater rafting. It didn't take very long for her to encounter disaster! She fell out of the raft in the middle of the first rapids and hit her hand on a rock. We managed to get her back in the raft, but her hand was hurting and starting to swell. We still had most of the trip ahead of us, so, from my vast reservoir of medical knowledge (and with precious little compassion) I told her to keep her hand in the cold river water to control the swelling and to keep paddling. She remained in the raft and paddled for five more hours, but when we completed the journey, her hand was quite swollen. After a six-hour drive home, she saw a *real* doctor, and an x-ray disclosed a broken bone in her hand, which required a metal pin for stabilization and healing. Whenever she needs a little leverage in a discussion with me, she mentions the time I made her paddle for five hours with a broken hand! A testimony of her courage, however, is that a couple years later, she went rafting again when we went down the same river with many of our kids and their cousins. She survived this time without injury and even went back for more the second day instead of going sight seeing with the other, much younger, wives.

Gloria & Bud
Rafting on the "Yough"
with Kevin & Alexis

In summary, our vacations were inexpensive and usually involved water, camping or both. My favorite comment, when we set out on a family journey, was, "The only thing I promise you is an *experience.*" We had plenty of those.

Chapter Fifteen

(Gloria)

CONFLICT, PANDEMONIUM AND ANGELS

Our life as parents began normally enough with the kinds of childhood misadventures many families experience. Neither Bud nor I saw them as portents of things to come. Let's start in Chicago with Ray.

Our second son had the wanderlust, even as a toddler. As soon as he learned to walk, he ventured off at the least provocation—or for no discernible provocation at all. It would happen quickly. A turn of my head, and Ray would be gone. I had attended a parenting seminar, held at our old parish of St. Michael's in Wheaton, where a mother of seven had suggested how we might cure Ray of running off. Her idea was to contrive an opportunity for him to be lost and scared, and then, just as he was overcome with panic, step forward to rescue him. It would be completely safe, of course—though Ray wouldn't know that—and it would be a great object lesson, encouraging him to stay close to me.

The idea sounded plausible, and I soon had a chance to

put it into action during a shopping trip to a clothing store near our neighborhood at Halsted and North Avenue. Predictably, Ray wandered off, and I remained out of his sight on the opposite side of a clothing rack watching how he reacted. Ray looked around and determined that I was nowhere to be seen. Did he panic? Did he cry out for his mother? Of course not. He headed straight for the door, and was on his way down the sidewalk before I came sprinting out and grabbed him by the arm ("sprinting" being a relative term, given that I was seven months pregnant!)

So much for the psychological approach of keeping my children under my wing. I bought two harnesses! It was an odd sight that met the stares of onlookers during subsequent shopping trips: me in my expectant state, dragging three-and-a-half-year old Steve by the hand, with 16-month-old Gay harnessed in her buggy and 29-month-old Ray bringing up the rear on a leash.

My mother, Kit, doubted that even a leash would be sufficient to restrain the children for very long, so she bought a batch of dog tags and had them stamped, "My name is (*first name*). I belong to Charles T. Vear," along with name, address and phone number, one for each of the children. Within the month, her system was put to the test.

On a beautiful warm afternoon in early September, I was watching Ray and Steve ride their tricycles on the wide Chicago sidewalk in front of our first floor apartment at 1663 N. Orchard, just ½ block from the Lincoln Boys Club where Bud worked. Gay was asleep in her buggy. The phone rang. What to do? I am a compulsive phone answerer, and Steve had only recently gotten out of the hospital with polio, so we were still in close contact with his doctors. As I rushed in the house, I called over my shoulder for the boys to stay right in front, where I could see them. The phone was near the front window, and a few seconds later I picked up the phone and looked out to check on the kids. Ray, age two and a half, had already disappeared from view. *"Oh, no!"* The caller was not the doctor, so I excused myself, hung up quickly and ran outside. Ray was out of sight.

I knew Ray could move quickly, once in motion, and I couldn't leave the other two kids to go combing the neighborhood; so I called Bud at the Boys Club. He recruited some co-workers, and they launched a search. Since Ray had been known to slip through the back yard fence to go to the street behind us, they searched around the block. No trace of him. They spread out to the adjacent blocks. Ray's tricycle was found abandoned at the corner of Armitage and Orchard, a very busy intersection, but there was no sign of Ray. An hour had passed, and we were becoming frantic, wondering if someone had kidnapped our adventuresome towheaded child. We contacted the police, but they had no report of anyone seeing a lost child.

This was our first experience with the terror that can grip parents when a child disappears. It also turned out to be our first encounter with an idea, which would present itself many times over the years. If traditional beliefs about guardian angels are true, then, that day, we had reason to hope that angels were protecting Ray. About an hour and a half after the search had begun, we received a phone call from a medical clinic located six long blocks away. "Do you have a son named Ray?" My stomach, already in a knot, felt like it had just been kicked.

"There's a child here with a tag that says 'Ray' and has your phone number."

The lady from the clinic paused for not more than a beat, but that was enough time for a string of horrific fears to go racing though my mind. Was our son badly hurt? Had our child been killed?

"He's perfectly all right," she said reassuringly. "He's been playing with the toys in our waiting room. People have been coming and going, so we didn't realize he wasn't with anybody until just a while ago. We looked closely at him and found the name tag."

When Bud arrived at the clinic, there was Ray sitting unconcerned on the floor, having a happy time with the waiting room toys. At the age of two and a half, he had somehow managed to cross several busy streets all by himself, (or with the help of some chance passersby). How he had avoided being run down, only God knows.

A year later, Ray tumbled seven feet into a cement basement stairwell behind our Chicago apartment, landing on his face. The resulting injury required no stitches, and his skull and neck were intact, but he looked like he was the victim of severe child abuse.

Moving to new locations didn't seem to change Ray's propensity to court disaster. In Elmhurst, his inquisitiveness placed him in jeopardy on numerous occasions. One time he sawed through a small, flexible tube that carried heating oil from its storage tank to the furnace. Disaster was averted when one of the other kids told us there was oil on the basement floor. Another time, he stuck a metal pipe into a light socket while standing barefoot on a metal chair in the basement. He shorted out the socket, receiving only a mild jolt to mark that experience. But there were other shocks and minor burns on other occasions—once from a knife stuck into an electrical outlet, and another time when he cut the cord of an operating electric fan with a pair of scissors (all this by age five). Where was mom? Usually in the next room—or the same room—but supervising Ray was like trying to follow a wave after it breaks on the shore.

One of our crises in Elmhurst could not be blamed on Ray. It sadly must be admitted that it reflected poor paternal judgment. When we were living in Elmhurst, we attended a church picnic, at a park where they had a miniature train ride. Of course, all of our children begged to ride on it. At Bud's insistence, and against my better judgment, I allowed 18-month-old Terry to ride the train, with assurance from Bud, that four and a half year old Gay could sit with her and keep her from falling out. Shortly after the train started moving,

Terry stood up, and Gay pulled her back down. Then, defiantly, Terry stood up again, just as the train was rounding a curve. She lost her balance and tumbled over the side of the car. A metal strut projecting out from the following car sliced her scalp as it went by. It took many stitches to close the wound. We were thankful it wasn't her face.

The kids' experiences with serious illness heightened our suspicions about angelic intervention. There was Steve and Gay's polio, of course, and Gay and Candi both survived cases of pneumonia that required hospitalization. Candi was a newborn when she was hospitalized, and she might not have made it through her illness, if my mother hadn't been at her hospital bedside just at the moment Candi stopped breathing. Grandma Kit alerted the nurses in time for them to take appropriate life-saving measures.

Grandma Kit functioned as the angels' earthly agent on more than one occasion, coming through at the critical moment each time. The reason she was in the hospital to provide life-saving intervention for Candi was her life-saving protection of Tony. While I was in the hospital delivering Candi, Mama had been taking care of Tony in her home in Wheaton. Tony remained with her in Wheaton for a few days after Candi and I returned to our home in Elmhurst. When Tony became ill with a fever of 105 and had a febrile seizure, mom realized his condition was serious and that he needed to be hospitalized. She had no car available, so she called the police, and they dispatched a patrol car to take them to Elmhurst Hospital, 20 miles away.

The officers radioed ahead to request that the main intersections be blocked off along Roosevelt Road, the busy route they were taking. However, one intersection wasn't closed in time, and a motorist, unable to hear the siren with his windows up (it was February), drove through a green light into the oncoming police car. The resulting crash totaled both vehicles. Kit suffered a broken back and ankle and her face was badly lacerated, but she had hung onto Tony (this, in the days before seat belts), preventing him from being killed. Tony did receive a broken collarbone, and the police officers, as well as the other driver, were injured. Fortunately, there were no fatalities. It was during mom's recovery in the hospital that she had intervened on behalf of Candi.

Tony had several other brushes with disaster. While we were living in Wheaton, Tony, at age 4, fell from a tire swing when the 25-foot rope snapped. He somehow escaped that fall without serious injury. However, a year later he suffered another fall, from a 30-foot magnolia tree and wasn't quite so lucky. He required stitches in his scalp and broke a bone in his forearm, but the result could have been a lot more serious. He landed in soft dirt, missing a railroad tie by inches! Where was his father? At the base of the tree, telling him to be careful. Tony loved to climb, and, since climbing had been a favorite childhood activity of Bud's, he didn't want to deprive his son of the same opportunity. Some weeks after, with his arm still in a cast, Tony was nearly flung from a moving car when an axle broke and the door flew open as we drove around the grounds of Wheaton's Loretta Convent, where he would be attending preschool. (If you're counting on angelic protection, you could hardly find a better place to get help than on the grounds of a convent.)

These events were only part of a long series of occurrences in which Vear children would court disaster, with near misses that sometimes seemed miraculous. Pam joined the disaster prone group at age 1 ½, when she fell down the back stairway in our Wheaton house and knocked out two front teeth. Her toothless grin persisted until her permanent teeth arrived at age six!

In Wheaton, Ray discovered the wonders of fire, and, at age seven, he nearly wiped out all of his siblings. The kids were in our station wagon, impatient to visit their Dad, who was taking a summer science course at Northern Illinois

University in DeKalb. Bud had been away for four weeks and had two more weeks to go, so the kids were eager to see him again. I was in the house taking care of some last minute items, and Ray was bored—a most dangerous state for any child. The car's gas tank had been over-filled, and some gasoline had leaked out and created a small pool in the gutter next to the car. Ray and a neighbor boy, Keith Carlson, decided to see if they could ignite it, by hitting paper caps with a rock. Keith didn't think it would work, but Ray wanted to try. He hit the cap hard and, YEP, IT WORKED! The resulting flames streaked along the trail of volatile liquid under the gas tank, heating up the fuel inside. Hot gasoline began spewing from the tank to enhance the fire. Once more, the angels were on the job. A passerby saw the blaze, hustled the kids out of the car and pushed the station wagon away from the flames. It was courageous involvement because he could have been a victim of a potential explosion. Had he not chosen to get involved, we might have lost our entire family that day.

Fire was a fascination for many of our children. One summer afternoon in 1961, I was cutting someone's hair in the kitchen of our Wheaton home (Practice for the cosmetology class I was taking in preparation for our move to Missouri to start medical school.) I noticed water dripping from the ceiling, so I ran upstairs to discover the source. A toilet was overflowing. The plunger was in the basement, so I ran down the two flights to retrieve it, only to discover the basement filled with smoke. I grabbed the plunger and raced back upstairs, hollering for someone to find the source of the smoke. My brother-in-law, Arnie, was there, and he traced the source to beneath the large front porch. Steve, then about nine, Ray, eight and their cousins, ten-year-old Jeff and seven year old Gary had made a pile of dry leaves under the front porch and had started them on fire. Arnie grabbed a hose and extinguished the fire before there was any serious damage to kids or property and before the fire department had to be called.

When we moved to Columbia, Missouri, we discovered that Ray wasn't the only child in the family who had a wanderlust gene. Two-and-a-half-year-old Rick wandered away from our college-girl tenants who had agreed to baby-sit the kids while I went grocery shopping. With no car during our medical-school years, I would walk to Wyatt's Market, a long uphill block from our house, and then push my groceries home in a shopping cart. I had gotten back home to unload the cart, and then returned the cart to the store, assuming all the while that Rick was with his brothers and sisters in the care of the students. However, he was really at Stephens Lake, about a mile away! Nearly every Sunday we would walk to the lake and enjoy picnics there. The Lake was located near the campus of Stephens College, my alma mater, and, apparently, Rick decided a mid-week visit would be fun—by himself! After several changes of address and the addition of more children, the dog tag system had been forgotten, so Rick didn't have one. However, he was able to direct the police back to his home, and, to everyone's awkward embarrassment, he came riding up in a patrol car, smiling and much pleased with himself. The police told us that someone had called them to report a toddler wandering by the lake without any evidence of parents nearby. No one, at home, had even noticed he was gone, but I didn't admit that to the officers. I was too embarrassed to even try to explain. Fortunately, the social agencies weren't so quick then to convict parents of child neglect.

Pam gained her own distinction as a firebug in Columbia, while Bud was attending medical school. She was about four at the time and was playing with matches in the half-bath off the kitchen. When a match burned her finger, she dropped it into a full wastebasket, and the contents quickly burst into flame. The bathroom had a curtain, instead of a door, for privacy, and Pam tried to hide behind the curtain. I was in my beauty shop on the other side of the house giving a manicure. When I smelled the smoke, I ran to find its source. Flames were leaping up the curtain, and I tried, unsuccessfully, to knock the blazing curtain down. I was startled to discover Pam hiding behind the curtain, cowering against the bathroom wall. If I had been successful in knocking the curtain down, it would have fallen on her. My client, Grace Curtis, rescued Pam as I poured water into the trashcan and soaked the now smoldering ceiling with wet towels. Grace was the Dean of Women at Stephens College who had written a letter attesting to my parenting reliability when Bud was applying to Missouri Medical School! Once more, we were blessed. Pam suffered no serious burns, the house was still intact and Pam never played with matches again.

The kids' antics were not without their humorous aspects. A large storm sewer ran under our house in Columbia, Missouri to carry off the excess water when it rained. It was large enough for a small boy to walk through and, except when it rained, contained very little water. One day, the kids were outside playing and their baseball rolled into the storm sewer. The only one who could fit through the opening was Tony (age 8), and his older brothers, Steve and Ray, convinced him that it would be perfectly safe if they lowered him down into the sewer to retrieve the ball. He retrieved the ball, but they discovered they couldn't get him back up. Steve tried lowering a folding chair into the sewer for Tony to climb on, but that didn't work. Eventually, they came to get Bud, and he went outside and discovered poor, pathetic little Tony, standing with tears in his eyes in ankle-deep water in the dark underground passage. His *helpful* brothers, of course, had told him that giant spiders, rats and other vermin probably inhabited the sewer, and Tony was appropriately terrified—sure he was on the lunch menu for some vile creature. It was one of those moments when a father wants to laugh but knows he shouldn't. How would we get Tony out? Bud tried opening the cover of a nearby manhole, but it wouldn't budge. He then suggested to Tony that he make his way through the sewer to the far side of the street, where there was a larger opening and they could pull him out at that end. Tony would have none of that idea! Better to stand and fight off the sewer creatures where he was, rather than creep even deeper into their lair.

Seeing an opportunity for adventure, however, Steve and Ray headed for the far side of the street with flashlights and climbed into the sewer through the larger drain. In the meantime, Bud had gotten a crowbar and worked the nearby manhole open, allowing Tony to escape. Steve and Ray, now fired with the spirit of exploration, and apparently unconcerned about the sewer creatures with which they had terrified their younger brother, insisted on going back the way they had come. They discovered that this sewer connected to a vast complex of underground passages—in fact, the citywide storm drainage network—the knowledge of which would prove to be irresistible. We didn't know it at the time, but, years later, Steve and Ray told us that they, and there friends, had explored the underground storm sewers of Columbia on more than one occasion.

The destructive capacities of our children were positively legendary. (We marveled at Judd and Rita's children, who maintained their toys and even kept jigsaw puzzles intact for years.) One Christmas, during medical school years, my sister, Louise, and her family repainted some old toy trucks and sent them to our kids with the note, "We make 'em, you break 'em." Not only did toys and furniture shatter under the onslaught; household appliances gave way as well. Michael's curious tinkering with an adjustment screw disabled the bathroom scale. Candi broke the handle off a Hoover upright vacuum cleaner. I found it could be repaired with the replacement of a screw, but unfortunately, before I could tell him, Bud, assuming it was useless, had already thrown it out. On another occasion, the irreplaceable glass bowl from a vintage stainless steel Sunbeam Mixmaster my mother had used for years was broken within minutes of arriving at our house—before I even got a chance to use it. Of course spills and miscellaneous messes were everyday occurrences. Whatever could be spilled usually was.

We faced flooded bathrooms and basements when socks, toothbrushes and diapers got flushed down toilets. We coped with clogged pipes and air vents when various articles were directed by the kids into the most unlikely places. Rick once dropped a curtain rod down a furnace flue (a large, old-fashioned, gravity-feed opening in the floor). It was retrieved when Bud held Ray upside down by his feet and lowered him into the flue.

Rick seemed to have a talent for creating unique messes. He once dumped a canister of tea on the floor behind a living room chair, and then dribbled cleansing lotion over the heap, creating a sort of "frosting" effect. Bud got his most vivid taste of Rick's talent after Rick spilled a whole box of salt on the kitchen counter and into some cake pans I was planning to use. I recovered the salt from the pans, placed it in a cup and set it aside. The next morning, half-asleep and in a hurry, Bud sprinkled what he thought was sugar on his cereal. He wasn't happy! (Perhaps there is a certain poetic justice in this episode since, as a child, Bud took unappreciated delight in reversing the sugar and salt as an April Fool's gag on his own father.)

Rick's antics figured prominently in one memorable day typical of my motherhood experiences. The morning started with Rick (then 3) climbing into our bed, his pajamas soaked. I rose to discover three other wet kids. I then set all four little bodies into the tub, stripped the wet beds (including our own) and gathered up the damp sheets for the laundry. When all but Rick, Candi and Pam were off to school, I briefly (and foolishly) entertained the idea of a leisurely breakfast. That notion was dispelled when Rick spilled an entire quart of orange juice onto the kitchen floor. As I was on my knees sopping up Florida's liquid sunshine, Candi spotted the eggs, which the milkman had left on the porch, and she began transferring them to the egg holder in the refrigerator. Jealous of his sister's helpful participation, Rick grabbed the egg carton from Candi. With alertness only mothers have, I managed to rescue all but one of the eggs. That egg reached the floor, but the inconvenience was minimal since I was already down there cleaning up the orange juice.

About this time, the buzzer on the washing machine alerted me to the fact that the load of laundry was done washing, so I entreated the kids to avoid making any more messes and headed for the basement. After transferring the clean sheets, I turned on the dryer, and it promptly made a loud noise and stopped running! Since my husband was not home, I decided to analyze the problem myself. (Like my grandmother would have done.) I pulled the machine away from the wall, found a screwdriver and removed the back panel to see if the drive belt was broken. The belt was intact, but as I was checking it,—"*POW!*"—There was a loud noise behind me. Startled, I quickly turned to see the remains of a broken light bulb on the floor and Rick, age 5, smiling innocently nearby. He was not hurt, so I scolded him appropriately, cleaned up the glass and returned to my research on the dryer. Meanwhile, Rick, trying to be helpful to get back in my good graces, decided to empty the basement dehumidifier. He did and emptied it all over the floor!

By this time my patience was wearing thin, so I gave up on my dryer repair efforts and went back upstairs to telephone the repairman. After relating my tale of woe to the service department and my desperate need for a working dryer, I hung up. Only then did I notice that the kids had made honey toast, a favorite breakfast snack. Unfortunately, the honey had been spread on slices of toast that were placed on a partially assembled, 600-piece jigsaw puzzle. Cleaning honey off of puzzle pieces as almost as difficult as putting the pieces together. Moreover, the kids antics did not end there because while I was cleaning up the sticky puzzle, the sticky table top and the sticky floor, the kids decided to do a bit of exploring in the floor furnace flue (the same one from which Ray had previously extracted the fallen curtain rod.) It was probably Rick's idea since he thought it was so neat the way Ray had retrieved the rod. The floor grate was removed and they had climbed inside. They were black! When I pulled them out of the flue, my patience was at an end. As I was about to launch into a fierce scolding, I was overcome with laughter at the three soot-covered "urchins" who looked like some weird parody of Buckwheat from the old "Our Gang" comedies. Back into the tub they went for their second bath of the morning. It was only 10 a.m.!

I usually manage to stay calm when responding to the various crises of our family life. However, the episode that shattered my coping ability was in Columbia, when three of the kids took a spill into a window well. Terry, Pam, Candi and Rick were sitting on the back of the couch, leaning against the storm window, when suddenly the pane swung open. Pam, Candi and Rick fell backwards off the couch, going out the window and into the cement window well four feet below. Only Terry, holding on by the tips of her fingers, managed to avoid falling. She came running to get me. I was eight months pregnant (with Lisa) and had recently suffered a fall, myself. I was trying to cope with severe back pain by resting on the reclining chair in my beauty shop. Bud was at medical school in the midst of semester exams and we had no car. Therefore, in tears and feeling helpless and unable to rescue the kids myself, I called the woman who helped clean our house. She came right over and took us all to the Missouri University Hospital emergency room. Pam's nose was broken, and Candi had a major bump on her head and two black eyes. Rick raised the biggest fuss and looked the worst because he was covered with blood. The blood turned out to be Pam's, and once Rick was cleaned up, we discovered he had only scratched a finger. Meanwhile, Bud was called out of his exam to calm his uncharacteristically hysterical wife. Fortunately, everyone including me recovered without permanent scars.

Even when they weren't being messy, destructive or otherwise challenging, it was rare for all the Vear kids to be well behaved and cooperative at the same time. To put things in proper prospective, however, I have realized that one of the blessings of a large family is that, when one child is acting up, you can generally find another who is doing something wonderful. Sometimes this was the only thing that preserved my sanity. Nonetheless, few collective undertakings ever proceeded without some frustrations.

A perfect example of the challenge we faced regularly in trying to coordinate the family was getting family photographs each year. Bud has often said that if it were not for my persistence we would have very few family photos. In our first 16 years of marriage we struggled through the process yearly so we could introduce our new family members through our Christmas card. In 1963, in Columbia, Missouri, we had only nine kids, so pulling off a group shot should have been a piece of cake. We got everyone dressed, primped and combed, piled the lot into the old pick-up truck Bud used in his summer house painting and drove down to the local hotel where Olin Mills was offering a family portrait special. After his initial shock at the size of the group, the photographer arranged everyone by height, tinkered with his lights and then made a few refinements in positioning. Suddenly, he looked up, perplexed.

"How many children did you say you have?" he asked.

"Nine."

He counted heads. "Where's the ninth?"

I took my own quick tally, got to eight, and then one of the kids asked, "Where's Ricky?"

Bud made a quick search, found Rick wandering around the hotel lobby and brought him back to the family portrait. At that point, Lisa (then four months) started screaming. After much fussing, fidgeting and time spent trying to get Lisa calmed down, our picture was taken. The kids were delighted that this yearly event was over—and so were Bud and I.

Early the next week, we received a call from the photographer who very apologetically informed us that he had had some technical problems, and the photo would have to be taken again! I suspect his supervisor had to withhold his paycheck to get him to make *that* call. We were not pleased, but again we trooped down to the hotel with everyone dressed, primped and combed, counted to make sure all were present and got the family arranged in front of the camera. As the photographer was making some final adjustments, Steve started swaying back and forth, looking ill. At the same time, Gay moaned, "I think I'm gonna throw up!" Lisa started crying once again, which started Steve (who was now feeling awful) crying too.

I suggested that the photographer shoot the next family group while we got Steve and Gay something to help calm their stomachs. I settled Lisa, and Bud went to buy some Coca-Cola for the nauseous pair. That started all the other kids complaining that they were feeling sick, in hopes of getting cokes of their own. Tony even went so far as to bang his head against the back of a chair several times to give himself a headache.

The portrait was eventually taken, but it must be reported that the representation of the Vear family, which appeared on that 1963 Christmas card, was less than flattering. The photographer was not to blame. The impression we made on that poor man was typical of what we showed to the world. Pretty much everyone who walked (or stumbled) into our life came away with a story to tell. One of these was a startled telephone repairman . . . .

Bud had managed to get two days off work at the hospital, so he could be home for Michael's baptism and a family celebration afterwards. Though he wasn't working, it was necessary for Bud to be available by phone in case he was needed at the hospital. The evening of his first day off we discovered that our phone was out of order. I called the phone company from a neighbor's house, explaining our urgent need for a functioning phone, and a repairman was dispatched. The house was in an unusually severe state of chaos—well beyond the usual state of disorder. We had just finished eating and the dining room table was still full of supper dishes. Sections of the evening paper were strewn about, and a pile of cardboard boxes were scattered around the floor. The boxes had held an assortment of clothes some relatives had sent to the kids, and some of the kids had already removed items to see if there was something they could wear to the Baptism. Those they didn't like were flung hither and thither around the living room. Some of our other kids were playing in the basement, where the acrid smell of stale cat litter wafted from an overflowing litter box. Tony decided to be helpful and empty the litter box, but while he was carrying the litter box up the basement stairs, he tripped, sending a cascade of smelly granules down the entire length of the stairway and onto the floor below.

About this time the repairman arrived at the front door! I led him through the maze of cartons in the living room and into the kitchen where the trashcan was piled high with a mound of food boxes, wrappings and assorted rubbish. As he started down the partially swept stairs, he caught a whiff of the kitty liter and stumbled against the trash can, whose contents toppled like a stack of dominos, sending milk cartons, empty cake mix boxes and used Pampers across the kitchen floor.

I forced a smile and quickly apologized for the mess before leading the repairman into the basement, where the sound of Vear children at play had risen to its customary roar. We located the telephone terminal box, and the technician (by now somewhat tense) was testing its wires when a call came through on his portable phone set. It was my mother. Since the call was long-distance, I smiled again and took the phone, leaving the man to observe a riotous game of keep-away then in progress. He had to dodge occasionally when the ball went whizzing past his head.

Grandma Kit had discovered a good buy on some surplus groceries available at discount (always an advantage on our limited budget), and, since she would be bringing them with her when she came to the baptism, she needed to know what kinds of canned goods the kids might like. The repairman waited, patiently, as my mother ticked off the list of items available, and I responded, "yes," "no" or "maybe". Suspecting the repairman was becoming impatient (if not outright fearful for his life), I promised to call mother back later and handed over the portable phone. Then I made a quick exit, leaving the harried technician to complete his task in as much peace as possible.

When he had finished in the basement, the repairman came upstairs to check the kitchen extension. At that moment, wild shrieking came from the second floor, followed by screaming children running down the stairs.

"Bat! Bat! There's a bat up there!"

Brave Tony to the rescue! He threw a football at the frightened creature, missing the bat and knocking a curtain rod off its bracket. The phone rang again. It was the mother of a neighbor boy, who had come over to play, telling him it was time to come home. However, when word of the bat reached the boy's older brother, he hurried over to join in the chase. A wild pursuit was underway, with the telephone repairman joining in. In the middle of the melee, Ray emerged from the shower, wondering at the fuss and wearing nothing but a towel. The bat was finally captured in a sack, and the neighbor boys took it home for use in a science project.

Shaking his head in bewilderment, the repairman went outside to check the exterior line. A faulty connection between the house and the telephone pole seemed to be the source of our erratic phone service. With confusing instructions from Terry, the repairman made his way through some bushes to the rear of the yard to where I was burning the trash from the kitchen. Along the way, a clothesline nearly strangled him and the handle of a rake came up and hit him in the face. Rubbing his face, he told me it was getting too late to work on the phone, but he said he would be back in the morning to repair the connection. He never returned! Someone else came to finish the job.

Fire prevention and safe handling of combustible materials became a regular subject of parental lectures in the Vear household, but I doubt that our entreaties did the least bit of good.

When Bud was interning at Saint Luke's Hospital in Saginaw, Michigan in 1966-67, Steve, then 15, survived serious burns to his face and hands while trying to make his own firecrackers. Unbeknownst to us, he was up in his third floor bedroom sifting chemicals in a metal sifter to get the lumps out of a mixture of phosphorous and magnesium, apparently unaware that phosphorous is highly sensitive to heat from friction. Suddenly, the mixture caught fire, engulfing him in a flash of about 2,000 degrees, burning his hands and face and catching the walls and ceiling on fire.

Bud and I heard the explosion, followed by blood-curdling screams, and we rushed upstairs. There was Steve, standing dazed at the top of the stairway, face and hands white with powder from the explosion, and the desk and bedroom wall in flames. He had been temporarily blinded from the explosion, so Bud led him down to the second floor where I put him under a cold shower. Bud then grabbed a wastebasket, filled it with water and raced upstairs to extinguish the fire. Unfortunately, the basket had a hole in the bottom and most of the water leaked out on the way up. One of the children had called the fire department, but the old frame structure would be burning out of control before they arrived, unless we could do something to slow the blaze. I started downstairs to look for a small aerosol fire extinguisher we had purchased in a school fundraiser. Ray—inquisitive, independent-spirited Ray—met Bud at the top of the stairs with the extinguisher in hand, asking, "Will this help?" At the start of the crisis, he'd had the presence of mind to run downstairs and fetch the small canister. Bud had time to spray the flames a couple of times before smoke and fumes drove him back downstairs. Amazingly, the fire went out. Ray's quick action had saved the house. (Shortly after this incident, the government, in their infinite wisdom, outlawed this type of small aerosol fire extinguisher.)

Were angels whispering in Ray's ear? Who can say? Earlier in the day, they might have been whispering to Bud and me. We'd planned a family outing to search for a possible replacement for our old station wagon, and Steve had begged to stay home to "work on my project." We refused his request. Had we allowed him to stay, he would have been there alone when the explosion occurred.

Steve spent a month recovering in the hospital, enduring considerable pain. His worst moments were the dressing changes, made bearable only by injections of strong pain medication. Bud and I shared in his suffering, as we watched our son go through these painful ordeals. His isolation in the hospital recalled the isolation he had experienced with polio years before. Because infection is such a major concern with widespread burns, isolation techniques are employed, and we had to put on gowns and masks when visiting. His room was lined with plastic to prevent stains from the silver nitrate dressings they used to treat the burns. Steve recovered, and— happy to say—in spite of extensive second-degree burns—avoided any scarring.

Shortly after we moved to Hillsdale, Michigan in the summer of 1967, to start Bud's medical practice, we completed our dozen with the arrival of twins, Kevin & Kelly on September 26. Therefore, our potential for family crises increased.

The dozen is completed
Hillsdale, MI 1967

Getting baby sitters for our large brood was a real challenge and usually involved unrealistic reassurance from us or outright deceit. ("The older children will help you!" or "Our children are very well behaved.") After experiencing our "well behaved children" once, seldom would a sitter return for a second exposure. Dennis and Cheryl Hrcka were the exceptions and they managed to survive many encounters with our twelve. In fact they still remain two of our closest friends. Dennis was a student and basketball player at Hillsdale College. He was also six foot eight and Cheryl, while considerably shorter in stature, was a firm disciplinarian with a great sense of humor. Their presence in the house while we were gone was probably more for control of our teenagers than for care of our infants. Dennis was in charge of the older kids and Cheryl the younger ones.

On one memorable occasion, Cheryl was changing one of the twin's diapers in the laundry room when she heard footsteps above her. She thought about this for a few seconds and then suddenly realized that there was no room above her—just the roof! She hollered at Dennis in the other room and told him he better check this out right away. He ran outside, saw a ladder propped against the house and looked up on the roof to discover some of the kids chasing each other over the peaks and valleys and 3 year old Michael halfway up the ladder on his way to join them! Dennis tried to remain calm so as not to alarm Michael before he reached him, but once Michael was safe, our tall baby sitter shouted at the other kids,

"What in blazes are you doing on the roof?" (This was a rather senseless question, since obviously they were *playing*!) All returned safely to ground level, and I don't think we heard the story until much later.

In fact, there were several other happenings that went on while we were gone which we didn't hear about until later. Dennis caught one of our adolescent sons smoking a cigarette and our wayward son, concerned about the consequences, assured Denny that he would tell us about it himself. Trusting this promise, Denny did not tell us. Neither did our son. I suspect he rationalized that he said he would tell us. He just didn't say when! Two years later we learned about it.

On another occasion the Hrckas were watching the kids while we were away at a medical conference. Before we returned, Tony, at age 13, broke his arm in a tumble from a half-completed tree house, located near Bud's medical office. He fell as he was very carefully inching backward to measure a piece of plywood that was not yet secured. The plywood flipped up, and down he went. Bud and I learned about the accident as we signed Tony's cast after our return. This same tree house project was the cause of a number of mishaps. Earlier that same day, Tony's friend, Mark Cantrell, had suffered a fall, breaking *his* arm, and, another day, Candi's hand was cut on a saw, when Tony asked her to catch it as he dropped it down from the tree. In addition, another friend, Kevin Pauken, suffered bruises from a falling 2-by-4. (Years later, as a father,

Tony did complete an impressive and sturdy tree house for his own children, but he curtails their climbing on anything less sturdy.)

Over the years, auto accidents have kept the guardian angels busy. As a teenager, Gay ran her first car into a tree after falling asleep at the wheel. She was unhurt, and the experience actually helped get her into great physical condition by making it necessary for her to bicycle six miles to work every day. Another accident occurred after she was married, and she was not so lucky. She and her husband failed to negotiate a curve. The car rolled, leaving Gay with a broken back. Six weeks in traction and a positive attitude pulled her through, and she has remained very active ever since, including working in her own landscaping business.

Lisa rolled our Chevette completely over one time on a snowy, slippery highway. She landed in a snowdrift, and was able to drive the car away with no damage to herself or the vehicle. A few years later she totaled that same car, sliding it under the back of a semi in similar weather conditions.

While Steve was attending Central Michigan University, he visited Frankenmuth during their annual beer festival and suffered a broken jaw when he slid off the front hood of a car. He had jumped on the hood, as the car was moving, to get a ride to the park entrance, but when he started sliding off, the driver slammed on his breaks and Steve shot forward onto the road, hitting his jaw as he rolled. He was taken to the hospital in Saginaw, from where we were notified, and we drove two and half hours each way to get him and transport him back to the Hillsdale Hospital where his fractured jaw was wired shut by Dr. Booth, an oral surgeon. For several weeks he took his nourishment through a straw and found he could liquefy most everything—including pizza!

On another occasion Steve ran into a deer, obliterating a Volkswagen shortly after spending many weeks taking the car apart, installing a new engine and reassembling it. Years later, he collided with deer twice within a two-week span and ran a rental car into some boulders at a "T" in the road when his vision was impaired by dense fog.

Our youngest daughter, Kelly, had what was probably the most miraculous highway escape. Driving to a meeting, in a torrential rain from her Washington, D.C. office—during rush hour—and praying that she would make it safely, she was sideswiped in the outside lane of the very busy D.C. beltway by a car that was merging from an incoming road. She went into a spin across the other two lanes, coming to rest alongside the left guardrail facing both the onrushing traffic and the car that had collided with her. Except for slight damage from the sideswiping, both vehicles were intact. In a hurry to go, the other driver left Kelly his address and assured her he would pay for the damage. He was faithful to his word, and Kelly made it to her meeting on time!

The most persistent firebug in the family was Michael. At age 3, the fireplace fascinated him. One day, when there was no one else in the room, he managed to get a hot glowing ember onto the fireplace shovel and very carefully place in on the couch. He repeated the process, transferring several more coals from hearth to couch. By the time we smelled smoke, the coals had burned through the fabric. The couch was smoldering and had to be carried outside so the fire could be extinguished. The couch had to be reupholstered . . .

The following year, Mike conducted more experiments with fire—only more secretively—starting two blazes behind closed doors. The first time, he lit some papers in the furnace room, closed the door as he left the room and hoped no one would notice. We discovered the fire when smoke began drifting into the living room—in time to call the fire department and prevent a more serious fire. The fuse box, located in the furnace room, had to be rewired because of fire damage. Mike's next experiment was in the bathroom, where he set a small fire in a wastebasket under the sink. This time he not only closed the door but also locked it (to conceal his mischief) and ran into the other room. When we smelled smoke, we forced the door open and were able to extinguish the fire, but a new vanity had to be installed to cover the hole in the floor under the sink.

It's easy to be critical of other parents, when you hear of someone's house, barn or trailer burning, due to a child's mischief or carelessness. However, we've been there (and our angels have, too), and we can testify that a kid bent on seeing what fire can do is one determined creature. You can't be too watchful—and, all too often, you can't be watchful enough.

We never did cure our children's' fascination with fire, a reality which was demonstrated in recent years, when son, Rick, who now lives in California with his wife and their four sons, nearly turned himself into a human torch by throwing gasoline on a burning fire. He wound up with extensive burns on his hands and face, which fortunately left no permanent scars.

Steve's closest brush with death did not involve fire, and was a somewhat humbling experience for Bud. It came when Steve was swimming with some friends at Baw Beese Lake, in Hillsdale one night, after the Park's curfew. He and his friends spotted a police car, cruising the area, and they scrambled for cover behind some bushes. Steve tried to jump over a cable, but his floppy sandals caught on the wire and, with his polio-weakened left arm unable to break his fall, came down hard on his belly. His stomach started hurting, and the pain became so severe that he came out of hiding and flagged down the police car. The officers took him to the emergency room.

When Steve arrived, Bud was in the hospital, waiting to deliver a baby. He came to the emergency room, checked Steve's vital signs, which were fine, and judged that Steve's condition was not serious. Bud gave him some pain pills and sent him home. (The hazard of being a physician's son is that doctor-dads often don't take the symptoms and complaints of family members as seriously as they should.) After Steve returned home, the pain became worse, so he called back to the hospital, and Bud suggested he take another pain pill. Finally, Steve became so weak, and in so much pain, that he couldn't even walk upstairs to wake me. We had two phone lines, so he was able to crawl to the phone and call me from the other line. I phoned the hospital—which was just across the street—and the emergency room nurse, Ella Cook, suggested I bring Steve over. She said she would keep an eye on him in the emergency room until morning. (This was before HMO's and insurance companies dictated care.) I drove him across the street to the hospital, dropped him off at the emergency room and then returned home to be there for the other eleven children.

By this time, Bud's OB patient was in the final stages of her labor, so he couldn't leave her. When Steve's blood pressure began dropping, Bud told the nurse to call Dr. Clark Smith, a friend and colleague of Bud's, for an evaluation. Dr. Smith checked Steve, and when he inserted a needle into his abdomen, he drew back bright red blood, indicating internal hemorrhage. Ed Henelt, a local surgeon, was called, and in less than an hour he operated and removed a ruptured spleen. Phil Fleming, the anesthetist (and also a friend) told us Steve's blood pressure had dropped to near zero during the procedure (which was about where Bud felt his medical credibility had fallen.) Steve's guardian angel must share the credit with Ella Cook, Dr. Smith, Dr. Henelt and Phil Fleming for Steve's survival on this occasion.

Sometimes angelic intervention seems to work so well that, not only is disaster averted, but also the mishap can actually yield unexpected benefits. Candi, at age 14, was walking home along a back road from a community theatre rehearsal for the musical, *Carousel,* in which she had a prominent role. Just as she was about to cross the road to walk facing traffic, an elderly driver with poor eyesight passed too close from behind, and his car hit her left arm. The arm was broken and put in a plaster cast for six weeks, eliminating her from *Carousel* and wiping out her plans to be a cheerleader and to participate in the marching band that fall. Candi was devastated, but the closing of these doors opened a window of opportunity two years later. The insurance settlement she received for the injury enabled her to spend her high school junior year in Belgium as an exchange student, which, in turn, enabled her to qualify for a foreign-language scholarship at Stephens College.

Illness and injury are part of childhood. If we had more than our share, it's because we had more than our share of children. However, our angels probably did special duty in the more creative misadventures for which the Vear kids seemed to have their own unique flair. Our survival secret for our children's escapades, in addition to angelic intervention, was maintaining a sense of humor. The ability to laugh at ourselves and our children, has softened many of our challenges, but the humor of a situation has sometimes taken days, weeks, months or even years to surface. Our children have given us both frustration and joy in abundance. We have enjoyed *most* of the journey, but please don't ask us to repeat it!

Chapter Sixteen

(Bud)

CREATIVE FINANCING

Today's parents probably base the size of their family on more rational financial logic than we did. Today we sometimes hear the following economic justifications for having small families:

"We can't afford another child. It takes two jobs just to survive."

"It costs $250,000 to raise a child to the age of 21."

"I want my children (or child) to have the things I didn't have, when I was growing up."

None of these applied to us. I'm not sure what formula was used to arrive at the $250,000 figure (which, actually, was the figure used 30 years ago), but, if it was accurate, our children were short-changed!

Finances were a continuous concern, of course, as we tried to feed, clothe and house our growing family on limited resources, but I can't recall the lack of money ever influencing our decision to have more children. When we married, I had $50 in a savings account and was a fulltime graduate student.

My income consisted of $110 per month from the GI Bill (our Government's education benefit for ex-service men and woman), and our rent was $60 a month. In addition, for the first eight months of our marriage, Gloria had a low paying clerical job with Meridian Mutual Insurance Company in Indianapolis. Since our medical insurance was not in effect long enough to cover maternity benefits for our first child, we had to pay these expenses ourselves. In spite of her low pay, Gloria was able to save enough money to pay the medical bills for her first delivery (about $150 for Hospital and Doctor). She was a stay-at-home-mom from then on, so we never became accustomed to a second household income. *My* mother never worked outside the home, nor did many mothers in her generation, so we just took it for granted that it was a man's responsibility to provide for his family.

My first job with the Chicago Boys Club, after six years of college and a Master's Degree in Social Work, paid me less than $300 a month ($3450 per year). We wanted a large family, and we entered parenthood with the innocent faith that God would provide a way for us to feed and clothe any children he sent our way. Gloria expressed a hope, at that time, that someday we might have an income of $1000 per month! I smiled and told her that she had unrealistic expectations. In Social Work, I could never hope to make *that* much.

A year and a half after starting my job with the Boys Club, our financial situation took on new urgency when I was hospitalized for 15 months with tuberculosis. Our income consisted of $75 a month from the Boys Club (Fortunately, they also paid for our family health insurance.) and an unexpected, but very welcome, monthly disability check of about the same amount from the Veterans Administration. Gloria and the kids went to live with her parents for six months and then with mine for the next six months. We had two children when I went into the hospital, but Gloria was also 3 months pregnant, so our family size increased during my hospital confinement. Katherine Gay, our first daughter, arrived on March 30, 1954.

In September, with three months remaining in my hospital stay, Gloria moved back into 1663 N. Orchard, our Chicago apartment, with our 3 children, ages 2½, 1½ and 6 months. She had survived twelve months of living with in-laws and parents and was anxious to return to her own home. With $25 a month from the Boys Club, $85 from the Disabled American Veterans and loans of $50 each month from each of our parents (all of which we later repaid), the household operated frugally. Had they been available, we would surely have qualified for welfare and food stamps, but we managed to survive the old fashioned way—with the help of friends and family. Occasional food baskets were dropped off as we approached the holidays, but our acceptance of them did not please my father. He considered accepting any charity as shameful, and he admonished us for not letting him know about our needs. We were up against it, financially, but we were too proud to ask our parents for any more help. We didn't want to be the recipients of charity even though we were in need, but we decided that refusing the help that was offered would probably offend the donors, and we would be doing it simply to protect our own pride. It was humbling to be on the receiving end of generosity, and we were made aware of how much easier it is to give than to receive. It also suggests that the kindest charity may be anonymous. We accepted the offerings. They were most welcome.

After I left the Boys Club and started teaching, our income increased a little, but so did our family, with the addition of five more children during the next six years. Tony arrived Sept. 28, 1955, Terry on March 17, 1957, Candi Feb. 23, 1958, Pam on May 8th, 1959 and Rick on Nov. 1, 1960. We continued to struggle to make ends meet. One benefit of teaching was that I could earn extra money during the summers to supplement my teaching income. My summer employment included factory work and painting.

For two summers, the father of one of my students obtained a job for me in the Quality Control Department of Motorola, where he was a Vice President. My task was to write an instruction manual for new employees. I would spend the day observing different workers operating their machines, and then write a step-by-step description of what they did. Since I am not very mechanically inclined, I asked many questions and wrote very simple instructions. The machine operators probably wondered how I ever got through college! I don't know if they ever used my manual, but it kept me employed for two summers.

Other summers I painted houses, a rather common summer job for teachers, but one summer I decided to create a niche business and received a memorable lesson in free enterprise. Locating house numbers on many houses in Wheaton was difficult or impossible, so I decided to solve that problem while generating some income. I painted house numbers on the curbs in front of residential dwellings. It seemed like a worthwhile endeavor with potential for good income, but it would be accurate to report that I spent the summer in the gutter. This produced bewildered stares from my students and their parents, who happened to pass by while I was sitting in the street working on the numbers. I'm sure my appearance did little to enhance my image as a teacher.

That summer gave me a new appreciation for entrepreneurs. Initially I made four stops at each house and charged $1.50. The first stop was to ask the homeowner if he wanted the number painted, the second was to paint the yellow background, the third was to stencil the black numbers, and the fourth was to collect the money. After a couple weeks, I decided this was not good time management, so I started painting the numbers, (hoping they wouldn't object—some *did*) and asking for a donation. This approach reduced the stops per house and enabled me to move from house to house more quickly. The donations averaged about a dollar, but the increased efficiency made it more profitable. Not profitable enough, however; so *that* experience with free enterprise ended after one summer.

We never ignored our creditors, but Gloria sometimes wrote them touching letters about our financial plight. This sometimes resulted in a reduction in our bill or a delayed payment schedule. In fact, just before I went to medical school, our pediatrician in Elmhurst graciously canceled our entire remaining balance.

Feeding a large family on our limited budget was always a challenge. We bought food in large economy sizes, went to day-old bakery outlets, seldom purchased snack food or pop, looked for sales, constantly compared prices and almost never ate out. We *did* discover that cheaper was not always better. We found that the bargain hand soap dissolved twice as fast as the more expensive variety and the cheaper off-brand breakfast cereal tasted like the cardboard box it came in.

Gloria learned to stretch food in simple but effective ways. She added more water to the soup, more breadcrumbs to the meat loaf or more beans to the chili. It was amazing the creative ways she could stretch a pound of hamburger to feed 14! Turkey carcasses were always good for at least one meal after a holiday, and any leftover meat, vegetables and potatoes would invariably end up in a pot of *super soup*. The soup ingredients were never the same, but it was nourishing, made good use of leftovers and, actually, was one of the family's favorite meals. Dessert would often be Jell-O, which, on an extravagant day, might include a can of fruit. Occasionally, we would have ice cream, and I became very skilled at cutting a half-gallon into 14 equal-sized portions. Of course, the kids always found small differences, so we established a method of distribution that I had learned at YMCA Camp years before. It was called "Horse 'n Goggle", and it worked this way: I called out "Horse & Goggle", and each kid would hold up one to five fingers. I would add the fingers held up, and then I would count around the table until I reached that total. Whomever I ended with, had the first pick, and the selection order would continue clockwise around the table until everyone had made their selection. Most of the kids will say that they never won, but it probably evened out. With 14 entries, the victories would not come often. Another system was used when only two kids were involved. One of them divided the item and the other picked which half he or she wanted. It was amazing how equal the portions became.

One of the advantages of having so many kids is that getting them to eat different kinds of food (even vegetables) was never a problem. Whatever one child didn't like, another would gladly consume. Moreover, since there were no snacks or replacement food available, you ate what was served or you went without. We seldom had leftovers.

Transporting a large family is difficult in the best of circumstances, but without a car, it is a *real* challenge. Today, most families have two or more cars, but for the first thirteen years of our married life, we couldn't afford *one*. Gloria's mother gave us her ancient Chevy coupe when we first got married, but a few months later, as we were returning to our home in Indianapolis after a trip to Dayton, the car threw a rod and could not be driven. We left the car at an auto repair shop on the east edge of Indianapolis and told the mechanic he could keep it because we couldn't afford to repair it. A short time later my father donated his old Buick to us, but it used so much gas and oil that we couldn't afford to keep it on the road. We sold it for $150 and gave the money, anonymously, to a couple, who had just lost their home in a fire. It was probably the most truly charitable thing we have ever done, and we were somewhat disappointed when, many years later, the recipients found out the source of the gift. I have the firm belief that heavenly rewards are reduced in direct proportion to the earthly rewards we receive, so their discovery probably eliminated most of our holy credits.

Once a week, during our years in Elmhurst, Gloria's mom

would drive the 20 miles from her home in Wheaton to take
Gloria shopping, and after our move to Wheaton, we were able
to borrow Aunt Edy's new Pontiac for trips to the store and
occasional picnics. We did a lot of walking, and probably were
healthier for it. During medical school, I rode my bike (a gift
from my family), and I became adept at carrying everything
from books to groceries to lumber in my rear baskets or balanced
on my front handle bar. The summer after our first year of
medical school, Larry Griffith, (a medical school classmate)
and I did purchase an old pick-up truck to use for our house
painting business, and, sometimes on a Sunday, Gloria and I
would load the kids in the back and go for a picnic.

Finally, just before the last year of medical school, we
purchased a four-year-old white Chevy station wagon, financed
by a friendly Columbia bank, with nothing down and a payment
of $25 per month until I finished my schooling. It provided the
transportation for our first extended family vacation; our twelve-
day trip to Colorado, with a rented fold-down camper and a
budget of ten dollars a day.

Shortly after starting my medical practice in Hillsdale, I
came home one day and tried to promote what I thought was a
wonderful idea for family transportation. I suggested that we
buy a used *airport limousine*. These were available for $6,000
in Battle Creek, just an hour and a half from Hillsdale, and,
with four seats, I thought it would be an ideal way to transport
our oversized family. We could all travel together in relative
comfort, and there would be a little less conflict over window
seats. The kids all groaned and unanimously declared, "*We're*
not going to ride in *that* thing!" So much for family unity!

We seldom had more than one car in Hillsdale while the
kids were growing up. This eliminated arguments over their
use of the car, since I needed to have it available in case I had
to make a house call. We also lived close enough to my office
and the hospital that I could walk or ride my bike, and this
meant that Gloria could use the car during the day.

New clothes were a luxury reserved for Christmas and birthdays, and at other times of the year Gloria had no hang-up about shopping at Good Will or Salvation Army outlets or accepting gifts of clothes from families whose children had out-grown them. Of course, hand-me-downs within the family were common, and Gloria tried to buy good quality clothes because she knew more than one child would use them.

Our second year in Hillsdale, the high school eliminated their dress code for students. Therefore, clothing consistent with the peer style of that time became very important, as far as the kids were concerned. Hip huggers and old jeans, preferably with holes in the knees, were "in". We partially controlled our kids' choices by making them pay half the cost of any clothing they bought after the age of 15. This gave them an incentive to get a part time job, to compare prices and to check out re-sale stores. Gloria thought the popular styles looked awful and insisted they dress better for church.

Handling the household finances became a rotating job between Gloria and me. When one of us became too frustrated with the monthly balancing act between available funds and bills, we would turn the job over to the other person. The problem, of course, was not with the person writing the checks; it was with the lack of funds. Finally, after I had criticized Gloria often enough for not keeping the bills paid, she turned the task over to me for good. I would give her a check twice a month with which to buy groceries and then try to pay all the outstanding bills with what was left. We still ran short of funds, and the children learned that bill-paying time was a very poor time to approach me for any extra money. Exhortations to turn off the lights, turn down the heat and to reduce phone usage were monthly pronouncements from me, as I struggled to make the income match the expenditures.

Another way to reduce expenditures was to do home maintenance work myself instead of hiring someone else to do it. Since my aptitude for such tasks was somewhat deficient, my attempts, not infrequently, would result in loss of time *and money*. Plumbing would probably qualify as my most deficient trade. Anytime I attempted a plumbing job, something disastrous was bound to happen.

On one memorable occasion, I decided to replace an old, leaky kitchen faucet. Although this seemed a simple enough task, I wisely set aside two full days to accomplish it. The first problem I encountered was that I couldn't remove the old faucet. I went to the hardware store, bought a hack saw and sawed it off! The next challenge was that the pipes under the sink were different sizes, requiring several trips back to the hardware store for different size connectors and some replacement piping. However, after *only a day and a half*, I had completed the job and was busy congratulating myself, when one of my sons shouted up from the basement and told me there was a leak down there. I said, "There can't be a leak down there. I was never down in the basement!" My investigation, however, revealed that with all the movement of the pipes in the kitchen, I had broken a sweat joint in the piping downstairs. Fortunately, I had two large home maintenance books for people just like me. I checked them to find out how to sweat a plumbing joint. I needed a blow torch and solder, which of course I didn't have. Back to the hardware store for more purchases. The process sounded easy. All you do is heat the joint with the torch and then touch the solder to the hot pipe and it will melt and flow around the joint to form a waterproof seal. I tried this for 30 minutes but couldn't get the solder to melt. In utter frustration, I went outside to reduce my stress level. My neighbor was outside and, although he was a bricklayer, I thought he might offer some suggestions. He did. He asked me if I had drained the water from the pipe before I tried to sweat the joint. Of course I hadn't. Neither of my marvelous home maintenance books said anything about draining the water. Apparently they took for granted that *anyone* would know that much! I called the plumber!

He came and fixed the leak quickly, but just when I thought my plumbing credibility had reached bottom, he managed to expose my ignorance one more time. There was a broken sweat joint in our garage bathroom, but the pipe was attached to a plywood wall, and I envisioned the wall burning if I tried to torch the joint. I had decided that sweating that joint would be a rather involved process, so I asked the young plumber (who happened to be a patient of mine) to take a look at it and give me an estimate of the cost to fix it. Within fifteen minutes he was back in the house, and I asked, "Well, what do you think?"

"Oh, I took care of it", he responded, "and it was such a small job that it won't cost you anything."

"What did you do", I asked with surprise?

"I simply slipped a piece of metal between the pipe and the plywood and sweat the joint."

That was the moment, I resolved never to attempt plumbing again!

*　　*　　*

While I don't pretend to be a financial wizard, after we moved to Hillsdale, I did adopt a little of the wisdom found in a little book, "The Richest Man in Babylon" by George S. Clason. He promoted the idea of putting some money in savings each payday *before* paying the bills. I set up three savings accounts; one for vacations, one for education and one for Christmas, and faithfully deposited $25 into each account from each paycheck. It wasn't much, but it was nice to have money available when those events came around. I incorporated my medical practice and put myself on a fixed salary, so I had a set amount to work with each month. Extra bonuses would be related to how well my practice was doing and would need to be shared with my other employees. I also employed my children to clean my office and most of them worked in this capacity for a year or more. I withheld 50% of their earnings and put it into a savings account from which they could withdraw only with my approval, (and my approval was not easily obtained). The kids initially grumbled about this arrangement, and they would present passionate appeals for withdrawal of funds. Usually their entreaties were not successful, but eventually they appreciated my reluctance to release the funds when they saw how their savings accounts grew.

We were inconsistent when it came to allowances. Periodically I would decide that they shouldn't get *any* allowance because I was providing them room and board. Then Gloria, to make *her* task a little more manageable, would work out an incentive system that would pay them for specific household chores. They didn't get much, but they received even less if they didn't make their beds daily or clean their rooms at least once a week. Most of the kids worked part-time outside the home during at least part of their high school years in order to supplement their income.

Paying for college for twelve children would have been impossible on my income, but I requested, and received, faculty status for my work at the Hillsdale College Health Service. This entitled my family to a tuition-free college education. Although most of our kids initially rejected any thought of attending college locally, financial reality soon changed their minds. I had agreed to pay half their college costs, wherever they went, but, since none of them could afford to finance the other half, eight of our children took courses at Hillsdale College, and seven of them, along with Gloria, are Hillsdale College graduates. Candi took some classes at Hillsdale College, but she graduated from Western Michigan University. The other four did not attend college; except for the one semester, Ray attended the Music School at Michigan State University. Three of our sons received partial football scholarships at Hillsdale, which paid for their rooms on campus; so we avoided most normal college expenses, without our children having to live at home while attending school. The campus became their home during their college years, and we didn't see them much more frequently than if they had been at school a thousand miles from home.

Our vacations were all low budget affairs, usually involving canoeing, sleeping in tents and preparing meals over a campfire. Today, without kids, we sleep in hotels and eat in restaurants.

A persistent insurance salesman—my brother, Dave, stimulated one financial decision that proved crucial. Shortly after I began my medical practice, he urged me to start putting money away into a tax-deferred Pension Plan. I told him, "I can't afford to." However, he convinced me that I couldn't afford *not* to. I was about 45 at the time, so I had fewer years than most to fund a retirement program. While my pension was modest, his persistence made it possible for me to retire from medicine twenty years later at the age of 65. Thank you, David.

Therefore, in our large family, money was never a problem. The *lack* of it was. Every year, I looked forward to our income tax refund to get our bills caught up, and twice we received unexpected small inheritance checks, that arrived just in time to take care of urgent financial needs.

So, how did we meet the financial needs of a large family? With much ingenuity, a little good fortune and a lot of faith. Moreover, we didn't spend $250,000 on each child!

Chapter Seventeen

(Bud)

SPORTS: HOW IMPORTANT?

Why do athletic events invoke such passionate response from parents and fans? They have little to do with most people's success in life, but their outcomes can create proud elation or disappointing depression unequaled by other events (such as performances in the classroom). Mature adults will wear cheese hats and stand on seats hollering expletives in condemnation of the coaches or officials. What is it about sports that brings out the worst in some people?

From fifth grade on, I was involved in some sport every season. My sports achievements through high school were less than noteworthy, but peer acceptance flows from just being a team member, and for an adolescent boy this was very important. I also followed the Chicago professional teams; the Bears, the White Sox and the Blackhawks with intense devotion. For most people, team loyalty is simply geographical. I lived in a Chicago Suburb at the time. We have now lived in Michigan for 35 years and I have acquired some affection for the Detroit teams. However, to the chagrin of my son-in-law, John Cool, I am fickle in my support, and the intensity of my loyalty is closely related to the teams' victories. Our daughter, Lisa, seems to have acquired some of my fickle genes. She participated in track and gymnastics in high school, but never really followed professional sports much until she moved to Dallas. She then became an avid and boastful Cowboy fan during their glory years. However, her enthusiasm seems to have waned some since they started losing. She no longer mentions them when I talk to her on the phone.

I recall the eagerness with which I looked forward to watching my sons and daughters participate in high school sports. I think most fathers view their children as extensions of themselves when it comes to athletics. With twelve children, I could hardly wait until the oldest ones reached high school. I looked forward to an endless stream of vicarious thrills and achievements. Instead, I was given a lesson in delayed gratification.

Our oldest son, Steve, in spite of having only one effective arm (because of his polio at age 4), surprisingly did compete with some success in swimming while in elementary school but showed little interest in other sports. He did go out for freshman football while I was interning in Saginaw, Michigan but I doubt that he really enjoyed it, and his participation in high school athletics ended there. Ray, our second oldest, was very competitive, and we hoped that sports participation might increase his interest in school; but he was declared ineligible for any high school athletics before his freshman year was two weeks old because he was caught smoking twice. Number three, Gay, showed encouraging gymnastics talent, so we sent her to a summer gymnastics camp with the expectation that she would make dramatic improvements and come back to star on the high school gymnastics team. Instead, after she completed the camp, she decided she would rather earn money. She got a part-time job and never competed again! I was still waiting for the vicarious thrills to start! And then came Tony, number four on our family tree. He was competitive, a good student, in compliance with the training rules and was eager to compete. Great! At last I was going to watch a son of mine perform on the gridiron. But no! Two weeks before freshman football practice started, he fell out of a tree and broke his arm!

These early disappointments certainly enhanced my appreciation for the athletic successes when they finally came, and our children did provide us with a stream of vicarious thrills for many years. For four of them, their athletic participation extended beyond high school and, since all four attended Hillsdale College, we were able to continue to enjoy their athletic achievements a little longer. Tolerate me, while I enumerate a few of the athletic accomplishments I enjoyed through my kids. (Remember, I did already share with you my disappointments.)

Tony recovered from his broken arm and in his junior year was a member of an undefeated state high school championship football team. A special highlight was watching him intercept a pass and score the final touchdown of the season. Terry and Pam provided us with some thrills in gymnastics and were qualifiers for the state high school gymnastic championships. Rick was the leading scorer (from his kicking) on a Hillsdale College football team that reached the NAIA National semi finals. A few years later our two youngest sons, Mike and Kevin, were members of a Hillsdale College football team in 1985 that tied for the national championship. And finally, our youngest daughter, Kelly, set several records and was on six conference championship track teams in high school and college. She was dubbed "thunder thighs" because of her powerful running style. (She has very feminine legs now!)

One of my most satisfying vicarious sports thrills was watching Mike win a conference tennis title by decisively defeating a cocky young player for the championship—just two weeks after this same player had beaten Mike easily in a dual meet.

I tried not to pressure our children to participate in sports, but I'm sure it was obvious I was pleased when they did. We attended as many sports events as possible, but I drew the line at cheerleading. Our daughter, Candi, insisted it was a sport and I think she still feels discriminated against because I didn't attend many basketball games at which she was cheering. I told her that true sports events were competitions, not demonstrations (this was before the advent of cheerleading contests) and besides, I did not like to witness the depressing losses by Hillsdale High School basketball teams. (In the 35 years we have lived in Hillsdale, the high school varsity men's basketball program has produced just three winning seasons!) However, I think Candi remains unconsoled.

I must admit that the performance of one of my sons or daughters in an athletic event usually produced a momentary high or low unmatched by their performances in the classroom. Is there any red-blooded father whose chest doesn't puff up when his son scores a touchdown or his daughter performs a flawless gymnastics routine in front of hundreds of other parents? In a small town it isn't necessary to announce, "That's my child!" You just stand up, look around and bask in the accolades. A good test score may mean more toward success in life, but it doesn't receive the same popular acclaim in an arena of approving fans. When my son or daughter performed *poorly* in a sporting event, I went to the concession stand!

Son, Michael, wrote the following story for his high school newspaper on his football struggles during his senior season. He was the quarterback.

*   *   *

"A lot of you have probably been wondering why some of the football players carry footballs around on Monday. I can tell you the reason. Coach Roy Dudas thought of this unique idea. He thinks that if you fumble the ball in the game, it means that you really don't know how to hang on to it. So, as a reminder of the ineptitude with which we handled the football, coach Dudas makes us carry it around all day. I would like to tell people it was because we won, but since we got annihilated 46-0 against Albion, I couldn't say that the following Monday. It's kind of fun carrying a football around all the time. It gives you a chance to make up some pretty wild excuses for carrying it. Teachers are always asking me, "Did you fumble again?" My clever reply is, "No, it's because it will get homesick if it's away from me for too long a time." Hopefully in the future, I will come to school on Monday without a football—but then people might not recognize me!"

* * *

An irony of my vicarious sports life is that I, unintentionally, missed seeing Hillsdale College's national championship football game. Not only were our two youngest sons on the squad but our daughter, Kelly, was their number one (and loudest) fan. The game was played in Conway, Arkansas, the hometown of Gloria's aunt, Ruth King, and we made elaborate plans to see the game with four of our children. I planned to make reservations to fly from Jackson, Michigan to Little Rock, Arkansas with the twins, Kevin and Kelly. (Kevin was on the team but not on the traveling squad). Son, Rick, (a former Hillsdale College football player) was flying down from Chicago, and Gloria was driving our daughter, Pam, home from Florida. They had planned to stop in Conway for the game and a visit with Gloria's aunt. Gloria was to pick up Kevin, Kelly and me at the airport in Little Rock, and we would drive over to Conway together. I had astutely predicted ten days before the title game that Hillsdale would win their semi-final playoff game in Colorado the week before the title game and qualify to play for the national championship. I checked for flights that would get me to Little Rock on time for the game, and was delighted to be able to book a Saturday morning flight from Jackson that would get us to Little Rock at 10:30 a.m. . . . . Jackson is a small city, closer to Hillsdale than Detroit, and the small Jackson airport was much more convenient than Detroit Metro. When Hillsdale won their game in Colorado, I felt smug because I already had booked my reservations to Little Rock.

Kelly, Kevin and I arrived at the airport 45 minutes early, carrying a large Hillsdale College banner and bursting with anticipation. My son playing in a National Championship game—wow! However, when we arrived and found the airport deserted, I called the airline to see if there was some mistake. The airline clerk on the phone assured me that there was no mistake. She confirmed my reservations from Jackson to Little Rock and suggested that perhaps I was confused because of different time zones. This did not make much sense, but I waited another half hour before calling again. This time I learned, to my bitter disappointment, that we had been booked out of Jackson, *Mississippi*! I was stunned and Kevin and Kelly couldn't believe it. The only reason they didn't complain more loudly was because they saw how devastated their father was. After recovering from our initial disappointment, we went home and listened to the game on the radio as Hillsdale tied for the National Championship. The rest of the family members got to the game as planned.

Vicarious sports thrills were certainly a highlight during my years of parenting, but I tried to keep their importance in proper perspective by remembering a bit of wisdom shared with me years before while I was teaching. Glen Heck, the youthful middle school principal when I taught in Wheaton, had earned *12* varsity letters in high school! (For those of you who never participated in high school sports, this is a remarkable and rare achievement.) I asked him which sport he chose to play when he went to college. He responded, "None", and told me, "I wouldn't have participated in my senior year of high school except that I was captain of two of the teams!" I found this astounding because he had obviously been an outstanding athlete. Why would he give it all up when he left high school?

His answer (while probably not popular with most sports-minded fathers) conveyed unusual wisdom. He told me, "I had satisfied my goals in athletics by the end of my junior year in high school and was ready to pursue other interests." This was a message I mentally recorded, but had difficulty understanding or accepting until after my children had started competing. When Gay, our eldest daughter, chose to work after school instead of competing in gymnastics, we were devastated. We had looked forward to watching her new routines and to hear the accolades from other parents. I was so upset that I was tempted to make her pay for the camp, but Gloria provided wiser counsel, and we accepted her decision without penalizing her.

On another occasion, when our son, Mike, told me he was going out for wrestling instead of basketball in his junior year of high school, I had to bite my tongue to hide my disappointment. Football and basketball are the most popular spectator sports in most high schools. For two years Mike had been the leading scorer on the Junior Varsity basketball team and would almost surely have been a starter on the varsity in his junior year. I was eager to bask in his accomplishments. But wrestling? His best friends were wrestlers (the reason for his decision), and as it turned out, he made the right choice. The wrestling team did very well that year, and Mike won half his matches; while the basketball team won only one game! Gloria and I both became avid and vocal fans at the wrestling matches. "PIN HIM, MIKE!" "TURN HIM!" "PUNISH HIM!" "FINISH HIM OFF, MIKE!" I couldn't believe that all of these aggressive statements issued forth from *Gloria's* lips!

While team sports involve more players and teach teamwork, I have found that individual sports offer some unique advantages. First of all, a boy or girl can earn his or her right to participate with head to head competition rather than depending on the coach's opinion. (Which parents usually don't agree with!) Secondly, you can focus on their own kid during his competition instead of trying to locate him under a helmet on a football field with 21 other players. And thirdly, success is not as dependent on others as it is in team sports. One of the finest coaches I have encountered is Pat Pastula, and he demonstrated the power of positive encouragement as well as anyone I have known. Pat has been the girls track and cross country coach at Hillsdale High School for many years (still is) and a couple of my daughters competed for him. His teams consistently won conference championships, but what impressed me most about him was the way he encouraged each girl to measure her performance against herself—always trying to improve on her best previous performance regardless of where she finished. He always found something positive to say to each girl after every event, and at the end of each season he compiled a booklet with an extensive summary of the year's accomplishments for the team and each individual. For some, it might be winning a championship. For others it might simply be reaching a new personal best. By encouraging each individual to do her best, he built a very successful program while helping individuals reach personal goals.

I think of Pat when I remember what was probably my most significant (probably my *only*) athletic achievement in high school. It occurred in track and was of significance only to me and the coach. I was slow (big feet), didn't have a lot of endurance or strength and couldn't jump very high, so I didn't win events or challenge any records. However, I enjoyed track because my improvement could be measured and I could set personal goals. I high jumped and ran the half-mile, but I was not the best on our team in either event. In my senior year, the smaller schools in the conference voted to limit entries to one per school in each event in the conference championship meet. (Previously each school could have two entrants.) Wheaton and Naperville were the largest schools in the conference and always dominated the meet, so the small schools thought that there chances would be improved if they limited participation. It did not accomplish their objective because Wheaton and Naperville still dominated. Our coach, Herb Hodges, who was a positive motivator and a legend in Wheaton High School track, was greatly disappointed because he realized that some of his seniors (including me) would not be able to compete in the final meet of their high school careers. He decided to have tryouts for the relay events in hopes that some of these seniors might qualify. Remarkably, in the try-outs, I managed to earn a spot on the half-mile *sprint* relay team. I was certainly not a sprinter, but on that rainy day of tryouts I was the fourth best 220 yard dash man on our team. Coach Hodges was delighted. The race itself was a little anti-climatic because I lined up to run against two top sprinters, the conference 220-yard champ on my right and the conference runner-up in the 100-yard dash on my left. Needless to say, I finished my leg in third place (I *was* gaining on the 100-yard dash man!), but for me, just qualifying for a sprint relay team was a significant personal achievement. Reaching goals doesn't always mean winning championships. The popular motion picture, "Rudy" certainly highlighted this fact.

While my athletic achievements in college were an improvement over my accomplishments in high school, my most publicized participation occurred while I was attending graduate school (Social Work) in Indianapolis. I was doing field work as part of my course of study in a Jewish Community Center, working with 8 and 9 year old boys. After being actively involved in sports for many years, I suddenly found myself with no competitive stimulation. A promotion appeared in the Indianapolis Star for a Golden Gloves amateur boxing tournament, and I decided to enter. My only boxing experience had been at home with my brothers, but I thought if I entered the heavyweight division, I might avoid the real boxers. I surmised that the serious boxers would all cut their weight to box in the lower weight classes. I also decided that I should enter the Novice division (for inexperienced boxers). My previous experience as a spectator with my Dad at Golden Gloves matches in Chicago (where the winners from other cities go to fight for the Midwest championship) had lulled me into thinking that I could compete on their level. I was long on confidence but short on wisdom.

When I arrived for the actual registration, I was informed that because of my age (25), I was automatically in the Open division which included the more experienced boxers! My attempts to convince them that I was a real beginner did no good. At the registration table was "Tiny" Bland, who must have weighed 300 pounds and who ran the largest boxing club in Indianapolis. His first question to me was, "What are you doing here?"

I told him I was starved for some competitive activity and saw the notice in the paper about the local boxing tournament.

"Are you in shape," he asked?

"Not really," I responded.

"Then you owe it to yourself to get in shape before you step into the ring. Why don't you come down to my boxing club and work out."

For the next three weeks before the tournament I worked out at his club, and this not only helped me get into better condition, but it also provided me with an opportunity to get acquainted with some of his younger fighters, many of whom fought at the club rather than on the street. "Tiny" probably helped a lot of kids stay out of trouble, and he developed some pretty good boxers. In fact, his fighters usually dominated the Indianapolis Golden Gloves each year. "Tiny" had a Master's degree in something and he and I became good friends. He enjoyed having someone educated to talk to, and I think he was hoping I would win so I could help him supervise the other winners who would be going on to Chicago. I came within one fight of doing just that.

I won my first two fights, even though both of my opponents almost knocked me out with their first punches. Neither followed up their early advantage—the first because he was too scared and the second because he was too out of shape. This put me into the championship match which was surprising enough, but the publicity I received far exceeded my talents. I became the new "White Hope" in the heavyweight division, and the Indianapolis Star (sponsors of the event) featured me in a promotional article for the event on their front sports page. Then the Chicago Tribune, sponsor of the Chicago Golden Gloves, featured me (with picture) on the front page of their sports section. They were looking for a human interest angle on possible winners from other cities who would be coming to Chicago and they promoted me as a 25 year old graduate student working with young kids who had just become a new father (Gloria had just delivered Steve.)

My older brother, Judd, was living in Chicago at the time and when he saw the paper, he couldn't wait to promote me to his Irish friends, and to encourage them to go out and watch me when I came to Chicago. I'm sure he also informed them that he could always whip me. Some of my youth center kids got their dads to come to watch me fight, and several of my fraternity brothers from DePauw were also in attendance.

Unfortunately, I never made it to Chicago! My analysis that the heavyweight division had fewer real boxers may have been correct in my first two matches, but my final opponent, Willie Crawford, was serious about his boxing and had won the light-heavyweight title the year before. He also worked out at Tiny's gym, so I had gotten to know him. The only thing I remember about the fight was getting up once after being knocked down early in the first round. I apparently didn't remain up very long because Willie knocked me out at 1:52 of the first round. I woke up half an hour later in the locker room! The ring doctor was there and he asked me if I knew what day it was. I didn't!

Bart Anson, my longtime friend and fellow graduate student,

brought me home. Gloria was sitting on the couch nursing our new baby.

"Guess what happened," I asked her.

"You got knocked out," she responded, with no appreciation for my macho image.

Fortunately I had no adverse after-effects and also no further desire to enter a boxing ring again. (Oh, I did occasionally have memory-lapse occasions when I said to myself, "I think I could whip that guy!") In my defense, let it be noted that Willie lost a disputed decision to the eventual Chicago champion. When I talk to my grandchildren about my boxing career, I simply tell them that I won twice as many boxing matches as I lost.

Sports did have educational value for three of our sons who attended college with the help of football scholarships, and I take partial credit for two of them. For about 14 years, one or more of our sons participated in the Pass, Punt & Kick competition sponsored by Coca Cola, and I spent many hours practicing with them to prepare for the annual event. Although none of them qualified to kick between halves of the Super Bowl, they did achieve some success on the local and district levels. More importantly, Rick & Mike both earned scholarships to kick field goals and extra points for Hillsdale College. Kevin also received a football scholarship, but he was a pass receiver so my influence on his career was purely genetic. I was also a pass receiver in college.

Let me list my order of priorities when it comes to my children's participation in sports. I suspect that many athletic-minded fathers share these priorities.

*　　*　　*

1. My child is the star on a championship team.
2. My child is a star on a non-championship team.
3. My child is a regular on a championship team.

4. My child is a regular on a non-championship team.
5. My child is a substitute on a championship team.
6. My child is a substitute on a non-championship team.
7. My child is a bench warmer on a championship team.
8. My child is a bench warmer on a non-championship team.

*　　*　　*

I freely admit that I attended school athletic events to watch my sons and daughters participate. It was an added pleasure when the team won, but it is my child's performance that I watched most closely. I suspect that most parents, if they answer honestly, would agree. The truly dedicated fans are the ones, who come to the competitions when their own children aren't involved, and the team isn't winning.

While sports can provide a healthy outlet for the competitive juices of youth and can teach some important lessons, we parents should probably accept the fact that our child's interest may be fleeting, and participation is not a lifetime commitment. We (especially fathers) sometimes place undue emphasis on the athletic accomplishments of our sons or daughters, and perhaps this is our way of vicariously prolonging our own athletic careers or of enjoying athletic achievements that we weren't able to accomplish ourselves.

Although I can sermonize on putting athletics in their proper perspective, the participation of my children in competitive sports was one of my parenting highlights. I can recall my anxious anticipation of Friday or Saturday football games and the many conversations I had with my children about their performances. I have been blessed with a cup filled with vicarious sports thrills, and I am now enjoying the athletic exploits of my grandchildren. While the demands of my medical practice occasionally interfered, I cherish the times I was able to attend. There is no instant replay button for the excitement of your children's achievements.

Chapter Eighteen

(Gloria)

SURVIVAL TECHNIQUES

"Cheaper By The Dozen", the book that provided the stimulus for our large family, was fascinating in part because of the carefully controlled organizational techniques of the father, Frank Gilbreth, and we had the naïve' confidence we could duplicate his efficiency with our own family. However, unlike father Gilbreth, we were not time-motion experts (He was a specialist in this field.), and God did not send us the same twelve children! We tried. Oh, how we tried. Moreover, we did have occasional successes.

One of our challenges was feeding a family of fourteen without running a cafeteria? Both Bud and I were raised in families where (without the aid of microwaves and frozen dinners) our mothers prepared the food, and mealtimes were family events at the same time each night. Bud's mom would use the supper table as a forum at which to hear reports from each of the four boys on their activities and their latest girl friends and his dad would talk about sports or assign jobs he wanted accomplished by the next Saturday afternoon.

Bud and I wanted to duplicate this family meal tradition with our children, and in the early years of our marriage we did pretty well. With the help of two high chairs, we continued to fit our family of four children (then five and six) around our kitchen table in our home in Elmhurst, Illinois. When we were expecting our seventh child, we moved into Bud's big old home in Wheaton. With the help of Aunt Edy, who was working at *Hahn's Storage and Moving* in Wheaton, we obtained (Edy bought it for us.) an old dining room table with eight chairs. It had been scratched in a few places, but we covered it with oilcloth, similar to today's vinyl cloth, and it was perfect for our enlarged family. It was much easier to wipe up spills of milk, juice and water, which seemed to be a daily occurrence. However, the chairs were another matter. These charming old chairs were probably valuable antiques, but with their rail backs they were a hassle to clean, and they soon became pock marked from the dried milk splashes. Also everyone (including Bud) couldn't resist leaning back in them, so they became wobbly and began to break.

I decided that benches would be much more practical, and my mother agreed. I decided to make them myself. I went to the Wheaton Lumber Yard, and they took pity on this housewife-carpenter and not only cut the boards to the proper lengths but also delivered them to the house. I reinforced the legs with metal brackets, and mom gave me stain and varnish to properly finish them. Building those benches was much more rewarding than washing dishes, making beds or doing the laundry, and the work didn't have to be repeated on a daily basis. The benches lasted for years, and I'm sure they saved me hours of cleaning. We moved them with us to Columbia, Missouri when Bud started medical school and then to Saginaw, Michigan for his internship. However, by the time we moved to Hillsdale in 1967 we were expecting Kevin and Kelly (numbers eleven and twelve), and the table was no longer adequate. Aunt Edy came to our rescue again. She called to tell us she had found a very large oak dining room table with eight chairs and three extension leaves plus a buffet to match. The set had been in Hahn's Storage for years, and since the family wanted to settle their estate, she bought the whole set for $40! The table was stained very dark, but several years later I refinished it. It took me several months to remove the dark stain and the decorative red, blue and green accents in the grooves on the legs, but the results have been appreciated these past thirty years. We had two more leaves made for the table by Mr. Casimer Safran, the father of one of Gay's classmates. Initially, the table would not extend far enough for the extra leaves, but Mr. Safran enlarged and stabilized the table to ten feet to accommodate all five leaves, and we have been using that table since 1968. I had to make longer benches in order to seat the whole family of 14 for supper. It is great for family gatherings, but no longer accommodates our extended family of 62!

Around the family table in 1970

Keeping the family together at the dinner table (most days our only time together) for any meaningful interaction was difficult, so we devised some activities that were somewhat educational and offered monetary prizes to the winners. One night we would go around the table naming the Presidents in chronological order. When people made mistakes, they were eliminated, and we continued until only one person remained. He or she won 50 cents! We would repeat this topic until it was pretty well learned, and then we would start on the Capitols of States or other Countries. These dinner table competitions might keep the family at the table for an extra five minutes! They also sometimes instilled excessive over-confidence in the winners. Our daughter, Candi, went to school one day prepared to show off her knowledge in history class by reciting the list of presidents. The impact of her accomplishment was greatly diluted when a classmate of hers, Mary Voorhees, not only recited all the Presidents but also the Vice-Presidents!

One stimulus for family togetherness came from an unexpected and unlikely source. Our small town of Hillsdale seems to regularly attract young Mormon men, fulfilling their two years of required missionary service. One year, when we still had eight children at home, I invited two of the young Mormons to come back and explain their program. Since we were devout Catholics, Bud was disbelieving when I told him they were coming. However, their visit proved to be a positive blessing. Their primary message was the promotion of a "family hour", an hour each week when the family would get together without interference from other activities. No television, no phone calls, no visitors and no other meetings would be allowed to interfere. The young Mormons provided a format for us to use which included a Bible reading, a discussion of events in our daily lives and a group game or activity of our choosing. Monday night from 7 to 8 became our "family hour", and the youngest six participated in this for almost a year. The sessions ended when sport practices and other school activities began to conflict. However, for several years afterwards our younger children would ask, "When are we going to have 'family hour' again?" I wish we had started the program sooner and had continued it longer. It is a sad commentary on family life today that it is so difficult to carve out one hour a week when the family can be together.

I had no role model for raising a large family, and we had discovered that *Cheaper by the Dozen* contained some unrealistic expectations. Bud allowed me much freedom of choice as long as it fit into the budget. My ideas usually resulted from some real or perceived needs, and in the early months of marriage I depended on Bud to carry out my requests. Usually he was agreeable, but I would often become impatient to get it done before he could get to it. I finally decided that I could become a first class nag, or I could learn to do the work myself. My Grandma, "M.G." Bagwell was a handyman way back in the 30's, so I decided that if she could do it, so could I. I bought a power drill, which enabled me to put up the hooks in the hard wood to hang clothes on, and then I bought a "Home Maintenance" book. I loved it! I replaced light switches and lamp sockets and rewired lamps. I even re-roped and re-attached window weights in the old windows in our Orchard Street apartment in Chicago, so the windows would stay up. After replacing the complete insides of a toilet that would never quit running, replacing washers in drippy faucets was a breeze. Once again, the best part was that these jobs stayed done. When Bud would come home and I had accomplished something other than laundry, cooking and cleaning, he always praised me. Moreover, if the house wasn't in perfect order or the dinner was not finished, then he helped complete those tasks. I was a happy wife. Remember the motto, "Happy wife = Happy husband."

I dreamed up ways to get organized and keep a neat home with as little effort as possible even though I shudder now at some of my solutions. Two particularly BAD creative ideas come to mind. In our lovely old apartment at 1663 N. Orchard St. on the near north side of Chicago the varnish had worn off the hardwood floors in the living and dining room except around the edges, so I decided to *fix* it. Today, I would have refinished the floors in a heartbeat, but back then my solution was to laboriously glue black asphalt tile over the entire two rooms! Surprisingly enough, we were actually pleased with the results! Every evening, before "daddy" returned home I would push all the toys into a big pile with my commercial size dust mop, and the kids would see who could pick up the most toys. As a result, sometimes when I was expecting someone else and asked the kids to help pick up toys, they would ask, "Is Daddy coming home?"

Another poor decision when we were still living in the same Chicago apartment was when I glued linoleum onto the surface of a lovely maple drop-leaf table my mother had given me. Since I had a piece of linoleum left after re-flooring our bathroom, I glued it on the table because I thought it would make the table easier to clean. (We also painted the wainscoting in the kitchen an ungodly shade of fuchsia and topped it off with a bilious lime green. UGHHH!) When we moved to Elmhurst from Chicago, my mother retrieved her table and probably questioned my intelligence as she struggled to remove all of the linoleum and glue and restore it to its original beauty. After mom died, I inherited that table and now use it in my home office.

Our children were indoctrinated into the dish routine the summer of 1959, when my sister, Louise, and her husband, Arnie, lived with us in Wheaton. Arnie had his PhD in Physics and was a professor at Kansas University in Lawrence, Kansas. He was on a summer assignment at Argonne National Laboratories near Chicago. This provided Louise and me a wonderful opportunity to become reacquainted as adult sisters and our kids a chance to know their cousins. Louise had three small children and we had just had our seventh. Up until then, none of my kids had ever routinely helped with the dishes. Our oldest, Steve, was only eight. Louise and I realized that our survival depended on establishing some system of sharing chores, so we decided on a division of household responsibilities. I took over the cooking and the washing of the laundry, and Louise took on the dish routine and the sorting and folding of the laundry. She also took on the ironing, a monumental task because not only were permanent pressed clothes not yet common, but I had a large basket filled with shirts, skirts, dresses and trousers that needed ironing. While my intentions were good, ironing was at the bottom of my priority list. Louise was a person who set goals and achieved them, and she focused on reaching the bottom of the laundry basket before the summer ended. When she finally did reach the bottom, she found a pair of eyeglasses I had lost a year before! Obviously, ironing had not made it to the top of my priority list for a long time.

Originally, only the five oldest children were to help with the dishes—Steve, Ray and Gay and their cousins, Jeff and Sandy—but Louise made it sound like so much fun that Gary and Tony whined, "It's not fair!" so they too were included. Gary was barely four and Tony was still three, but by standing on chairs at the sink, they could help. Fortunately, we had wonderful unbreakable Melmac dishes, and washing dishes became a rotating job in our family from then on. Using Tony as the benchmark, the youngest children started helping when they could stand on a chair and reach the sink. After Louise and her family left, our family continued to grow, and I realized that if I were going to survive, the kids were going to have to share more of the housework. The luxury of having a mother who can accomplish all tasks in a family this big was impossible.

While the kids were still in grade school, although the house was noisy and chaotic, family life was mostly enjoyable and the pressures of parenting would be relieved by funny episodes. I would think to myself, "Some day this will make a good story." Finding humor in their behavior became more difficult when we moved to Hillsdale. This was mostly because we now had teenagers in the house, but another unexpected event expanded our responsibilities.

In July 1967 Bud was just setting up his medical practice in Hillsdale, and I was expecting a baby October 1. We had just moved into our new home at 209 S. Howell Street. Our home was in a perfect location! It was a block from the hospital and two blocks from his new office. I had my first visit with Dr. Clark Smith, who I had chosen to deliver our new baby. "I don't understand why I am so tired" I complained to him. He just smiled at this mother of ten who was complaining about being tired and then added, "You've miscalculated your due date." I knew that was impossible because Michael was only nine months old. Dr. Smith then appeared a little concerned and said that we might be having twins. He immediately ordered x-rays. (This was before the advent of medical ultrasound.) I really didn't get my hopes up, but I had always wanted twins. When the presence of twins was confirmed, both Bud and I were ecstatic. Later we heard that Dr.Stein, the radiologist, had quipped, "I thought they were a little crazy to have ten children, but to be happy about having twins, now I know they are crazy!"

Dr. Smith immediately put the damper on our enthusiasm. He began to give me instructions and warnings, "If you want to have *live* twins then you have to do absolutely nothing!" He reminded me that the greatest danger for twins is prematurity, so therefore, "No more house work or strenuous activity of any kind." I thought he must be kidding, but he wasn't, and he made sure to get this point across to Bud.

Obviously, we needed to find someone to help me. The kids could help until school started, but then what? I still had Lisa and Michael at home. We advertised in the local paper and received a call from Shirley Curtis on Hoxie Rd in North Adams. Instead of giving references she said, "Come and check out my home any time. I know I can fill your needs, but I have several requirements. I can only work when my husband works and I must bring my little preschooler with me."

We visited Shirley and were immediately impressed with

her home and her personality. Her work ethic was excellent, but I had never had outside help before, so I could not *direct.* She came several days a week until school started and then every school day. I think I was in a fog shortly before the twins were born, because I don't recall giving any directions. Shirley just knew what to do. The twins were born healthy September 26, 1967, just one week early. Michael turned 1 the next week on October 3rd. Shirley washed clothes, cleaned the house, made breakfast, baked birthday cakes, polished mirrors, changed sheets, put out the garbage, and still had time to sit down for her *soaps* while she ate her lunch. She also managed to start dinner before she left each day. She just did what needed to be done. She helped me though the winter months and into early spring.

I knew my physical and emotional strength was returning when I realized that the kids were slacking in their responsibilities. Bud had been more than generous to me, even borrowing money so that I could have the needed help. *"Let Shirley do it"* was said once too often by our kids, and I knew the time had come to once again take over my household.

We had achieved our dreams; we had our twelve children, and Bud was now a doctor. I had envisioned peace and harmony in the household. Not so! We had three teenagers and two more entering adolescence and instead of harmony there was rebellion. My vision of a household of willing cooperation was replaced by the kids' frequent challenges to my requests and suggestions, and Bud could offer little emotional support because he was so busy in his practice. After dealing with his patients' problems all day, he was not interested in hearing about my problems with the kids when he returned home. While I just desired a listening ear when I related the kid's transgressions and problems, Bud felt he had to fix everything I mentioned—a daunting assignment at the end of his workday. I had not read Gary Smalley's books on marriage and gender differences at that point, but I knew something had to change.

I left home (with the four youngest children) and spent five weeks with my mother in Wheaton and a week with my sister in New York. I returned home emotionally refreshed and with the realization that I couldn't control how the children responded to me, but I could control my response to them.

On one memorable occasion I blunted son Rick's anger and left him speechless with a simple response to his outburst. He was a defiant 17 year old at the time—complaining bitterly about something I asked him to do. I finally commented, tongue in cheek, that he really was lucky to have such a doll for a mother. He looked at me in total frustration and quipped, "You're not a doll, you're a DOG!" I quickly retorted, "And you know what that makes you?"

I read and adapted ideas from books on child rearing and tried a new system about every six months to motivate the children to set goals, accept responsibilities and complete household chores. After six months, a system would no longer generate much response. My impression of a clean and peaceful home was often not the same as the children's.

"But mom", they complained. "You didn't tell me I had to do that!"

"Why make the bed? It'll just get messed up again tonight".

Other favorites were, "That's not fair", "That was Terry's job." or "It's not my night to do dishes. I traded with Candi?" or "I can't do it after school. I have to be at *basketball . . . gymnastics . . . football . . . , play . . . . tennis . . . track, (any activity would do)* practice." The old book P.E.T. (*Parent Effective Training*) gave me many good ideas.

I finally bought a HUGE wall calendar. Every kid was to write their schedules on the calendar, and then I assigned the work schedule to fit their schedules. In addition to the assignments on the calendar, I also posted my expectations in the appropriate areas of the house. I divided the house into five areas because at that point only five kids remained at home. The kids' chores were rotated each week. I was actually getting organized! I recently found the following instructions still posted (after 20 years) on the back of the closet door in the front entryway at 209 S. Howell, our old home where our son, Mike, now lives.

#5 HALLWAYS, ENTRY WAYS, STEPS.
DAILY . . . . B4 School
> *Straighten front entry hall——the slate tile area.*
> *= Coats hung, shoes or boots in order, sweep*

WEEKLY . . . . Friday B4 you go anywhere for the evening, or Thursday night (Not Saturday A.M.).
> *Scrub front entry with Mop and Glow. Be sure to vacuum space between tile and front door.*
> *Vacuum all steps (and hallways in front of bathrooms).*
> *"409" any door jams that are dirty. (Or Murphy's oil soap, Spic & Span, etc. may be used.)*
> *AFTER above is done, you may collect your $5. Thank you.*
> *Mother reserves the right to make exceptions for extenuating circumstances.*

Each of the school age kids received a dollar a day for lunches and five dollars on Saturday for their allowance. I rationalized that this was less expensive than hiring a cleaning lady, and they all learned to clean well. For each day they didn't make their bed one dollar was deducted from their allowance. At one point I even made up slips, which they turned in at the end of the week because without the slips I found it impossible to remember who had made their beds each day.

Andy Eicken, our first Youth for Understanding exchange student arrived before we put the last system in place which included eight sets of chores that were rotated through the eight children still living at home. There was not much left to do, but we wanted to include him on the schedule, so he would feel more a part of the family. He was raised like an only child, following his sister's death, and was blessed with a mother, grandmother and maid who did everything for him. After he tried several different tasks, such as washing dishes, sweeping down the steps to the basement and taking out the trash, he finally ended up with the job of sorting the socks in the laundry room. More than once he announced, "This is dumb work!" He was a delightful son, but he never quite adapted to household chores.

Originally, the kids worked together on the dishes each night; Eventually, however, their eagerness to help was replaced by more and more arguments about who was doing the most; thus a decision was made to take turns doing it alone. This meant they would only be responsible for the dishes about once every week and a half. Because some of the kids would dawdle for a long time when they were on dishes, I found it necessary to establish some guidelines. They were allowed an hour after dinner to finish cleaning up the kitchen. If they didn't finish in time, they were on the dishes for another day. During Bud's first year in Medical School, Ray really stretched the limits and at one time had penalties totaling two months! This delighted his siblings but had little impact on Ray. He figured he had nothing further to lose. He never did work off the penalty, and we forgave his debt as a Christmas present.

Some of our sons took great pride in their efficiency at cleaning the kitchen, and at family gatherings it became a tradition for the men (without prompting) to clean up after each meal. They did a super job and their sisters and wives wisely never criticized their work. Mike became a popular dinner guest because he usually washed the dishes and cleaned up the kitchen after eating.

One of the more amazing transformations in our household would occur before meetings, parties, family gatherings or other events where a clean (and organized) house was desirable. No amount of coercion, bribery or threats would stimulate activity toward this goal until an hour before people were to arrive. At that point, the kids moved into a *crisis-cleaning mode,* and a full day's worth of house cleaning was completed in 59 minutes! If people arrived early, they would simply be swept into the cleaning whirlwind. Daughter, Pam, earned the title, "The White Tornado", because she could accomplish twice as much in half the time. She later turned these skills into a house cleaning business, and because she works so fast, she always works by the job rather than by the hour. Bud recalls one time when she was starting to clean our house and he went out to do something in the garage. He came back into the kitchen 45 minutes later, and she had not only finished cleaning the kitchen, living room and dining room, but had also washed and waxed the kitchen floor and had a cake baking in the oven!

Probably the biggest organizational challenge in a family of 14 is the laundry room. It was overwhelming even for me and any flat surface, including the floor, was quickly covered with clothes. Differentiating the clean clothes from the soiled clothes was a near-hopeless adventure. The washing machine and dryer worked overtime every day. One day, trying to be helpful, Bud suggested to me that it would be more efficient if I just had one or two laundry days a week! I can't remember whether I laughed, cried or threw something, as I described to him how the laundry room would look and smell with a week of dirty cloth diapers (much cheaper than the disposable ones). He got the message!

He deserves a crown, however, for not complaining about the poopy diapers I often left soaking in the toilet, waiting to be rinsed out. This went on for 18 years! In those hectic days, I thought I'd never see a time without diapers, but now it has been over thirty years. Praise the Lord!

In Hillsdale, the challenge of the laundry room lured more than one into its clutches. Bud would occasionally tackle it out of necessity (to find some clean clothes to wear), but his efforts were only temporary, and a few days later the room would show little evidence that he had been there. One time my mother, who couldn't understand why the laundry room could not be kept neat and organized, decided to get things under control. She attacked the room with a vengeance, but after two weeks she gave up, shut the door and never again entered that room. Now in retirement, Bud has taken over the laundry room and it usually looks wonderful. But in fairness to me, the kids are no longer at home.

At 209 S. Howell in Hillsdale, I did develop a system that lessened the chaos. We converted a bedroom into the laundry room, and I built large shelves in the old clothes closet. The kids had individual laundry baskets for their clean clothes. They were supposed to take these to their rooms and bring back the dirty clothes to be washed. It sounds simple, but often the little (or big) cherubs would simply leave their dirty clothes in their rooms, go into the laundry room, grab the clothes from their baskets that they needed at the moment and never move the rest of the clothes off the shelf. The system was laudable, but its execution was so deficient that we probably could have gotten by without ever putting dressers in their rooms!

Frank Gilbreth was a time-motion expert. We weren't! So we stumbled through many attempts to organize our brood in order to produce a measure of peace and tranquility. I read many books on child rearing, but the one that probably gave me the most peace and comfort was Peg Bracken's humorous account, *I Hate To Housekeep*. She gave a name to my condition. I was a *Random Housekeeper*. Sometimes I was good and sometimes I was bad. At last I had a diagnosis. Thanks, Peg.

My Advice for Survival: Always wear a Smile and Laugh Every Day!

We got a chuckle when Lee Droeger, a "48" Wheaton High School classmate of mine sent us this E-Mail. I don't know the author, but thanks, Lee! We think it is an appropriate way to end this chapter.

CHILDREN

>*You spend the first 2 years of their life teaching them to walk and talk.*

>*Then you spend the next 16 telling them to sit down and shut up.*

>*Grandchildren are God's reward for not killing your children.*

>*Cleaning your house while your kids are still growing is like*

>*clearing the driveway before it has stopped snowing.*

>*Mothers of teens know why animals eat their young.*

>*I asked Mom if I was a gifted child?*

>*She said they certainly wouldn't have paid for me.*

>*The main purpose of holding children's parties is to remind yourself*

>*that there are children more awful than your own.*

>*We childproofed our home 3 years ago but they're still getting in.*

>*Be nice to your kids. They'll choose your nursing home.*

>*Advice for the day: If you have a lot of tension and you get a headache, do what it says on the aspirin bottle: "Take two aspirin and keep away from children".*

Chapter Nineteen

PEOPLE and PROJECTS

PART I: Bud's Comments

Who we are, is often defined by what we do. As with most people, our involvement in activities outside the family has been related to causes about which we care deeply. Although my interest in medicine was based on a desire to help people, Gloria is more truly people-oriented than I am. Whenever anyone asks for her help, she will stop what she is doing to give a haircut, alter a dress or counsel a distressed mother. Although she would ask for my approval, Gloria was the one who invited most of our overnight visitors. If entrance to heaven is dependent on what we do for others, then Gloria should be able to walk right in.

Many of her involvements have been with activities that relate to her role as a mother. LaLeche League, an organization established to provide support for breastfeeding mothers, has been an important part of Gloria's life for over 40 years! She first became involved when we were living in Wheaton, Illinois, a couple years after she had met Mary Ann Kerwin, one of the founders of the organization, which is now International in scope. She continues to use LaLeche as a forum from which she can counsel young women, and has helped many women improve their marriages with her support and suggestions.

When I was in active medical practice and delivering babies, Gloria taught Gamper childbirth preparation classes for my patients and the expectant patients of the other doctors in Hillsdale and the surrounding towns. Although she turned that responsibility over to the local hospital years ago, she still occasionally gets requests from expectant couples who want help in preparing for their deliveries. She is always willing to give them some individual preparation, and they never question her qualifications!

At the request of Linc Miller with the Hillsdale Intermediate School District, Gloria started a Gifted Student Program in Hillsdale that continued for 20 years.

At *my* request, she became involved in community theatre, and, although this was a lifetime avocation for me, she actually involved herself in more aspects of the theatre than I. She functioned as the Producer or Director of several big musicals, raised money, cleaned the bathrooms, served on the Board and was particularly good at getting other people actively involved. (One year she converted a vocal critic of the community theatre into a very effective Board Member!) Her optimistic attitude was a motivating factor, when the Hillsdale Community Theatre Board voted to purchase an old movie theatre in the neighboring town of Jonesville and convert it into a performance theatre. There was little money in the Theatre treasury at the time, but Gloria helped convince the majority of the Board members to submit a bid to purchase the building, and if the bid was accepted, she assured them that the money could be raised. The bid was accepted, the money raised, and the resulting Sauk Theatre has been a wonderful addition to the community for the past 29 years!

Although Gloria has helped our community theatre in many ways, the most vivid example of her positive optimism occurred when she was directing the beautiful, heartwarming musical "The King and I", and the leading man, Bill Shannon, developed a life-threatening form of skin cancer. Bill was a very popular, charismatic Hillsdale High School principal, who possessed a special gift for relating to the rebellious teens of the 70's during our early years in Hillsdale. He was also one of my closest friends. After serving as high school principal for a few years, Bill was removed from that job and returned to his previous position as a middle school history teacher. It was a great disappointment for Bill and for the students, whose fondness for him is expressed beautifully in the following testimony, which was given on Class Day in June of 1974, after it had been announced that he would no longer be the high school principal.

Mr. Shannon
Quietly he came with little adieu, sharing himself
and his beliefs with us, as well as his time, his patience
and his love—always treating us as mature and
responsible individuals. It is our misfortune that he is
leaving us. Remaining will be fond memories and halls
filled with his legacy ... that enduring legacy ... the
ability to evaluate self—resulting in inner acceptance
and the heightened awareness, sensitivity and respect
for other people and their ideologies. Through this one
man, a little more light and truth, a little more love and
goodness have come into our world. We appreciate all he
tried to do for us.
Class of 1974, Hillsdale High School

"The King and I" was sold out for the eight performances to be presented on two successive weekends. However, Bill had to go to a Cancer Center in Houston, Texas on Monday of the second week, and his availability for the second weekend performances was uncertain. What should we do? This was a community theatre where everyone was a volunteer, and most of the people working on the production had fulltime jobs. Understudies seldom exist in community theatre, and they certainly didn't in ours. It would be impossible for someone else to learn the role in such a short time, and most community theatre directors probably would have canceled the second weekend. Not Gloria! She checked with the Hillsdale College alumni office to get the phone number of Doug Harvey in New York. Ten years previously Doug had played that role while a student at Hillsdale College. She called Doug and asked him if he could possibly come to Hillsdale to fill in—with the understanding that when Bill returned, the part was his. Doug agreed to come and Gloria appealed to some community theatre supporters to provide the money to cover the cost of bringing Doug and his family to Hillsdale. The necessary funds were raised, and Doug arrived with his family on Sunday in time to watch a Sunday matinee performance of the show (Bill was still there). That evening, Gloria and Karen Veurink (the female lead and music director) worked with Doug, as he learned his lines, his songs and his movements on stage. The intense rehearsing continued on Monday and Tuesday. Doug even shaved his head for the role! He did two excellent performances, before Bill returned for the final two. It was the most emotional production ever performed at the Sauk. (The King dies at the end.) Two months later, on October 25, 1975, Bill died. The church was filled for his memorial service with many of his former students in attendance, and the student testimony shared previously was one of many presentations made in his memory. He touched many lives and left an unforgettable legacy.

Bill Shannon

My own involvement in community theatre was certainly a reflection of my father's interest, plus the enjoyment of being on stage; but I was also motivated by the important contribution a community theatre makes to a small town. It provides an available forum for latent talent to develop and bloom, and many outstanding performances are seen on community theatre stages in towns and cities across the Country. Gloria and I (along with many others) have invested much sweat equity in helping to keep community theatre going in Hillsdale County, and we take pride in the fact that with nothing but volunteers the Sauk Theatre has survived and prospered for three decades.

My favorite role: "Tevye"
In "Fiddler on the roof"

My other major involvement in Hillsdale has been in a cause, about which I feel very deeply. For the past 24 years, I have served as president of our local Right to Life group, promoting the Sanctity of Human Life. In spite of my strong feelings about abortion and euthanasia, it still took me several years before I was willing to back up my beliefs with any real commitment. After two years of talking about it and doing nothing, I became actively involved after I was challenged by a Catholic nun.

Sister Mary Rita Sayers was the principal of our local Saint Anthony Catholic School during our early years in Hillsdale, and she taught me a valuable lesson when I served on her School Board. There was a referendum in Michigan at the time in support of educational vouchers that could be used in private schools, and I was strongly in support of the proposal.

She said to me, "If you truly believe in something, don't just talk about it. *Do* something about it!

"What do you suggest I do?" I asked.

"You should set up a phone-calling tree to get out the vote."

"But that sounds like a lot of work," I responded.

"Do you believe in this cause, or not?" she challenged.

I set up the phone tree!

Although the referendum was decisively defeated, I felt good that I had *done something*. This was a lasting lesson for me, and I recently attended Mary Rita's 50th Jubilee and thanked her for it. She could not remember imparting this message to me, but she did remember most of our children when she attended our 50th wedding anniversary celebration.

My pro-life views actually started when I was in high school and were certainly influenced by my Catholic faith; although at that time (the early 40's) there was general agreement that abortion and euthanasia were wrong. I can recall many discussions on the street corner with my non-Catholic friends, and we often differed in our views of birth control, mixed marriage and divorce, but we were in agreement on the pro-life issues. I am still puzzled by the change in attitude that has taken place since Roe V Wade in 1973—even among some of my high school friends. For the past 25 years I have been involved in the grassroots educational and political efforts to change people's hearts and minds about the sanctity of life and to offer non-abortion help and support for women with unplanned pregnancies. We have not been spared from some difficult challenges with abortion in our own family, so we *do* understand how difficult and emotional the decisions can be.

In my medical practice, I delivered over 2000 babies, but, thankfully, never had to choose between the life of the mother and the life of the baby. ("Life of the mother" is the one exception I will make in my opposition to abortion.) Fortunately, Gloria has been supportive of my pro-life views, and she and one of my daughters have both spent time counseling at our local Alpha Omega Crisis Pregnancy Center.

Shortly before my retirement from medicine, we decided to develop a home-based marketing business. Even in this endeavor, Gloria's focus was to help people, while mine was to generate additional income for my retirement. She sees this business as a way to help people get through life's challenges in their marriages, their jobs and their parenting. For her, the business is a *mission* to help other people, and it has enabled her to touch many people in very meaningful ways. She has truly helped save some marriages and has been a strong supporter for many people, who are going through struggles in their lives. Although the business has produced some financial rewards for us, I cannot begin to claim her level of altruistic motivation.

Our other significant involvement has had an International flavor. When our daughter, Candi, after her sophomore year in high school requested permission to participate in a foreign exchange program sponsored by Youth for Understanding, she opened the door for many enriching experiences for our family. She wanted to spend her junior year of high school in a foreign country where she could improve her French. We didn't realize at the time that this would open our own door to students from other Countries. Candi actually ended up in Belgium, not in the southern part, where they speak French, but in the northern part near Antwerpen, where they speak Dutch. She had to learn a brand new language and was very homesick for the first month. She spent much of that first month writing letters and reading long novels like "Gone With The Wind", "Winds of War" and "War and Remembrance". After school began, however, she met her classmates, adapted well and by midyear had become quite fluent in Dutch. Candi's experience prompted Gloria to become involved with YFU, and she served as an Area Representative for ten years, placing over 75 foreign students in area homes. Eight of these students lived with us, five of them for a full year. While it was Gloria's idea, our children and I shared in the benefits of interacting with young people from other Countries. It made the world a little smaller and people's differences less significant.

Andy Eicken

Andy Eicken, from a small town in the southeastern corner of West Germany, was the first to join us, and he faced quite a challenge in adapting to a large family. He came from a home where he was raised as an only child after his sister was tragically killed in an accident when she was very young. Before he came to the U.S., his parents told him to adapt and not to cause any problems during his year in the U.S. Because of this, when he first came he would never openly disagree with anything we said. This bothered Gloria, and she finally told him that she didn't mind if he disagreed, but he should be willing to discuss his disagreements. She told him to stop *pretending* he agreed with everything. After that, our relationship was much more open, and he was a truly delightful son. He exerted his independence when we had our family picture taken that year. He refused to wear a tie! We visited him twice in Germany after his year with us, and we found it interesting to note his change in attitude about money between the two visits. During our first visit, he was a college student in Munich. He thought money was unimportant, and that it should be shared equally with everyone. (Socialism) At that time, of course, the State paid for his education, and his father provided his other support. When we visited him again a few years later, he was married, had a child and was struggling to establish a medical practice. He did not think everyone should share equally in the money he earned and sounded much more like a Capitalist.

Mich Van Put

Mireille "Mich" Van Put, from Belgium, came to live with us, when her first home placement didn't work out. (In Gloria's experience, about one-third of the exchange students she placed didn't finish the year in the home where they started.) We thought our home would work out well for Mich because Candi had just returned from Belgium, and they would both be seniors. Candi tried to include Mich in her circle of friends, but Mich formed relationships instead with other students who weren't much interested in school. At Christmas time she wanted to go home, but we discouraged that, and she did finish the year with us. The school year ended in early June, but she didn't return to Belgium for another month, and during that month her attitude changed and we got along much better. In fact, she even expressed sadness when it was time for her to leave. Only years later, when we visited her in Belgium, did we understand the reason for her initial attitude while in the U.S.. She had actually completed high school before she came over as an exchange student, so she was more mature than her American high school classmates and not much interested in high school studies—thus her relationship with other kids, who were also not interested in school. Her attitude changed after school ended because she no longer had to pretend to be a high school student. At the time of our visit in Belgium, she was married, had a small child, and was effervescent and delightful—totally different than she had been during most of her year in the U.S.. We were delighted to meet again on her "turf".

Chris Potrafke

Chris Potrafke's arrival in our home marked the beginning of our multiple relationships with a delightful German family

from Balingen, a city, near Stuttgart, in the southwestern part
of West Germany. Chris was a very bright and outgoing high
school senior who fit into our family quickly and became
involved in many activities. He was advised that the best way
to meet other students was to get involved in after school
activities. Therefore, he went out for football (a game he had
never played). He *had* played soccer, so I suggested he try out
as a kicker. I took him out to the football field to practice. The
first time he ran up to kick the ball, his feet went out from
under him, and he fell and broke his wrist. That ended his
football aspirations, but later he did join the basketball team.
He didn't get to play much in the games, but he must have
learned something because when he returned to Germany, he
was considered a good basketball player. His favorite sport
was tennis, and he excelled as the number two player on the
high school team. He also was involved with me in community
theatre, where he played the part of a Russian soldier in our
production of "Fiddler on the Roof". Our second trip to Germany
was to attend Chris's wedding to Dagmar, a beautiful, tall
German fraulein, and we were treated like honored guests. It
was a wonderful experience. We were even given English
translations of the talks given by the two fathers at the reception.
An awkward moment occurred when the groom couldn't locate
his wife after she had been "kidnapped" following the wedding
ceremony. We learned that after weddings in Germany it was
common for the bride to be "kidnapped" by the other girls in
the wedding party, and then the groom's friends would set out
with the groom to locate her. They would take him to a pub,
where he would be instructed to dance on a table or perform
some other stunt before they took him to the next location.
Someone with the groom would know where the bride could be
found, but several pubs would be visited before the two would
be united. In Chris and Dagmar's case, however, there was a
mix-up in communications, and the groom never found the bride!
An hour after the search had begun, the unhappy bride returned

to the reception without the groom, who appeared a half hour later. They were not a happy couple at that moment, and the members of the wedding party were very apologetic. While this wedding tradition backfired, the marriage has survived very well. Both Chris & Dagmar have law degrees and recently traveled to the U.S. with their two children to attend our 50th wedding anniversary party.

Tilman Potrafke

Three years after Chris left, his brother, Tilman, joined us and provided us with a marked contrast in personality. He was delightful and bright but very quiet. He was a great listener and enjoyed sitting in on our conversations but so seldom expressed his thoughts, I sometimes kidded him about being a German spy. He was an excellent tennis player and was the number one player on the high school team. Although usually very stoic on the tennis court, I do remember one time when he became so frustrated during a match, that he let loose a volley of German expletives. Fortunately, no one else understood.

Tilman was a wonderful addition to our family, and when he left, it was doubly sad because he took our daughter, Kelly, with him! Kelly was only fourteen at the time and had just finished her freshman year in high school. She wanted to spend a year in Germany, and, since she would be on the same flight with Tilman and staying with his family, we agreed to let her go. When we look at fourteen year olds today, we wonder how we could have agreed to that. Shortly after the plane took off, Kelly became homesick and shed some tears, for which Tilman was little comfort. He didn't say more than a few words during the entire flight, and when she asked, "What do I say to your parents, when I first see them?" his response was, "Hello". Kelly ended up enjoying her year in Germany. She was the only daughter in a family of three boys, and her German parents treated her like a princess. She certainly didn't get that treatment at home.

Anna Aguilar

We had three other students, who came to us for part of a year, when their first homes didn't work out. Anna Aguilar from Argentina arrived just in time to join us for a *24 hour* marathon trip from Hillsdale to Washington, D.C. and back (about 1000 miles) on a school bus! We were participating in the annual Right to Life March with 100,000 other pro-lifers. I'm not sure she even understood the purpose of the event, but we told her that it would be an opportunity to see our Nation's capitol. The bus was very uncomfortable with people trying to sleep sitting up or lying down in the aisles. Anna got sick during the journey and really had little time to see the tourist attractions in Washington. After her survival of that experience, Anna adjusted very well and was a very pleasant addition to our family.

Grandma Kit & Kayo

The other two students were from Japan, and neither was with us very long. Kayo Fujioka spent several weeks with us after all of our children had left home, and she tried very hard to adjust in a household without any other young people. She didn't want to move, but we convinced her that she would be better off in a home with a daughter her age. She was a wonderful, caring person, and the other home did work out better for her. In spite of her short time with us, she has been very diligent about keeping in touch, and both Gloria and I on cool evenings use the lounging jackets she gave us as a parting memento. Kayo is married now and has a family of her own.

Our international relations are still expanding because as I record these lines we are hosting Katia Noskova, a Hillsdale College student from Russia. She came to us (as you might suspect) because of the efforts of Gloria. A year and a half before Katia came to live with us she worked with Kristin Pauken, one of our 37 grandchildren, at the Kimball YMCA Camp in Hillsdale County and joined us for Thanksgiving dinner. She also spent a week with us over Christmas that year when the camp was closed. Katia is from a poor family with divorced parents, and toward the end of her work visa at the camp she expressed a desire to spend more time in the United States. Gloria suggested that perhaps she could attend Hillsdale College on a student visa. Katia was excited about that possibility, even though she had already completed four years of college in Russia, so Gloria contacted some people she knew at the College, and Katia was not only admitted, but she was awarded a full scholarship! However, there was one major obstacle. She could not obtain a student visa in time to start classes that January and was told to return to Russia to get her visa through the American Embassy there. The Embassy was not very helpful and initially turned her request down because they said she had over-stayed her work visa. This was not true, and Gloria contacted the offices of our Congressman, Nick Smith and our Senator, Spence Abraham for help. It took nine months (and $500) before Katia was finally able to get her visa. She returned to the U.S. and moved in with us in December of 2000 and started her classes at Hillsdale College the following month.

Katia
Our gift from Russia

Katia has been a true blessing. She is a serious student and very grateful for the opportunities provided to her in this Country. The freedoms she enjoys here were only dreams in Russia, and she helps so much with chores around the house, that we often call her "Cinderella". Her life here is so much different than her life in Russia that her favorite expression is, "Oh thank you so much." In reality, she has given *us* much more than she realizes. She is a wonderful example of the goodness and ambitions of people regardless of their country of origin, and she serves as a constant reminder to us of the unusual opportunities we have in this Country. She is a pleasure to have around.

We have been unusually blessed by the people, both here and abroad, who have impacted our lives, and in this book we have only brushed the surface of that list. We have come to realize that most of our friendships and relationships are temporary—related to events or activities as we progress through life. Although we attend reunions with hopes of resurrecting these friendships, our attempts usually fall far short of our expectations. I thank Gloria for the people she has brought into our home. They have enriched our lives greatly, and I hope that we have been able to touch them in some meaningful way.

PART II: REFLECTIONS BY GLORIA

I have been given the opportunity to witness many births via my role as a childbirth educator, and each birth is such a miracle. Equally awesome is being present as one transcends from life to death. Three such experiences in my life especially stand out.

I will forever be grateful to Judy Shannon for allowing me to be with her when her husband Bill died on Oct. 25, 1975. Bill had many friends and none of us could fathom that he would die so quickly. Judy was teaching school and wanted to be there for him at the end. She didn't know he would go so soon, so she continued to teach, and several of us volunteered to drive him to his daily treatments in Adrian about 40 miles from Hillsdale. Bill had been such a supportive visionary for so many young people, we all wanted to be there for *him*. During his final days, we each had quiet moments with him to say good-bye. Judy and I were with him at the end. It was a spiritual experience for me. I felt like I was truly witnessing the miraculous transition of Bill from the suffering of this life to the peace and beauty of his spiritual life. It is difficult to put into words, but it was similar to experiencing the miracle of birth. Thank you, Judy, for allowing me to share this experience.

My next experience was with Aunt Edy, as she made her transition from life into death at 2 P.M. on February 3, 1985 at the Hillsdale Medical Care Facility. Both Bud and I were with her. Aunt Edy had always been a big part of our lives. Since she had no children and was divorced, she spent most holidays with us, and after her retirement she had come to live in the apartment over our attached garage which we had built especially for her. Aunt Edy was fun! The children all enjoyed her great sense of humor and her love of the holidays. Christmas just wasn't the same without Aunt Edy. She had a habit of opening gifts before Christmas to see what she was getting, and then re-wrapping them so she could enjoy the gift twice. However, after her hip replacements and her stroke which left her unable to speak she became grouchy and impatient with the kids (Never with me). We converted the north part of our house into a handicap accessible apartment for Edith. She had been a smoker for years and refused to quit. We rationalized that it was not worth it to try to make her stop. However, when she began to burn holes in the carpet and her clothes, we did take her cigarettes away and only allowed her to smoke if someone was with her. This made her very defiant; so hardly able to walk or talk, she would sneak out of the house and hobble across the snow covered yard in her nightgown to beg cigarettes from the neighbor. She would even stop the mailman and ask him for cigarettes. At this point we felt that in order to protect her from injuring herself, we had to put her in a nursing home. This decision was an emotionally draining experience for me, and I felt guilty for failing to fulfill her needs after all that she had done for us. I cried for a week, and even wanted to bring her back home, but Bud convinced me that the nursing home was the best place for her. They took good care of her, and I visited just about every day. The Sunday she died, they called to let us know the end was near. We were able to be with her and pray with her and tell it was OK for her to let go and let God take her. She died peacefully, and I also felt at peace.

My last personal experience with the transition from life to death was when Mom died. Mom had moved to Hillsdale three years after my adoptive Dad, Clark, had died on January 7, 1970 while he and Mom were still living in Wheaton, Illinois. Clark was 24 years older that Mom, and I found it interesting that she died 24 years after he did. A few years after Clark died, the church across the street in Wheaton offered to buy Mom's home for $67,000 to make a parking lot! What a blessing. The home needed many repairs, which Mom did not have the skill or the money to make, and she was lonely. There was no family in Wheaton any more, so we encouraged her to move to Hillsdale. With added encouragement from my sister, Louise, and a lot of prayer, Mom finally made the decision to move, and she bought a small house in Hillsdale with a big back yard. She moved to Hillsdale on July 4, 1973.

What a great opportunity for all of us. She came, and with her came her front door! We had the front door removed from 319 N. Cross Street in Wheaton before Mom's house was torn down, and we installed it in our Howell Street home in Hillsdale. When Ray built our present home, we took the door with us, and he designed our main entrance around that 110-year-old solid *cross-grained* oak door. It still has a mail slot and the original beveled glass and hardware.

Mom's new home was across the street from the Hillsdale College football field, at 184 Oak Street. It gave us a convenient private parking space for all of the home football and basketball games. This was doubly beneficial because through the years she was there we had three sons who played football for Hillsdale College. It was also nice for the boys because she did their laundry and baked cookies for them while they lived on campus.

Our daughter, Terry, also benefited when she returned to Hillsdale College to finish her degree because Grandma Kit could take care of Terry's daughter, Kristin, while Terry was in class. Grandma Kit loved the opportunity, but she insisted on being free to discipline Kristin. Mom used a ping-pong paddle labeled *"moral persuader"* but seldom actually used it because Kristin usually behaved.

Mom was never shy about giving advice. As many mothers are prone to do after their children are grown and have moved out on their own, she called frequently and complained that no one came to see her. She would comment, "I could be dead and no one would know it," or "Why did I bother to move to Hillsdale?"

While we were building our marketing business, we traveled a lot, and this worried her. "What will I do if something happens to you?" she asked with every announced trip. I tried to reassure her that God would make sure that we were home when we needed to be—and we were. On one occasion, while watering her plants, she fell into the bushes and could not get up. I was visiting her at the time and was able to help her. I was around many other times when she needed me, but eventually I suggested that she consider moving into the apartment over our garage. She thought about it for a couple of seconds and said, "OK". It took awhile for her to sort through her belongings and decide what to take with her. She sold the house, gave lots of stuff away and moved into the apartment on August 7, 1989. The timing was perfect. Our final Hillsdale College children had graduated, so the need for her convenient private parking space and her laundering efforts had ended, and the apartment over the garage was empty. She loved her new home and the close proximity to me, and, at the age of eighty-one, she immediately took over our yard work and the gardening! In the summer, she supplied us with fresh green beans and tomatoes, grown in *her* garden. She mowed the lawn and started four compost piles for the rakings. She encouraged the neighbors to do the same, and she sometimes mowed their lawns because she didn't like the way they did it! Mom was an organic gardener and a charter subscriber to Prevention Magazine, from whom she received a lifetime membership for just $100. Some of her ideas on health appeared to be a little far out, but many are now being accepted and supported by the medical profession. She was a lady ahead of her time.

Mama was not brought up in a family that outwardly showed affection, and she felt uncomfortable saying, "I love you." There was never a doubt in our minds that she did, but her life had not been easy. She was a survivor. I think my sister, Louise, expressed it very well in this 1952 Mother's Day letter.

Dearest Mama,

    You know, Mama, sometimes I wish you didn't pretend to be so unsentimental and cold-hearted. After all, there are times, such as Mother's Day, when a gal would like to tell her mother how much she loves her, and what a wonderful mother you are and have been.

    Since I can't be gushy and yet would like to get the ideas across to you, let's see if we can attack this problem scientifically and see if we can find out whether you have been a good mother or not:

1.   *When my sister and I were babies, our mother gave us enough cuddling to store up the feeling of security and love when we grew too big for cuddling.*

2.   *As we were growing up during the depression, you worked long and hard to provide for us, giving up many things in order that we could get proper vitamins.*

3.   *When we were still very young, you became separated from us (which must have hurt you deeply) in order to take a better job and therefore provide a better living for us.*

4.   *You fell in love and married a man who became a father to us and for the first time in our lives we had a real family unit in our home.*

    a. You will never know how much it meant to your daughters to feel that they were like other families and had a real home where they could bring their friends. (Thanks.)

b. I am not forgetting that much of the credit for this goes to Dad, (Clark)

But after all you married him, and just catching and holding him is a fact worthy of admiration. (I agree, Clark was one-in-million . . . there will never be another . . . they broke the mold when they made him.)

5. *You allowed us to grow up with as much freedom for expression, learning, and growth as two girls should have had.*

6. *You put yourselves into debt in order that we could go to a nice college (Stephens College)*

7. *You left us free to choose our own marriage partners and accepted our choices as though they were your own.*

8. *You are continuing to prove your unselfishness by showering gifts upon your two grandsons.*

9. *You haven't fooled your daughters at all about being cold hearted.*

CONCLUSION: A pretty darn wonderful mother, and you will always get an A+ from me

I Love you, Louise

This was sent to Mama in 1952 but the copy I have was typed in 1976 when Mama retyped the hand written note from Louise and sent it back to her, saying, "I hope you still feel the same way."

Years later, when she was hospitalized with congestive heart failure; she commented to our daughter, Terry, "Why doesn't God just let me die?"

Terry laughingly told her, "He won't let you die until you tell your daughter you love her.'"

The next day, when I came to visit Mama in the hospital, she proclaimed, "I LOVE YOU, I LOVE YOU, I LOVE YOU. Now can I die!?" The Lord must not have felt she was sincere, because she lived a few more years.

Mom always worried that I would not be home when something *"happened."* However, it seemed I always was. I was there when she fell in the bushes, I was there when she had her stroke and I was there when she almost died after emergency abdominal surgery. When she needed me, I always seemed to be there for her. Thank you Lord.

Mama was diagnosed with lung cancer in April of 1992 and was given six weeks to four months to live. We notified all of our children and they all made special trips with their children to say good-bye. She loved it. The last four months of her life were pleasant ones. Since I had alerted the family and friends, she received many cards and visits. At first Mama was short of breath and fatigued, but she had no pain. She slept a lot. Hospice was wonderful, and they arranged for us to have oxygen and suitable pain medicine available during the last month of her life. More importantly, they encouraged Mom and I to talk about her impending death and to share our thoughts and our feelings. They also helped her to write a letter to me, which I was given after she died.

My final days with Mom were special. Our youngest daughter, Kelly, quit her job and came home to help. She was wonderful and could be less emotional in dealing with Mom than I could. Mom became very appreciative and considerate during those final few months, and we spent much quality time together. She died peacefully on August 1, 1992 just before Kelly had to return to work.

I thank the Lord for giving me the opportunity he has given me to minister to the needs of others during their final days of life and for the privilege of witnessing a glimpse of their transition from earthly life to spiritual life.

Chapter Twenty

(Gloria)
PARENTING SUCCESS
OR SURVIVAL?

To what extent are parents responsible for their child's behavior? We cringe when we hear suggestions that parents should be punished for the misdeeds of their offspring. Psychologists, counselors, and teachers often suggest that crime, school violence and sexual promiscuity can be traced to unstable, abusive and unloving homes. Before we had children, we believed this. We intended to be perfect parents and have perfect children. Neither occurred. We believed that childhood behavior was totally under the control of the parents. Now, we prefer to think it is *genetics*. We may be responsible for both, but we can't be blamed for the latter.

Most parents don't start out being mean, short-tempered, unfair, stingy, selfish, not with it (old-fashioned) and strict, but as the child/parent ratio increases, and the children get older, these characteristics become survival techniques. It took us a little longer (12), than most, to accept our limitations as parents. To those of you who always thought we were nuts; *we are,* and to those of you who thought we were marvelous; *you are* (nuts!). Judge for yourself.

*   *   *

We are at home on a typical weekday morning with the twelve children ranging in age from 2 to 17. Another day begins:

The twins (2) just shared a jar of honey and a box of Cheerios . . . on the kitchen floor! Mother (38) speaks:

"Michael (3), where are your clothes? Who wants to get Michael dressed?"

"Kelly (2), you took your shoes off again. Where did you leave them? If you don't find them, you are going back to bed."

"No, Steve (17), you can't use the car this morning. I'm sorry you're late, but I can't drive you, and your Dad is doing surgery this morning."

"Somebody wake up Tony (14)."

"Ray (16), didn't you go to bed at all last night . . . AGAIN! I appreciate the fact that you like to be clean, but would you please pick up the five towels you dropped on the bathroom floor . . . and put the top back on the toothpaste."

"Gay (15), get out of the shower. Your Dad still has to shave and there is no hot water left."

"Is Tony up?"

"No, Pam (10), you can't have a slumber party. I know Terry (12) had one last week. I know it's unfair but don't bug me . . . And change Kevin's (2) diapers, will you?"

"Terry, will you stop dancing and help Michael get dressed?"

"Lisa (6), I know you have tights in your drawer. I just sorted the clothes, so go look again."

"Candi (11), get Kelly's shoes on."

"Did anyone get Tony up?"

"I don't have any change, Candi. Borrow some paper from your sister."

"Will *someone* get Kelly's shoes on?"

"Ricky (9), I don't have time to check your workbook and sign it. Why didn't you ask me sooner? . . . Well, I was busy then, too."

"Is Tony up?"

"I'm sorry, Pam, but you can't use the Spam for your sandwich. It's for supper. Try bologna . . . OK, try peanut butter."

"Who spilled the milk? . . . Well, it didn't spill itself, so someone wipe it up."

"Kelly, your shoes are on the wrong feet."

"Where is Tony? TONY, Get up! You have ten minutes to get to school."

The twins (2) just dumped a pan of water and completely soaked themselves—fighting over the rag to wipe up the spilt milk.

It is now 8 a.m.!

*   *   *

When our kids reached their teens they struggled to be independent—to test their wings—to find their own direction, sometimes in defiance of our wishes.

Most of our children left the nest when they finished high school but two of them were gone by the time they were 15 and 17—either by request or as a way of announcing their independence. By the age of 19, some of them had moved back in! They had discovered that room and board is not free. The conversation, on their return, would go something like this:

*   *   *

Offspring: "Hi, folks."

Parent: "Nice to see you again, son. How long do you plan to stay?"

Offspring: "Just until we get things set up. It won't take long."

Parent: "WE!"

Offspring: "Oh yeah, this is Joe Longhair. You won't mind if he crashes here for a few days will you? He's a friend I met at Independence Hall and we're planning to go into business together—got some great ideas that can't miss."

Parent: "Now wait a minute. We already have a houseful, and it wouldn't be fair to make any of your brothers or sisters move out of their rooms. There just isn't any . . ."

Offspring: "Aw, we won't need a separate room. We'll be glad to sleep on the floor. I've told Joe what great parents I have. He was raised in a Youth home and never knew what a real home was like. Besides, we won't be staying very long."

Parent: "Well, maybe for a few days it would be okay, but . . ."

Offspring: "Great! See, Joe, I told you what great parents I have. What's for supper?"

*   *   *

Toward the end of 1972, our home population ranged from 13 to 18. Our two oldest, Steve and Ray (20 and 19) had just returned home after brief attempts at independence. Gay (18) was working in Wheaton, Illinois, living with her aunt Edy. Tony (16) still appreciated the benefits of living at home and was diplomatic enough to tell us what we wanted to hear. The other eight were still at home, and we had temporarily taken in a two-month-old premature baby whose mother had died of Lupus shortly after her delivery. The child's father sometimes spent evenings with us, and our son, Ray, had a working partner who enjoyed our free room and board. Kim Henry, another teenager upset with her parents, also moved in with us. We would often tell parents that their children could spend the night at our house, but we might not notice them until breakfast!

Ray exemplified the striving for independence more defiantly and persistently than the other children. One year he balked at joining us for our annual Thanksgiving family gathering in LaGrange, Illinois with Bud's brother, Dave, and his family. Ray was not around when we were ready to depart. He was 17, with an already well-established reputation as a free spirit, and we were concerned that if we left him home alone, he might have a party in our house with some of his similarly independent friends. We were angry at his defiance, so we locked the house, notified the neighbors and the police that our son was not to be in the house and went off without him. He did manage to get into the house after we left but was promptly evicted by the police.

When we returned a couple days later, we found this note from Ray:

"It's a sad thing when I am no longer welcome in my own home and you find it necessary to send the police to throw me out."

While we were being consumed with guilt for being such callous parents and wondering if we had made the right decision, Ray was hitchhiking to California! He made the 2,000-mile trek (with no money) in three days, and was enjoying surf, sun and sand when the police picked him up. (At 17, a non-Californian without parents was considered a *vagrant*.) He was taken to a youth facility, and the authorities contacted us. We were given two choices. Either we could pre-pay his air fare home and they would put him on the plane or Ray would remain a guest of the State of California in the youth facility for three months—until he turned 18—for which *we* would pay $25 a day. Bud's initial feelings of parental guilt were replaced by frustration and anger, and he suggested we leave Ray in California! However, a cooler head prevailed—mine.

"Ray is our son", I pointed out, "and, besides, compared to $25 a day, airfare is a bargain." The cost-comparison convinced Bud, so we paid for the plane ride home.

We often speculate about the effects of the large-family experience on individual children, and Ray caused us the most speculation. Ray probably would qualify as an authentic prodigy. He is remarkably gifted as a carpenter and musician, and we have often wondered whether he would have thrived better in a small family where his talents could have been more individually cultivated. We *did* recognize his talents and creativity early on and tried our best to offer him opportunities for creative growth, even enrolling him in a private school for gifted students at one time (Wawasee Prep School in Indiana). As it turned out, the aspect of his personality, which came to dominate, was his rebellion against conformity that he exhibited early on when he toddled into the waiting room of a Chicago medical clinic at age two and a half.

Shortly after we flew him back from California, Ray moved to Toronto and except for some intermittent stays at home, has been pretty much on his own after his 18th birthday. ("On his own" being a relative term with Ray.) Surprisingly, family has always been important to Ray, and seldom does he fail to return for the holidays. He always (with the exception of his California trip) kept in touch and let us know where he was. Moreover, his brothers, in spite of their frustration with him at times, admit that they have all learned home building skills from him.

The Sixties wreaked havoc on Ray. The rebellious spirit of the time (which actually spans a period starting the last three or four years of that decade and running into the mid-1970s) pandered to Ray's inherent craving for freedom from any kind of limits or restraint. How Ray has survived, we cannot say. He was far more than we could handle, and his avoidance of total destruction seems even too much to attribute to angelic protection. Perhaps there is simply some God-given core of strength and perseverance within him that has brought him through. He is still a free spirit and continues to struggle against conformity. However, he did design and build a beautiful new home for us, which we are now enjoying. It took a year and a half to build, and was built on his own bizarre, non-traditional schedule, but it represents a dream of his (and ours) and is a magnificent testimony to his talent, creativity and love of his parents.

Ray has helped us to understand the biblical account of the prodigal son, a story whose message is very difficult for non-prodigals to accept. Not long ago, we had an interesting conversation with him. We asked him to recount the sequence of his escapades because they all blur together in our memories. After he had gone through a quick synopsis, we suggested that perhaps he would have been better able to develop his talents in a home with fewer siblings. He smiled and told us we should quit beating ourselves up about our parenting.

"You are great parents. I just chose to live my life differently. I have no regrets and neither should you."

As is usually the case with Ray, we are not sure whether this comment should reassure us or baffle us.

Our family in 1973
Tony, Candi, Bud, Gloria, Pam, Rick
Kelly, Kevin
Lisa, Mike, Ray, Gay, Steve, Terry

Some years later we handled another son with wanderlust differently. During the spring of his sophomore year in high school, Rick told us he had to get away. He was having difficulty in school and wanted a break. Would we let him hitchhike to Florida, a thousand miles away? This was a disturbing request. He was only 15, and our first inclination was to say, "Absolutely not!" However, his problems were real and spring vacation was near. We decided it might do him good to be off on his own for a few weeks. Bud had done quite a bit of hitchhiking when he was young and was not as apprehensive about the dangers as others might have been. I followed his advice in making our decision, and, setting our misgivings aside as best we could, we allowed him to go.

Rick's trip began safely enough. His Grandma Kit drove him the first 60 miles and dropped him off in Ohio. He then began hitchhiking and made it to Kentucky where the State police, suspecting he was a runaway, stopped him and called us. We told them he had our permission to travel, so they let him go with instructions to keep off the main highways. Rick slept under a bridge that night, and survived a night by himself in the out-of-doors without falling prey to spiders or snakes.

At one point is his journey south, he had a stroke of good fortune when a generous family gave him a ride for a day and a half and took him all the way to Fort Lauderdale. That evening he was searching along the beach for a place to sleep when it started raining. An empty beach house looked like a handy shelter, and Rick was preparing to spend the night there when the local police confronted him. They offered him a choice between going to jail and relocating to the municipality on the other side of the river. He chose the other side of the river.

A couple days later, Rick struck up a conversation with a young man who had a place to "crash." He said Rick could stay in his guestroom, and Rick gladly accepted the offer. During the night, our 15-year-old son awoke to find his benefactor in bed with him—with a hand very inappropriately placed. "What do you think you're doing?" Rick exclaimed! The man made some lame excuse about sleepwalking, at which point Rick decided the living room floor might be a safer sleeping place. In the morning when his host was out buying juice and doughnuts for breakfast, Rick quickly departed.

Rick found some temporary work during his time in Florida and eventually made it all the way to Key West. By this time he had been gone for three weeks, had run out of money and was ready to come home. As it happened, Bud and I were celebrating our 25th wedding anniversary in Saint Thomas (Virgin Islands) and were to fly back home through Miami. Rick got in touch with us before we left Saint Thomas, and we arranged for him to stay with some friends, Karen and Kenton Wood, who lived near Miami. They let him stay with them until we got back to Miami and then they brought Rick to the airport, and we flew back to Michigan together.

In spite of the potential dangers of such an adventure, the journey proved to be a positive one. Rick got a taste of freedom, but more importantly he learned how to deal with a variety of people and challenges. Moreover, since part of his four weeks away had coincided with the school's spring vacation, he hadn't missed much class time and was able to complete his sophomore year with passing grades. Overall, his attitude toward school was much improved, and we felt our judgment in letting him go had been vindicated. Rick, now the father of four boys, is appalled that we would have allowed him to make that journey at such a young age. He states emphatically that he would never allow one of his sons to do the same. His point is certainly legitimate but everything turned out well, and we no longer feel obliged to defend our decision.

Why did these things happen? Having twelve children was at the very heart of our vision of marriage; it was, in fact, one of the shared goals that brought us together. However, if we are short of definitive answers, our experiences have at least provided us with some valuable thought-provoking observations.

One of our observations suggested that our sex education talks with our children did not always transmit information correctly. When our daughter, Lisa, was 12, she and two of her older sisters, Candy and Terry were talking about topics of interest while sprawled on our king-sized bed with me. Lisa related that Lynn Moes, one of her best friends, had told her how babies were made. She found this hard to believe, but was sure that all the "seeds" must have been planted with one act of intercourse. Her mature sisters smiled and clarified that each baby was the result of a separate sexual encounter.

Lisa, with innocent disbelief, looked at me and responded, "You mean that you and dad had to do it 12 times!?"

Needless to say, her sisters doubled up in laughter, and I was also unsuccessful in maintaining my composure in spite of Lisa's obvious embarrassment.

As the parents of twelve children we would concur that in a large family dynamics are multiplied. There are more individual lives in motion—all in close quarters—each bumping up against the movements (and emotions) of the others. Each child brings his own personality to the mix, and the interaction of these personalities creates challenges. There is the need to share, the need to help, the need to be heard, the need to adjust, and the need to compete for attention. These dynamics are not exclusive to large families of course. Raising children is never easy, and challenges arise in all families, large or small.

The hubbub in a large family, of course, is also not without its positive side. The adventurous soul understands that a challenge is also an opportunity for growth, and in a large family, each day offers plenty of those. You can cry in frustration or look for solutions. While not always successful, we've tried our best to come up with suitable solutions. Along with the sheer number of kids in the household, there's no doubt that we interacted differently with the older children than we did with the younger ones. Largely this is due to the reality that each child entered our lives at a different point in our own growth as parents.

1989
Kevin & Kelly become our 7th & 8th
Hillsdale College graduates
Steve (38) Ray (37) Tony (34) Bud (63) Rick (29)
Mike (23) Kevin (22)
Gay (36) Terry (32) Candi (31) Gloria (58) Pam (30)
Lisa (25) Kelly (22)

Initially we had high expectations of perfect children and a family life of happy interactions and uninterrupted bliss. When misbehavior or childhood rebellion disturbed that bliss, it was the kids' fault and required appropriate discipline. This reflected our early assumption that we were born to be the mother and father of a large brood (the influence of *Cheaper By The Dozen* again), natural parents filled with love. We felt that our love would triumph over every adversity. We held the line, stuck to our guns and punished when necessary. (Yes, this sometimes included a whipping on the bottom with dad's belt). We weren't entirely inflexible. In fact, we saw early on that our initial assumption that all children could be treated alike wasn't realistic. We switched to a more customized approach, trying to meet the particular needs of each child as we thought most appropriate. Still, we insisted on at least minimum adherence to our standards of proper behavior, and when our methods didn't produce the expected responses, we were perplexed and frustrated.

Our older children arrived in their teens during the '60's, probably the most culturally tumultuous era of the 20th century. Bud and I were not prepared for it. We had both been raised in times and homes where *respect* was the norm. While neither of us were perfect children, we rarely intentionally disobeyed our parents or our teachers. Bud's father demanded respect and Bud had neither the desire nor the courage to challenge his father's authority. He found life much more pleasant when he obeyed his father's wishes. Our parents, quite simply, expected us to do what was right.

Bud remembers one Saturday afternoon in his early teens when he had remarked that he planned to go to confession that day. He didn't recall what sins he had committed, but confession always instilled an element of anxiety, and his enthusiasm for going dwindled as the day progressed. He was in the living room at home, and his father was sitting in his favorite chair reading; when he suddenly looked up and said, "Bud, I thought you said you were going to confession." Bud mumbled some excuse for deciding not to go; at which point his father got out of his chair, and told Bud he would drive him to church. He was not Catholic, seldom went to church and never had gone to confession, but he apparently understood that Bud's earlier statement about going to confession meant that he needed to go. He waited in the car for Bud to finish.

The era, in which Bud and I were raised following the depression and in the midst of the very patriotic World War II, gave way, twenty five years later, to the social and political turmoil of the 60's and 70's. *Rebellion* replaced *respect*, and our attempts to use the same methods in raising our children that our parents used with us, produced much different results. Our oldest two boys were old enough to be eligible for the draft during the Viet Nam conflict, but Steve's residual weakness in his left arm from polio exempted him, and Ray received a high draft number and was never called. Whether either would have agreed to serve, I do not know. Since at their age Bud had willingly served two years in the U.S. Navy at the end of WW II, he not only could not understand the reluctance of young people to serve in Viet Nam, but he also tried hard to justify our Country's involvement there.

The war, of course, was only one aspect of the rebellious generation. Our children, like many others, got caught up in the music, the dress, the sexual freedoms and the drugs, and we reacted to these parental challenges in many different ways. We tried stricter discipline (like giving our 12-year-old son a crew cut whenever we caught him smoking. This proved ineffective because once his hair was short; he didn't have anything to lose.) We tried to improve communications with our teens. I read book after book on teen behavior in an effort to discover ways to develop positive relationships with our children. We helped start a teen center in town because a similar experience during our high school years had been very meaningful to both Bud and I. The Center failed to provide the same stimulation for the teens of the 60's, and it lasted only a short time. We became involved in activities with our children whenever we could. Not only did we help chaperone school dances and attend most of their extra-curricular events, but we purchased an old style coke machine to go with our ping pong and pool tables and opened our home as a gathering place for friends of our teen aged children. We enrolled our children in Catholic school, attended Mass every Sunday and participated in Christian retreat weekends (T. E. C.) with teens. We even became involved in a high school production of "West Side Story" with our rebellious 17 year old daughter in hopes that it would improve our relationship with her. It didn't! We took family camping and canoe trips each summer as "bonding" experiences. We sought the help of counselors, but they usually reinforced our feelings of inadequacy as parents. We were too strict or not strict enough. We were too rigid or too relaxed. We were too controlling or not involved enough with our children. When we were told by one counselor that our problem was, "You are too perfect, so your children can't hope to measure up." we decided that the counselor needed counseling!

Bud's reaction to our children's problems was often denial. While I wanted to be informed of everything, he didn't; so I screened what I heard because if Bud knew of the problem, he felt obliged to do something about it—often with authoritative measures. Later we were to learn (from Gary Smalley's "Hidden Keys To Loving Relationships") that a common distinction between women and men is that women usually just want a sympathetic listening ear at the end of the day, while men feel obliged to *fix* every problem mentioned. With some of our children, nothing worked, and as our dream of being best friends to our teenagers gave way to conflict and frustration, the realities of parenthood took on new meaning. I left home for six weeks at one point for visits with my mother in Wheaton and my sister in Long Island, telling Bud it was either that or an institution! I took the four youngest children with me and left the teenagers with Bud. They had driven me to my emotional limit! I had tried very hard to be a loving and understanding mother, and our teenage children appeared not to respect or appreciate me. The time away was beneficial. I finally accepted the reality that I could not control how the children behaved, but I *could* control how I responded. Bud and I both decided at that time that we were no longer going to blame ourselves for our children's behavior. We felt that we had done the best we could with the twelve God sent us. We certainly made some mistakes, but we did not *intentionally* do anything to impair their development. What they chose to do with their lives was our concern but not our fault. Perhaps because the motherly buffer was gone, the teens treated Bud royally during the six weeks I was away, and this produced some censured comments from me when I returned.

The rebellious '60's and '70's produced more serious behavior than simple disobedience, and our family was not immune. Setting a good example did not seem to work with our brood. Neither Gloria nor I smoked, and yet, at one time or another, ten of our twelve did. We are not drinkers, but we have several alcoholics and others who have encountered problems because of alcohol. We have never used illegal drugs, but many of our children experimented with them, and two have spent some time in drug and alcohol treatment centers. The sexual revolution was in direct conflict with our beliefs and the message we tried to give our children, but it produced a lifestyle adopted, at least for a while, by some of them. We have been actively involved with the Pro-Life movement for more than 20 years, but our family has not escaped the trauma of abortion. So much for setting a good example!

How did we two "traditional" parents cope? Poorly at times. I recall one time when Bud asked the high school principal to let him speak to a high school assembly about drugs after 2000 amphetamine capsules were stolen from his office. He felt that in order to get the attention of an auditorium of teenagers and perhaps to soothe his own parental conscience, he should personalize his message by sharing his concerns for his own children. Without giving names, he explained that he had two children who had experimented with drugs and another who had helped an older boy get into his office to steal the amphetamines. Whether this had any impact on any of the students present, we do not know, but the next day we received a phone call from a local lawyer telling us how stupid we were to announce in public the transgressions of our children. At the time Bud felt he did what was appropriate, but now we suspect the lawyer may have been right.

Experimentation with drugs became almost a rite of passage in those days, and few families escaped the impact. One of the factors that added to the stress for parents was that at first they were too embarrassed to talk about their children's use of drugs because they thought this would be an admission that they were not good parents. Finally, when it became apparent that the use of drugs affected the homes of even good parents, information was shared more freely. At one point we talked about forming a support group for us and other distraught parents. (With a bit of irony, we thought we might call the group "POT" (Parents Of Teens).) It was a laudable idea but it lasted only a few meetings. Perhaps it was too painful for parents to share stories about their own children's use of drugs. Some teens told their parents that they couldn't understand drugs because they had never used them! A few parents, in their attempts to better relate to their teenaged children, fell victim to this ruse. Thankfully we didn't.

We struggled with the long hair, the loud music and the protest messages on T-shirts because they were symbols of rebellion, but the sexual revolution bothered us much more. Our desire of course was for our children to remain chaste until marriage, but the reality was much different. Looking back now, we made some moral compromises in our attempts to communicate with our teens while defending our own conservative moral standards. Even though our approval was not required for our daughters to obtain birth control pills, we gradually relaxed our objections (rationalizing that an unplanned pregnancy would be far worse). The pill, of course, did not effectively prevent unplanned pregnancies.

For two people who set out to be perfect parents, we have been humbled often. God, in his infinite wisdom, has given us what we needed. While we had some disagreements on the proper decisions in child rearing, Bud and I were able to communicate our frustrations to each other and hang on until we could accept the reality that we could not control our children's lives. They were separate individuals, and what they chose to do was our concern but not our fault. In short, we achieved a certain balance. We realized that, as parents, we have the power to guide, to influence and to limit. However, ultimately our children were accountable and responsible for their own behavior. We had to let go—a difficult, if not impossible, process for parents.

After agonizing through the challenges presented by the older kids—fighting our fiercest battles with the destructive cultural forces of the sixties and seventies—both Bud and I began to feel more comfortable with ourselves as parents. We behaved much less punitively toward the younger children, and by the time we got to the last four, we *really* backed off (so much so, that the older siblings suggested we were getting soft.) By then we recognized that certain tendencies are inborn, and certain patterns will take hold no matter how much you try to resist them.

Consequently, things went a whole lot more smoothly in the Vear household during the closing phase of our active parenthood than they had a few years before. We were able to gain a new perspective on the parenting experience, which turned out so differently from expectations instilled by our reading of *Cheaper by the Dozen*. Reaching that perspective was challenging, there's no denying it. Our adventure as parents had been launched with naïve certainty that our children's lives would unfold along the lines of our serene expectations; that they would grow up according to our idealized vision of family; that they would marry and bring forth their own children in uncontested joy. It concluded with a much clearer understanding of parenthood. We have not been perfect parents. *We* have made mistakes. Moreover, we have not had perfect kids. *They* have made mistakes.

The passage through our tumultuous family life has been a truly humbling experience. Actually we feel a genuine sense of gratitude for that, as in the end humbling experiences can be beneficial. The blithe confidence with which we embarked on parenthood was, after all, a certain kind of arrogance. God knew what we needed and has been quite thorough in making us confront our pride. Our children have humbled us.

Summarily, we thank God and the many angels for the journey that has taken us to where we are now in our lives together. We are not unscarred by all the conflict and pandemonium. However, we have survived.

Blessedly, so have all twelve of our children.

**Bud walks into retirement
with a grandchild
March, 1991**

Addendum: A Tribute

to Our Children

THE VICARIOUS REWARDS
OF PARENTHOOD

Each of our children has enriched our lives in a special way and we thank them for that. Therefore, this addendum is a tribute to them for their accomplishments, both in childhood and in adulthood. We are proud of whom they have become, and we will continue to bask in the reflections of their successes. We love each of them in a special way.

STEVE, our eldest, continues to provide exciting surprises for us in the political arena, and with the strong support of his wife, Mary, has twice survived difficult campaigns to win elections as a Michigan State Representative. He is now launching a campaign to win a seat in the Michigan Senate. Steve possesses three traits that serve him well in the political arena. First he has a broad range of knowledge, secondly he seldom gets flustered or loses his composure and thirdly he almost never says anything unpleasant about other people. He

also has been a good father to his own son and his two
stepchildren. We are proud of his achievements, but we are
even more proud of the quality of his character.

Our kids born between 1952 and 1967 in chronological order
Back: #6 Candi, #1 Steve, #7 Pam, #2 Ray,
#9 Lisa, #5 Terry, #8 Rick, #3 Gay
Middle: #4 Tony, Glo & Bud, #10 Mike
Front: #s 11 & 12 twins, Kelly & Kevin

RAY has enriched our lives in many ways. He has built us
a house, which is far beyond our wildest dreams, but, more
importantly, he has taught us how to love more completely and
to be more tolerant and forgiving toward him despite his free-
spirited independent lifestyle. He introduced us to classical
music, by taking us to hear the Chicago Symphony, and we
still marvel at the way he customized a piano keyboard, so the
black and white keys would alternate, and it would make it
possible to play in a different key without changing fingering.

While he has presented us with many challenges, we have never doubted his love for us—nor ours for him.

GAY has blessed her own family and us with her positive upbeat attitude toward life in spite of her many trials. Her ambitious work habits started in high school, and we admire her courage in recently starting her own lawn care business. More importantly however, she and her husband, Jeff, have allowed us to share their parenting challenges and the achievements of their three sons. We have great respect for them as parents, and appreciate the fact that they seem to share many of the same family values as we do. We thank them for letting us be so much a part of their lives.

TONY gave us thrills on the football field, as a member of the finest high school football team I have seen in our 34 years in Hillsdale (My apologies to Rick, Mike and Kevin.), and Tony's leadership and scholarship in high school were sources of much pride for us. However, most special, was Tony's willingness to converse with us, and I cherish the late evening discussions he and I had in my office, when he came up to do the cleaning. We also are proud of how hard he has worked to succeed in his job as a salesman, and the parenting that he, and his wife, Sherry, do with their children.

TERRY, our fifth oldest, is a survivor of many struggles in her life, but she maintains an upbeat attitude, cares deeply for her children, and we are continually impressed by the dedication she has in serving the needs of seniors, as director of the Hillsdale Senior Center. She is currently pursuing a graduate degree in Non-profit Administration while organizing a major project to build a wonderful new Senior Center complex. She has had to successfully negotiate through a maze of regulations, politics and financial challenges to bring this building project to fruition. Terry has always had an artistic flair and her artistic talents surfaced on the stage in high school and in interior decorating and landscaping in recent years. She has often blessed us with the benefit of these talents. In the midst of her very busy schedule, she also found the time to review this book and she offered many helpful suggestions. (She even corrected some of my punctuation—a reversal of the role I played when she was writing papers in school.) Thank you, Terry.

CANDI introduced us to exchange student programs and enabled us to expand our horizons internationally when she had the courage to spend a year in Belgium at the tender age of 16. She also later turned a disappointing educational experience into a positive, when she lost her opportunity to be a Physician's Assistant but gained a wonderful husband, Bill Neal, in the process. They have been dedicated parents and have provided a loving home for four of our grandchildren. They, along with Rick and Marie, also give us a reason to travel to California each year.

PAM provided us with some enjoyable gymnastic moments in high school, but far more importantly, in her adult years she has helped us to understand alcoholism and to separate the person from the disease. She has also helped us develop unconditional love that continues despite unacceptable behavior; and, although she will have a lifetime struggle with her addictions and her recently diagnosed lung cancer, her energetic ambition and her generous nature have been bonuses for others and us. Pam likes to serve—whether in making pies or cookies for the holidays, cleaning a house or cutting a friend's hair, and we cherish the opportunity she has given us to be an important part of her life and the lives of her children.

RICK, who had to speak loudly at home in order to be heard, provided many vicarious thrills for us in football, basketball and other sports, but we are most amazed by his creativity— whether in constructing furniture from willow branches, renovating his house or collecting beautiful stones for a wall around his front yard. Rick is intense about everything he does (and there is little that he hasn't done), and we admire his ambition to pursue a teaching career at the age of 41. We also respect the parenting he and his wife, Marie, are doing with their four rambunctious and affectionate boys.

LISA offered us parenting relief. She was quiet and, without a doubt, the easiest child for us to raise. In fact, on more than one occasion teachers expressed surprise when they learned she was *our* child, because she was so obedient and never caused any problems in the classroom. Because of her passive nature, we were concerned about her ability to survive on her own, but at the age of 18, she left home, moved south and has never returned except to visit. She was the youngest of our children to permanently move out on their own, and she is now a loyal Texan. In spite of her quiet demeanor, she recently received recognition as the top inside sales person in the company for whom she works. While her mother would like to help her find a suitable husband, Lisa seems to be surviving quite well without one.

MIKE has furnished us with many athletic highlights in football, basketball, wrestling and tennis, including playing on a National Championship football team at Hillsdale College in 1985, but his pursuit of a career in the medical field, which required going back to school at the age of 26, has been a most pleasant surprise. He is the only one of our children who has pursued a medical career, and he has earned much respect as a paramedic in our local hospital emergency room. We take great pleasure in the frequent complimentary feedback we get from patients he has taken care of, and Mike is now doing very well in classes he is taking to earn his RN degree. We have enjoyed watching him and his wife, Nancy, pursue their parenting roles.

Kelly, one half of our final tandem, has achieved many athletic accomplishments in track, and she was the most vocal fan in support of her brothers' exploits on the football field. However, probably her most courageous decision was to spend a year in Germany as an exchange student at the age of 14. She not only survived the experience, but she became fluent in German and majored in this language in college. After her involvement in Spence Abraham's campaign, when he was elected to the U.S. Senate from Michigan, she met Jon Cool, who is now her wonderful husband. They are raising a fine family, and we are pleased that the two of them have become actively involved in helping women find alternatives to abortion. Perhaps her most loving contribution to our lives was when she left her job the summer of 1992 to come home and help care for her Grandma Kit, the summer Kit died of lung cancer.

KEVIN, the second of our final tandem and also a member of the National Championship football team at Hillsdale College, has provided thrills for us in several sports, but he also demonstrated musical talent in the choir and acting talent on the stage. Just before his junior year in high school, he was given the opportunity to play the part of Ali Hakim in our community theatre production of "Oklahoma". Because of his age, we had concerns about his ability to handle the part, but he did a marvelous job and must have some of his grandfather's theatrical genes. However, more important than his exploits in sports and live theatre, (two activities very dear to me), he has displayed unusual focus in his work career and his parenting. He has drawn much recognition for his accomplishments in advertising sales for the telephone yellow pages, and he and his very talented wife, Alexis, are raising two wonderful children.

We offer thanks to God for entrusting us with the parenting of twelve of *His* children and for giving us the graces and the strength to help us survive the challenges they have presented. They have enriched our lives greatly, and we feel abundantly blessed; but we have neither the strength nor the desire to repeat the experience.

OUR DOZEN

Stephen Anthony Vear   Jan. 16, 1952
State Representative, Accountant and Father

David Ray Vear   Feb. 27, 1953
Carpenter/Builder, Musician and Father

Kathryn Gay Godfrey   March 30, 1954
Landscaper and Mother

Anthony Allen Vear   Sept. 28, 1955
Salesman and Father

Theresa Marie Vear   March 17, 1957
Senior Center Director and Mother

Candace Ann Neal   Feb. 23, 1958
School Secretary and Mother

Pamela Sue Hannel   May 8, 1959
Factory Worker, House Cleaner and Mother

Richard Fitzpatrick Vear   Nov. 1, 1960
Teacher and Father

Lisa Louise Vear   July 2, 1963
Inside Sales Representative

Michael James Vear   Oct. 3, 1966
Emergency Room Paramedic and Father

Kelly Carson Cool   Sept. 26, 1967
Volunteer and Mother

Kevin Henderson Vear   Sept. 26, 1967
Outside Sales Manager and Father

BVG